ORIENTING HOLLYWOOD

CRITICAL CULTURAL COMMUNICATION

General Editors: Sarah Banet-Weiser and Kent A. Ono

Orienting Hollywood

A Century of Film Culture between Los Angeles and Bombay

Nitin Govil

NEW YORK UNIVERSITY PRESS

New York and London

NEW YORK UNIVERSITY PRESS
New York and London
www.nyupress.org

References to Internet websites (URLs) were accurate at the time of writing. Neither the author nor New York University Press is responsible for URLs that may have expired or changed since the manuscript was prepared.

Library of Congress Cataloging-in-Publication Data
Govil, Nitin.
Orienting Hollywood : a century of film culture between Los Angeles and Bombay / Nitin Govil.
pages cm. — (Critical cultural communication)
Includes bibliographical references and index.
ISBN 978-0-8147-8587-4 (cl : alk. paper) — ISBN 978-0-8147-8934-6 (pb : alk. paper)
1. Motion picture industry—California—Los Angeles—History 2. Motion picture industry—India—Mumbai—History. 3. Motion pictures—India—Influence. 4. Motion pictures—United States—Influence. I. Title.
PN1993.5.U65G6355   2015
384'.80979494—dc23   2014040536

New York University Press books are printed on acid-free paper, and their binding materials are chosen for strength and durability. We strive to use environmentally responsible suppliers and materials to the greatest extent possible in publishing our books.

Manufactured in the United States of America

10 9 8 7 6 5 4 3 2 1

Also available as an ebook

CONTENTS

ACKNOWLEDGMENTS

No matter what we are carrying across a border, most of us avoid the "something to declare" checkpoint. In ferrying this book across the finish line, I would like to linger for a moment and declare my thanks to those who have made the journey possible.

The initial research for this book began at the Department of Cinema Studies at New York University. I am deeply grateful to Richard Maxwell, Anna McCarthy, Manjunath Pendakur, George Yúdice, and most importantly Toby Miller, for their engagement and encouragement. These smart people helped to assemble scattered ideas into an argument. I'd also like to thank the rest of the Cinema Studies faculty and staff for their many kindnesses during my time at NYU, especially Richard Allen, Ventura Castro, William Simon, Robert Stam, Chris Straayer, Ken Sweeney, and Zhang Zhen.

I was fortunate to develop the research for this project with the generous support of colleagues at the University of Virginia and the University of California, San Diego. Thanks to Patrick Anderson, Gayle Aruta, LoriAnne Barnett, Lauren Berliner, Aniko Bodroghozy, Bethany Bryson, Lisa Cartwright, Sharon Corse, Johanna Drucker, Rita Felski, Gary Fields, Liz Floyd, Susan Fraiman, David Golumbia, Dan Hallin, Val Hartouni, Sharon Hays, Robert Horwitz, Krishan Kumar, Kate Levitt, Jamie Lloyd, Carl McKinney, and Pawan Singh. At UCSD, the Hellman Fellowship Program and the Faculty Career Development Program supported writing during the latter stages of the project.

As the book neared completion, my new colleagues at the University of Southern California welcomed me into a collegial and productive atmosphere for research and writing. I would especially like to thank Christine Acham, Jade Agua, Sarah Banet-Weiser, Elizabeth Daley, Mike Dillon, Kate Fortmueller, Larry Gross, Anikó Imre, Priya Jaikumar, Rick Jewell, Kara Keeling, Neetu Khanna, Akira Lippit, Tara McPherson,

Shana Redmond, Michael Renov, Ellen Seiter, Laura Serna, Alicia White, and Bill Whittington.

As with most projects with an extensive archival component, only a fraction of the consulted material appears in the notes at the end of this book. I would like to acknowledge the library staff at the following institutions for their generous help in researching well over fifty newspapers, periodicals, and trade journals, as well as providing access to innumerable memoranda, policy documents, trade reports, letters, and other ephemera: Anwar Jamal Kidwai Mass Communication Research Centre, Jamma Millia Islamia, Delhi; Asiatic Society, Mumbai and Kolkata; National Archives of India, Delhi; Nehru Memorial Library, Delhi; and V. Shantaram Foundation, Mumbai. I would especially like to thank Barbara Hall at the Margaret Herrick Library, Ned Comstock at the Warner Brothers Archive, and Moslem Quraishy at the Sarai Archives for their assistance. I must express my deep gratitude to Debashree Mukherjee for her diligent research support and expert advice during the course of research.

This project benefited from talks and presentations in North America, Europe, and South Asia. I would like to thank Michael Curtin, Lars Eckstein, Greg Elmer, Joe Karaganis, Suvir Kaul, Purnima Mankekar, Allison Perlman, Kevin Sanson, Anja Schwartz, Shuddhabrata Sengupta, Paul Smith, Michael Szalay, Rosie Thomas, and Ravi Vasudevan for their generous invitations.

Many artists, practitioners, policy makers, trade and industry representatives, and journalists generously granted interviews accompanied by drink and the occasional armed guard. Special thanks to Saleem Ahmadullah, Javed Akhtar, Madhusudan Anand, Fayyaz B., Shailaja Bajpai, Simrat Brar, Yash Chopra, Uma da Cunha, Kunal Dasgupta, Siddhartha Dasgupta, Blaise Fernandes, Jacinto Fernandes, Ashutosh Gowariker, Ravi Gupta, Nina Lath Gupta, Jiten Hemdev, Karan Johar, Jyoti, Nikhat Kazmi, Aamir Khan, Farah Khan, Pankaj Khandpur, Amit Khanna, Alex Kuruvilla, Manish Malhotra, Gul Nanda, Rahul Nanda, A. M. Padmanabhan, Anjum Rajabali, Sharmishta Roy, Kapil Saha, Supran Sen, Shankar, Aditya Shastri, Shravan Shroff, Sarabjit Singh, Uday Singh, D. F. H. Sidhwa, Shridhar Subramaniam, and Prakash B. Verma.

The wonderful folks at New York University Press helped steward the project as it traveled from initial proposal to final manuscript. I'd like to thank Ciara McLaughlin, Alicia Nadkarni, Kent Ono, and Eric Zinner for their support. Above all, the inimitable Sarah Banet-Weiser trusted in this project from the beginning—I so appreciate her enthusiasm and engagement. In addition to thanking the two anonymous reviewers for their careful feedback, I would also like to thank Anikó Imre, Priya Jaikumar, Carl McKinney, John McMurria, Denise McKenna, and Shawn Shimpach, who all generously offered detailed comments on the manuscript in various stages of completion.

So many friends have offered help, collaboration, and inspiration along the way. I'd like to thank in particular: Paula Chakravartty, Matthew Fee, Tejaswini Ganti, Michael Gillespie, Roger Hallas, Jennifer Holt, Eric Hoyt, Brian Larkin, Nancy Kwak, Sudhir Mahadevan, Neepa Majumdar, Mia Mask, Debashree Mukherjee, Roopali Mukherjee, Kartik Nair, Lisa Parks, Aswin Punathambekar, Ken Rogers, Bhaskar Sarkar, Jessica Scarlata, Lorca Shepperd, Rosie Thomas, Ravi Vasudevan, and Federico Windhausen. Special thanks to Ira Bhaskar, John McMurria, and Shawn Shimpach for their friendship, warmth, and encouragement.

Ravi Sundaram's camaraderie, playful cynicism, and tremendous insight have sustained me throughout the project. Ranjani Mazumdar has remained my dearest confidant and sparring partner during a time when I so needed both. Ravi and Ranjani's East Delhi apartment has been a home away from home for almost fifteen years. This book is simply unimaginable without them.

My extended family in India—especially the Govils in Gurgaon, the Parmars in Noida, the Mohans in Saket, and the Golerias in Andheri—kindly put me up and helped me whenever they could. I would also like to thank Ela Prakash and Monika Prakash for their support. I will always be so grateful for Denise McKenna's unwavering confidence. More than anyone else, our daughter, Anya, will be glad that the book is finally done!

When I was very young, my parents told me that I was made in Japan but born in India. As I surreptitiously polished off their last remaining drops of Johnnie Walker Black—some childhood habits are hard to break—I would repeat that joke to the grownups at our family parties and wonder why they laughed naughtily. I have thought a lot about that transnational origin story while writing this book. "Home" has only ever existed as an orientation, but writing this book has helped point the way. This book is for those loved ones who know what I mean, and for Bhagwan Prakash most of all. And yes, in case you're wondering, I think I finally get the joke.

Introduction

Narrating Encounter

Do we need *another* book on global Hollywood? Is there really anything new to say? After all, Hollywood remains the most well-documented media industry in the world. Setting the standards for success and failure across the international media trade, Hollywood is so omnipresent that much of the history of cinema seems captive to its domination.

This is a different kind of book about global Hollywood.

This book is different because its starting point is a place where Hollywood *doesn't* seem to matter much—India. Let me explain. A lot of writing on Hollywood acknowledges its powerful global reach. Nevertheless, the Indian market disrupts the uniformity of Hollywood's international domination. With massive domestic industries and a popular culture beholden to various regional cinema practices, India has been, and still is, a relatively minor territory for American film distribution. In the popular imagination, Indian cinema—especially the Hindi industry centered in Mumbai—is seen as the industry that survived Hollywood, assimilating and defeating it on native soil as far back as the 1930s.

Here's a case in point. The trade magazine *Hollywood Reporter* recently featured an interview about inter-industry relations with one of Hindi cinema's biggest stars, Shah Rukh Khan. His film *Chennai Express* is a coproduction between Khan's media company, Red Chillies Entertainment, and the recently launched Disney–UTV. With its US$454 million acquisition of the Indian media and entertainment company UTV in 2012, Disney's foray into locally branded film content in India remains one of the few places where it is directly involved in non-Hollywood production. Commenting on the Red Chillies and UTV–Disney tie-in, Khan notes that "I think that it's fantastic that the Hollywood studios are here. At first the studios wanted to popularize Hollywood films here but our cinema is deeply rooted in Indian culture. So it's good to see them producing Indian films. We also learn a lot from the experience of working with an international studio . . . it's a sign of changing times and will benefit Indian films to go international faster."[1] What remains unspoken in Khan's statement, however, is the sheer ubiquity that surrounds press and industry accounts of alignments between the Bombay and Hollywood industries. Khan's story, and innumerable others like it, have become part of a generic textual practice that references contemporary global media's fascination with Hollywood in India.

Everyday, we are surrounded by images and stories that highlight the proliferating ties between American and Indian media, most commonly seen in the remarkable conjoining of Hollywood and Bombay cinema.[2] So ubiquitous are these figures of contact that they seem auto-generated by a cottage industry of connection.

A relatively new but not unprecedented trope of contact has Hollywood stars breathlessly extolling the pleasures of working in Mumbai or expressing platitudes that laud the success of a wonderful industry "over there." Major Bombay cinema stars coyly play with the possibility of Hollywood exposure while steadfastly refusing ethnically stereotyping in minor film roles. At the same time, Indian technicians—their labor characterized by outsourcing stereotypes—work at home and abroad to invigorate and subsidize Hollywood formula. All the while, Hollywood and Bombay film stars mingle at film festivals, on red carpets, and at industry parties, dining out on future associations. As standard publicity practice in both industries, these tropes of connectivity rely on the cult of celebrity to put a glamorous face on industry alignment.

There are, of course, many other connections. Indian tourist brochures reference the lucrative global exposure offered by Hollywood location shooting. Film schools in the United States and India sign agreements of understanding, committed to training the next generation of international media practitioners. Glittering industry confabs, glossy management consultancy studies, and drab commerce and trade delegation reports all testify to a gloriously collaborative future. Moving beyond promotion but announced with equal fanfare, Indo-American media mergers and coproduction agreements solemnize industry alignments.

Globalization's oracles and spin-doctors work hard to document and celebrate these proliferating associations. Commentators publicizing these collaborations seem transfixed by the possibility of two strikingly different media industries seeking common ground. For some, editorial enthusiasm for industry cooperation deals with a perceived inversion of power relations in the international media economy, with Hollywood toppled from its position of global mastery. Affinities between Hollywood and Bombay cinema are taken as a sure sign of Indian media achievement. Furthermore, proliferating Hollywood–Mumbai connections testify to a globally relevant India. In story after story about Indian economic success, the pervasive rhetoric of industry connections take on world-historical significance. In the press nowadays, the magic of contemporary associations has clearly cast its spell: entrenched postwar asymmetries between national media are brushed aside as globalization reconciles existential contradictions between the West and "the Rest" in a new media order.

Admittedly, this turnaround in fortune is remarkable given the history of Hollywood in India. In the 1910s, India was often the last stop in the global trade of Hollywood film prints, which arrived scratched, worn, and marked by the transit of use. Nevertheless, Hollywood built on an established European distribution infrastructure in the subcontinent and rose to prominence through the 1920s, despite competition from British colonial cinema. As it reached a compromise with British cinema, Hollywood had reason to look forward to a long period of domination in the subcontinent, yet it never recovered the majority market share it enjoyed in the mid-1920s. Hollywood's market fortunes were derailed, in part, by the emergence of sound cinema and an Indian studio production culture, particularly in Bombay. Hollywood's subsequent decline was steady if not precipitous. Even as late at the 1930s and early 1940s, India remained the most lucrative market for Hollywood in South and East Asia and the only market in the region besides the Philippines where an American film could expect a theatrical return in the US\$ thousands. Still, the erosion of Hollywood's distribution network, the consolidation of regional Indian film studios, and a clear audience preference for vernacular-language cinema sealed Hollywood's fate in India.

Though its market share declined, Hollywood remained immensely popular among Indian audiences throughout the country. This popularity extended beyond the films into a wider public culture as images of Hollywood stars regularly anchored print advertisements for beauty and health products in Indian periodicals and newspapers.[3] When it came to the films, existing prints remained in constant circulation and Indian media artists accessed Hollywood as an archive of narratives and styles. For Bombay directors, writers, and technicians, Hollywood offered a way to study and occasionally appropriate film technique. For the Bombay industry, Hollywood film marked the horizon of technological achievement. Its marketing and promotional machinery was the envy of newly institutionalizing Indian industry organizations. However, when it came to its star system and bloated budgets, Hollywood was both a model and a cautionary tale. As Sumita Chakravarty and Ravi Vasudevan note, Hollywood functioned as both "a crucial marker of film form" and the "locus of both envy and resentment" in the Bombay film industry.[4] While "Hollywood" specifically denoted American film production, it also referenced a broader semantic field that engaged the discourses of innovation, imitation, and institutionalization *within* the Indian media economy. Hollywood's placement within the Indian mediascape belies the monolithic conception of domination sometimes adopted by historians, economists, and social theorists in presenting the univocal application of power by global American media.

After Indian independence in 1947, a series of dramatic shifts altered the relationship between Hollywood and Bombay industries. These included growing protectionist measures like rising import duties, censorship, Cold War mentalities that degraded Indian political relations with the United States, and a crisis in foreign exchange reserves. A postwar alignment between Hollywood and the U.S. government increased overseas revenue by organizing distribution to the mutual benefit of the American film studios, which effectively functioned as a cartel under the aegis of the Motion Picture Export Association of America (MPEA). However, trade disputes between the MPEA and the Indian government in the late 1960s and 1970s severely curtailed new Hollywood releases in India. The Indian government called for reciprocity in American distribution of Indian cinema, "higher quality" Hollywood product, and American investment in the Indian film sector. In turn, Hollywood asked for lifting restrictions on repatriating profits out of India and increasing the number of prints in circulation. Hollywood embargoes inevitably followed in the wake of stalled trade talks during this period.[5]

Hollywood's fortunes looked up as the television and home video boom of the early 1980s transformed India's relationship to global audiovisual culture. After decades of frustrated attempts to tap into India's enormous media audience, Hollywood's reanimation flickered briefly with the success of *Jurassic Park* in the mid-1990s. Since Steven Spielberg's genetically reconstructed CGI dinosaurs lumbered across screens in India, market reforms, including a rationalization of imports and a relaxation on foreign ownership, have brought Hollywood in closer contact with Indian media. Now, Hollywood shoots more films on location in India, sends its films to Indian studios for postproduction and dubbing, and seeks alliances with Indian media companies.

Over the past ten years, every above-average American film opening in India has been taken as a sign that the tide has finally turned for Hollywood. While the Indian market is still small in terms of Hollywood's global box office, an array of synergies, co-ventures, and points of institutional contact now intertwine the fortunes of the two remaining global film industries. Indeed, state and market transformations ensure that Hollywood is not incompatible with the industries that were once its competitors.

Clearly, there is an interesting story about this "other" global Hollywood. After all, the story of Hollywood in India only partially corresponds to accounts of dominance pervasive in critical media studies. Until relatively recently, Hollywood remained a minor economic force in India, stuck for decades in a single-digit market share, anywhere from 3 to 8 percent of the annual box office. Clearly, Hollywood in India must be understood beyond the conventions of mastery and mimicry that structure accounts of economic domination. A compelling alternate story about Hollywood in India would add depth to the general conception of Hollywood's subjugation of other "national" cinemas, whose resistance is heroic but ultimately futile. Breaking with such conventions usually entails a loosening of conceptual orthodoxies. In this case, Hollywood hegemony is an insufficient account of inter-industry relations between the United States and India.

Before I explain why this book doesn't tell *that* story, where political economy plays the lone starring role, let's play out the script as if it did.

Hollywood's placement within the acceleration of Indo-American economic encounter after the Indian economic liberalization policies of the late 1980s and early 1990s reads like a narrative of inevitable victory. In other words, before liberalization, Hollywood and Bombay's encounter is akin to small-scale globalization, where collaborations are somewhat irregular and largely under the international economic radar. But *now*, after economic liberalization, things were different, right? It would be as if all the diverse historical constellations of the Hollywood–Bombay encounter could be swept up, blown through, and reassembled in a cosmology of contemporary economic interdependency.

As I began the research for this book, I sometimes felt beholden to contemporary events, as if they conspired to force me to write precisely *that* book about transnational economic victory. As I've already noted, the new millennium ushered in countless press accounts that spoke of Hollywood and Bombay cinema in one breath. Indeed, over the past five years, inter-industry contact has proliferated in all directions.

The first decade of the new millennium ended with an Indian theatrical strike that crippled domestic Indian exhibition. Faced with a restricted flow of new Bombay films, Hollywood focused its Indian release schedule on technological spectacle and mega-budget films like *2012* (US$12 million gross in India) and *Avatar* (US$16 million). Both films were among the biggest box-office draws of 2009. In the last few years, a number of American films have done well, beating out Hindi-language counterparts during opening weekends. For example, in its first week, *Pirates of the Caribbean: On Stranger Tides*, released by Paramount in India in May 2011, grossed 50 percent more than *Haunted 3D* (Vikram Bhatt, 2011). Indian releases of Hollywood sequels built on the strong starts of their franchise predecessors; films like *The Hangover Part II*, *Fast Five*, and the sequels to *X-Men* and *Transformers* all roared out of the gate.

Hollywood's agents in India took notice, suggesting targeted strategies to reach Indian audiences. For example, in late April 2012, *The Avengers* was released in India one week before its American launch. Opening in English, Hindi, Tamil, and Telegu across a record eight hundred screens (including 3D and IMAX versions), the film is now among the top-grossing Hollywood films in India. Domestically, *The Avengers* was distributed by UTV, an Indian entertainment conglomerate acquired by Disney in 2012. While the film's Kolkata scenes introducing Hulk alter ego Bruce Banner (Mark Ruffalo) were filmed in New Mexico, reportedly in association with the city's Indian community, the film's producer claimed that "the idea was to introduce our characters to Indian audiences in a manner that they can relate to them."[6]

In June 2012, the *Spider-Man* reboot was released in India a week ahead of its U.S. release. With Indian actor Irfan Khan in a cameo role, the film was released in 1,150 prints—almost doubling the release volume of the third film in the *Spider-Man* franchise in 2007. The film opened to the best showing by a Hollywood film in India, and went on to collect almost US$15 million. The Indian arm of the Motion Picture Association, representing the six major Hollywood studios distributing in India, strengthened its antipiracy enforcement actions in anticipation of the wide release. The film released to 90 percent occupancy in Indian multiplexes, resulting in double the opening take of most Hollywood films. Some reports suggested that Hollywood was back to double-digit market share in India, although most claimed only 8–12% of overall box-office revenue.

Hollywood's rising stake also buoyed the confidence of Indian media conglomerates, which moved toward acquiring American media interests. Most significant among these was Indian media conglomerate Reliance Entertainment's joint-venture investment in the Hollywood studio DreamWorks. In July 2009, Reliance contributed US$325 million toward a new partnership with DreamWorks, along with Disney and a syndicate of international banks, to finance new production projects over three years. As part of its "Hollywood strategy," Reliance ended up holding 50 percent of the American studio. Reliance added to its 170 US cinemas by announcing a BIG-branded five-screen multiplex in Chicago that would transmit films over fiber-optic cable, thus circumventing the need for film prints. Just a few months later, in the fall of 2009, rumors swirled that Reliance Entertainment and another Indian conglomerate, Sahara India Pariwar, were putting in separate bids for the venerable Hollywood studio Metro-Goldwyn-Mayer (MGM), the studio behind the *James Bond* films. MGM had been in financial difficulty, struggling with billions of dollars of debt and narrowly avoiding bankruptcy before a debt-restructuring rescue deal was announced in late 2009. Despite the failed deal, Indian interest in Hollywood remained undiminished. In early 2010, a Los Angeles–based producer of Indian origin, A. V. T. Shankardass, floated a US$100 million equity fund in India called

Global Entertainment Partners (GEP). Comprising thirty-three Indian investors, GEP was designed to support American film financing in the wake of the global recession.

The reasons for Hollywood's renewed interest in India are numerous: its cinema-driven popular culture; its well-developed and varied regional industries with intricate histories of collaboration; the ongoing relaxation of the regulatory market and the availability of capital for media investment; a growing middle class with money to spend; the presence of English speakers as well as well-established dubbing practices into "local languages" like Hindi, Tamil, and Telegu; the proliferating multiplex boom; well-established diasporic audiences; and the growth of Indian ancillary markets, especially in postproduction and back-office services. The relative theatrical underdevelopment of the small cities and towns—the Indian "B" and "C" circuit—present an appealing, variegated market for innovation in exhibition. The movement of Indian broadcasters toward becoming horizontally and vertically integrated studios also creates opportunities for Hollywood collaboration.

What do the Indian media industries gain from Hollywood collaboration? Indian distributors use Hollywood alignments to leverage production agreements in other countries, while Hollywood becomes a way of driving and showcasing world cinema in the Indian context. Hollywood's interest in India also spurs British, German, and Italian coproduction treaties with India, even as Indian producers work outside the state's ambit. Strangely enough, the predominance of high-profile U.S.–Indian collaborations has created opportunities for "independent" film production in India, supported by a resurgent Indian National Film Development Corporation, which took advantage of the curtailing of foreign imports in the early 1970s to help fund new art cinema. The Bombay film industry generally assumes that Hollywood's economies of scale can help stabilize the 90 percent failure rate of Indian film production by guaranteeing financing and international distribution.

Such contemporary transformations demonstrate how "national" media culture is implicated and legitimated by an array of transnational networks. That Hollywood can be located in the transactions between domestic Indian industries tells us that the older forms of differentiation in the media industry need rethinking. No longer imagined as an aspirational goal, Hollywood is now seen as a "starting point" for Bombay media's global ambitions.[7] This inversion of the traditional story of media development suggests the need for a new historiography of global Hollywood.

Should such a study be directed by contemporary events, focusing on the increasing profitability of American cinema in India and the accelerating institutional connections between Hollywood and Mumbai? As world media became captivated by Hollywood's rising fortunes in India, my own more modest interests in Indo-American media encounter were in danger of being overwhelmed by the juggernaut of economic inevitability. As accepted wisdom began to speak of Hollywood and Bombay together, this book was in danger of devolving into a story about India's transformation in a relatively short period from a Hollywood outpost to a frontier of opportunity. It was as if contemporary financial proximity between the industries was conspiring against more nuanced and even contradictory accounts.

Of course, many industry collaborations are documented according to the rhythms of rising and falling profits, but that didn't mean that an account of encounter needed to follow the same tune. *Orienting Hollywood* is an attempt to engage with textual politics and social forces to avoid substantiating boosterist accounts and box-office successes and failures. This book aims to texture the contact between Hollywood and Bombay cinema by digging into the reality and the imagination of encounter.

I have taken some disciplinary and methodological license during this project. As part of my research, I wanted to visit archives, watch movies, analyze data, and talk to people. My intention is to enliven rather than abandon traditional media analysis. In engaging empirical and conceptual methods, I have drawn on my intellectual roots in literature, cinema studies, communications, and critical cultural studies. Drawing on the humanities and social sciences, *Orienting Hollywood* takes a transhistorical comparative approach that engages equally with structure, discourse, and practice to argue against a fixed notion of industry. In other words, I want to pay closer attention to the ways media industries are produced, conceptualized, and sustained over time. How have "Hollywood" and "Bombay cinema" been produced in the history of encounter? How have the varied trajectories of circulation that constitute media industries—the movements of material objects, knowledge, expertise, personnel, capital, ideas, and images—organized relations between global medias across time?

To answer these questions, I decided to look further back and farther afield. While I have acknowledged contemporary transformation, I have refused to neglect historicizing breaks and ruptures. For that reason, *Orienting Hollywood* traces the encounters between Hollywood and Bombay cinema from 1913 to 2013. Over this period, which maps roughly onto the first century of feature film production, there have been multiple dimensions to the relationship between the two global media industries. From competition to collaboration, contestation to coproduction, Hollywood and Bombay cinema have been brought into contact, catalyzing mutual forms of influence. Considering Hollywood and Bombay cinema synoptically, this book is a genealogy of cross-contamination, with India and the United States as both real and imagined stages of encounter.

Missions: Possible?

In the 1950s, the Indian magazine *Filmfare* featured a column called "A Film Letter from Hollywood" written by its "local" correspondent Sylvia Norris. Describing life in Hollywood for her Indian readers, Norris's column combined gossip and travelogue to create a postcard from the land of glitz. Her breezy prose conveyed the casual exoticism that was part of *Filmfare*'s regular engagement with Hollywood. At times, however, *Filmfare* departed from these relaxed engagements in favor of windier pronouncements on Indo-American encounters. For example, in March 1958, *Filmfare* featured a different kind of Hollywood correspondence, this time written by Eric Johnston, the president of the Motion Picture Association of America (MPAA), the film industry's powerful lobbying arm. In the article, which exemplifies the technocratic subgenre of Cold War literary poetics, Hollywood's chief booster declares Hollywood fit for the task of global liberty, insisting on the stabilizing power of the motion pictures during precarious times: "I believe that if we could transplant the entire population of one country to another country for a long visit, and repeat the process over and over again among all the countries, we would see an end of international doubts, mistrusts, misunderstandings and wars. We cannot do that of course. But I know of no better substitute than the motion picture."[8]

Johnston's Cold War felicities sum up four decades of Hollywood faith in the power of American cinema to civilize, to act as an international ambassador of goodwill, and to serve as an agent for the betterment of humankind. Since the early 1920s at least, Hollywood's world ambitions had articulated a leading role in coordinating intercultural encounter within a broadly ecumenical vision. Johnston's sentiment in *Filmfare* was yet another expression of global Hollywood's inaugural feint, upgraded for new times.

Similar reports of inter-industry encounter, rooted in the comparative assessment of film industry practice, were perhaps less craftily utopian but nevertheless shared some underlying features with Johnston's account. Written a year after Johnston's article, *Time* magazine's January 1959 "Movies Abroad" column describes Bombay film as "the zaniest movie industry on earth . . . a montage of pomp, profit and speculation."[9] Most of the story focuses on the rising power of film stars in Bombay's Hindi cinema, the "new maharajahs of the film industry," but special attention is given to the "cash and curry" mobility of female stars like Madhubala. The closing lines of the article shift toward the possibilities of Hollywood encounter, stated in more dramatic terms than Johnston's dry diplomacy of the year before. *Time* noted that producer–director's Mehboob Khan's next step after the success of *Mother India* (1957) was to get "Hollywood itself to lend a co-producing hand with an even more lavish film fetchingly titled *Taj Mahal*. What will happen when Hollywood and Bombay meet, Siva only knows."[10]

Some fifty years later, with the Cold War safely behind them, two new maharajahs of Indo-American film encounter did meet (at the Taj Mahal, no less). The Associated Press (AP) documented the encounter in the photograph below, which shows two major international film stars shaking hands against an iconic backdrop (fig. 1.1). Fifty years after Eric Johnston and *Time*'s predictions, Anil Kapoor and Tom Cruise's gesture seems to reconcile a clash of civilizations with a simple assertion of friendship. Media worlds are conjoined with a momentary clasp of hands. Here, in the affective charge of a physical gesture, popular representation shifts from an earlier register of mystery to a new image of

Figure I.1. Bollywood star Anil Kapoor and Hollywood star Tom Cruise in Agra, 2011. Nyay Bushan, "2011: When Hollywood Connected with India," *Hollywood Reporter*, January 1, 2012.

correspondence. In *Time*'s earlier account, inter-industry contact is improbable, beyond mere mortal imagination; in the new narrative visualized by the AP photograph, contact is affirmed and celebrated—though it's not clear why the guy behind Tom is holding his nose.

One of the biggest Hindi film stars of the 1990s, Anil Kapoor catapulted to fame as the lead in Shekhar Kapoor's 1987 film *Mr. India*. But he is perhaps better known internationally as the president of the fictional Islamic republic of Kamistan in the American television series *24*—the Indian version of the show premiered in October 2013—or as *Slumdog Millionaire*'s game show host. Hollywood star Tom Cruise first met Anil Kapoor at the American Golden Globes award ceremony in 2009 when he handed out the Best Motion Picture award for *Slumdog*. Two years later, Tom and Anil had completed *Mission: Impossible—Ghost Protocol* and were visiting the Taj Mahal together as part of an Asian publicity junket promoting their new film.

Standing in for national as well as industrial encounter, the AP photo performs a double function. In the first instance, India and America's long political, cultural, and economic engagement is telescoped into the frame of the photograph. In the second instance, Cruise and Kapoor stand in for the *real* star of the scene: the connection between Hollywood and Bombay cinema. The transaction represented in the photo anthropomorphizes industry relations, suggesting fraternity and partnership: interpersonal intimacy functions as a metaphor for institutional

cooperation and coexistence. In making a picture of inter-industry relations, the photo epitomizes what Ulf Hannerz famously called the global
ecumene, the "interconnectedness of the world by way of interactions,
exchanges and related development, affecting not least the organization
of culture."[11]

Pointing the way forward for Hollywood in India, the 2011 Kapoor–
Cruise AP photograph is a tantalizing image of affirmation and promise.
Taken during a hasty twenty-five-minute trip to the Taj Mahal during a
publicity tour for *Mission: Impossible—Ghost Protocol,* the photo shows
Anil Kapoor and Tom Cruise shaking hands in front of the Taj in Agra.
The Taj serves a number of symbolic functions here. It haloes Tom, en-
capsulating and augmenting his otherworldliness as a film celebrity. At
the same time, the majesty of the white marbled mausoleum affirms
the monumentality of encounter between Hollywood and Bombay cinema and reframes the actors' "bromance" against a globally recognizable
symbol of timeless romantic love. But because the Taj is already so familiar as a national metonym in countless tourist and advertising images,
the backdrop is also an example of *filmi* kitsch, which is why Anil wears
that mock expression of seriousness.

Commissioned in the seventeenth century by the Mughal emperor
Shah Jahan, the Taj was constructed as a tribute to the memory of his
third wife, Mumtaz Mahal. It stands now both as a monument to the
majesty of South Asian imperial culture and as a potent symbol and
index of Indian accomplishment. Its contemporary relevance is not
without contestation, however, as in the last fifteen years Indian courts
have dismissed revisionist claims that a Hindu king constructed the Taj.
As the singular image of the nation, the Taj has also been appropriated
in the twenty-first century as a sign of globalized connectivity between
the United States and India, as the following advertisement for AT&T
suggests (see fig. 1.2). Images like the AT&T ad are increasingly in vogue
now, as market "liberalization" and the increased buying power of the
urban middle class have fomented a mutual country-crush between
India and the United States.

It was in this spirit of Indo-American connectivity that Anil shook
hands with Tom in front of the Taj in December 2011. Accompanied by
his *Ghost Protocol* costar Paula Patton, Tom Cruise arrived in India as
part of an Asian promotional tour with stops in Tokyo and Seoul. The

Figure I.2. The Taj Mahal reimagined in American pennies in a 2009 AT&T ad. *Entertainment Weekly*, April 3, 2009, 13.

India leg of the tour was scheduled just before the film's December 7 world premiere at the Dubai International Film Festival. With stops in Delhi and Agra before arriving in Mumbai for press and fan screenings and Bollywood parties, Cruise's visit represented the first time that a major Hollywood star had come to India to promote a film. In Mumbai, Cruise was put up at the presidential suite at the Taj Mahal Palace Hotel in Mumbai (which had also hosted Barack Obama), accompanied by an entourage of chef, trainer, and assistant, along with instructions that his suite's air conditioning be set to precisely 73 degrees Fahrenheit.

Ghost Protocol was released in India in 2D and IMAX 3D on December 16 across a thousand screens in four languages. Without any major Hindi film competition, *Ghost Protocol* set the record for highest opening weekend gross for a Hollywood film in India, collecting over US$5 million, about 20 percent more than *Avatar*. In order to "position" the film among Indian (and it was hoped, Asian) spectators, Paramount released a new poster for *Ghost Protocol* that prominently featured Kapoor. In addition, India's largest selling cola brand, Thums Up, featured as an in-product placement in the Indian release of the film, replacing shots of Coke Zero in the "original" release. The indigenous replacement didn't cause much of a corporate ruckus. After all, while Thums Up was a hugely successful response to the expulsion of Coca-Cola during the import-substitution policies of the 1970s, it had been acquired by Coke in 1993 and relaunched as a competitor to Pepsi in India.

In *Ghost Protocol*, Anil Kapoor plays an Indian entrepreneur named Brij Nath, with Cruise reprising his role as Ethan Hunt, an agent for the Impossible Missions Force (IMF). For twenty minutes toward the end of the film, the action shifts from Dubai to Mumbai, as Hunt's team works to take over Nath's telecommunications network and his prized possession, an old Soviet military satellite. Described as a tycoon possessing "state of the art technology built on Cold War knockoffs," Nath is all debauchery and *filmi* flash: a veritable amalgam of Hollywood's Asian stereotypes. Smarmy yet fey, Nath is a pirate entrepreneur with a technology network that leapfrogs the developmental presumptions of modernity. He ends, predictably, facedown and unconscious after ceding control to the IMF. Ironically, all this sounds like an allegory about the structural adjustment policy of another, more powerful IMF—the International Monetary Fund—that sought to bend the economic will of developing nations with its draconian lending policies.

Mission: Impossible began as an American television show in the late 1960s, but by the time it was reintroduced as a Hollywood film franchise, it had exchanged its Cold War subtext for a fascination with stateless, globalized criminality. Paramount's *Mission: Impossible*, released in 1996, was a response to the collapse of the Soviet Union, whose demise dismantled the narrative justification for Hollywood's arch antagonist in thriller, action, and crime films of the Reagan 1980s. By the time of *Ghost Protocol*, the fourth installment of the film series, the action had returned to the Cold War stage, featuring secret Soviet archives and the destruction of Moscow's Kremlin.

First announced in 2009, the fourth installment of the *Mission: Impossible* series was inevitable given the worldwide successes of the first three films in the series—released in 1996, 2000, and 2006—which earned US$400–US$500 million per film. The first three films had earned Rs.40, 100, and then 150 million in India. The year 2009 also turned out to be a good one for Hollywood in India, with *Harry Potter and the Half-Blood Prince* opening with 350 prints released on more than four hundred screens in English and Hindi and Telegu versions and in IMAX 3D as well. More than half of *Half-Blood's Prince's* opening collections came from Mumbai theaters, but the Hindi-dubbed version was a big hit in Lucknow and Aurangabad, and the sixth *Potter* installment was the biggest opening for an English-language film in India that year. The same year, the successful Indian release of films like *Ice Age: Dawn of the Dinosaurs* and *X-Men Origins: Wolverine* represented an upswing of Hollywood's confidence in the Indian market. At the end of 2009, *Avatar* was released with seven hundred prints in India in English, Hindi, Tamil, and Telegu, and also a 3D version in Tamil.

A year prior to his promotional tour for *Ghost Protocol*, Tom Cruise was already solidifying ties with an Indian fan base, tweeting thanks to Indian fans who had posted birthday wishes to him on Facebook and Twitter. Cruise wrote, "A huge THANK YOU to the wonderful people of India for their birthday wishes and kindness," adding, "I'll 'see' you at the movies Friday." He was referring to *Knight and Day*, released in India in July 2010 in English and a dubbed Hindi version. Later that year, in October 2010, Anil Kapoor confirmed that he had accepted a role in Cruise's latest film. After the success of *Slumdog* and the international exposure facilitated by his role in *24*, Kapoor was looking to build his presence in Hollywood and had signed with the Los Angeles–based talent agency International Creative Management, the first of a group of Bollywood stars looking for American representation as a way to build a global presence.

With filmmaking planned for Rajasthan at the end of October 2010, Paramount's *Ghost Protocol* was part of a crowded slate of some forty foreign film projects seeking the Indian Ministry of Information and Broadcasting's permission to shoot in India over the preceding two years. Responding to this high demand, in November 2010, the Los Angeles India Film Council was set up to coordinate location shoots between the United States and India. Anil Kapoor noted that this declaration of cooperation between Hollywood and Bollywood was an important step toward ensuring "that our industries collaborate commercially and creatively."[12] Although *Ghost Protocol*'s India shoot was delayed, with scenes eventually shot in April and early May 2011, none of the principal actors shot any scenes in India. A Bangalore street scene featuring Cruise was recreated in Vancouver and interior scenes that placed the stars in Mumbai and Bangalore were shot in Dubai and Vancouver. For second-unit acting and chase scenes that were actually shot in South Mumbai, Cruise's double stood in for him, with crowds packing in to see the specially designed BMW "supercar" as it moved through Prabhadevi streets.

Tom Cruise did see fit to personally attend the two-day Indian promotional tour for the film, in a visit that was rumored to have cost Paramount over US$300,000. *Ghost Protocol*'s publicity managers strictly controlled press coverage, allowing few interviews, though Indian fans were encouraged to post photos on social networking sites. *First Post Bollywood* claimed in a widely cited story published during Cruise's visit that the fan adulation upon his arrival in Mumbai was staged:

> When the world's biggest star and possibly the most famous Scientologist on earth, Tom Cruise, stepped out of the Mumbai domestic airport on Saturday with his entourage, little did he know that the screaming crowds he was waving out to were not his Indian fans at all! In fact, the 200-and-odd people gathered there didn't even know who he was and they couldn't care less. They had been hired at the rate of Rs.150, or $3 per person approximately, by a model coordinator to do the same! "Tom *kaun*? [Tom who?] I don't know who he is or what he does. We were told to come here by 1pm today and wait for a foreign VIP to come out of the airport gate and scream and shout when he came. None of us know who Tom is. There was a buffet lunch also for us and we were paid Rs.150 for this job today. We do this for television shows and other such events where crowds are required," said one of the junior artists at the airport, who was hired as an excited Tom fan.[13]

In a cover story on the controversy, the *Mumbai Mirror* claimed that extras were paid between four and eight U.S. dollars, depending on their "cheering experience." Assembled hours before Cruise's arrival, the paid crowd was a benefit for local security, as one officer noted that "mobs that randomly gather to see celebrities can be extremely unruly and tough to control. A hired crowd is better. It behaves itself and listens to us."[14] Paramount and Wizcraft, the Indian event management company coordinating Cruise's visit, vehemently denied the staged adulation by hired extras, known as "junior artists" in industry parlance. Both companies, along with Anil Kapoor, claimed that the enthusiasm for Cruise was "pure."

The accusation of paid compensation and any possible corruption of adulation destabilize the authenticity suggested by the Cruise–Kapoor photo's expression of friendship. The photographed handshake demonstrates the careful manufacture of contact, while the cheering fan connotes a spontaneous burst of emotion. One is enacted, the other supposedly real. Of course, both are socially constructed forms of expression, staging the dramaturgy of encounter, but the danger in accusations of fan compensation is that they suggest an atrophying closeness between Indo-American media ecologies. That is why Paramount's publicists pushed back so hard on the newspaper reports. After all, the 2011 AP photo forwards a pedagogical imperative, instructing us in the way to look at the relationship between media industries. The Cruise–Kapoor handshake celebrates reciprocal engagement, framing comparison as contact. The photo suggests a meeting between equals: industries in balance, met in a gesture of equivalence. That much seems obvious. But what else does the handshake between Tom Cruise and Anil Kapoor suggest about Indo-American media relations? Sociologist Erving Goffman's work on symbolic interaction is instructive here.

A handshake can mark the initiation of a relationship or the culmination of one. In other words, a handshake can embody a moment of initial contact or the reaffirmation of an existing social bond. This dynamic temporality affords something both new and old for the parties involved. A handshake is a reciprocal gesture that implies mutuality, equality, friendship, and partnership, a greeting, a mutual decision, the conclusion of a successful negotiation and the sealing of a new deal. These gestures are all part of what Goffman terms *facework*: those dramaturgical efforts that define social interaction.[15] For all its gestural reciprocity, however, a handshake also implies an obligation; as Goffman notes, in polite society, "a handshake that perhaps should not have been extended becomes one that cannot be declined."[16] As orchestrated gestures, handshakes preserve what Goffman calls a "strict situational solemnity," a superficial appearance that effectively shields the true relations between participants.[17]

The Cruise–Kapoor handshake, carefully managed for the cameras in a staged display of spontaneity, speaks to the myriad theatrical enactments that perform the "facework" of industry. The handshake affirms a certain kind of sociality predicated on prior personal contact at the same time that it seals the possibility of future interaction. Part of the allure of the photo op is that it stages the much-lauded rebalancing of global power in the contemporary political economy. Sustained popular and scholarly engagement with the economic triumphalism of the BRICS nations—Brazil, Russia, India, China, and South Africa—has suggested a fundamental challenge to Western economic hegemony.[18] This "reorientation" of the global economy marks the brief passage of European hegemony and the restoration of an "Asia-centered world."[19] This "rebirth" of the East, staged against the decline of the West, has been widely disseminated in popular economic discourse.[20] Film, media, and communications studies scholars have taken this rebirth as an occasion to de-Westernize the field, shifting accounts of media globalization away from North American and Western European perspectives.[21]

Taken at "face" value, then, the handshake between the two film stars reaffirms an underlying principle of the global political economy: a rebalancing of the power dynamic between East and West (though this rebalancing is thrown slightly off-kilter by Cruise's prominence at the center of the frame). However, the Cruise–Kapoor bromantic encounter is not just a complement to industry; it configures a site where industry is anchored and performed. Paying attention to the social, political–economic, and affective forces that produce "industry" as form and practice, *Orienting Hollywood* takes seriously this idea that industry is the product of encounter. The task of the book is to capture the texture of encounter, examining trajectories of connection and itineraries of exchange and conflict. *Orienting Hollywood* delves into the history and quality of encounter between Hollywood and Bombay cinema, offering not just a window into their relationship but framing a critical comparatist politics in film and media studies.

To return to our photo: connections are affirmed in the handshake at the same time that promises are being made. This begs a question—does the handshake attest to the *restoration* of fraternity, founded at the onset of the feature film history? Certainly some have suggested as much, as we shall see below.

Orienting Hollywood, Part 1

In what is perhaps the first full-length academic study of the Indian film industry, Panna Shah offers 1913 as the shared date for the founding of the Indian and the American film industries: "It is a strange coincidence that *Harischandra* should have been presented at more or less the same time as Adolph Zukor presented the first multiple-reel feature film *Queen Elizabeth*, which paved the way for the future feature films. Thus apparently as far as the origin of feature film goes, both East and West started together. The West, however, advanced rapidly, while India lagged far behind."[22] Shah's founding narrative is a bit off historically. D. G. Phalke's *Raja Harischandra* was preceded as a feature in 1912 by Ram C. G. Torne's *Pundalik* (not to mention Hiralal Sen's "lost" features, dating back to the early 1900s). Also, what she calls *Queen Elizabeth* was actually a French production titled *Les Amours de la Reine Elizabeth*, directed by Louis Mercanton, which Zukor partially financed and distributed in the United States by obtaining the rights to the film.

Furthermore, Panna Shah's apocryphal rendering of the mutual origins of Bombay cinema and Hollywood acknowledges the question of development but underemphasizes D. G. Phalke's call to link film with the nativist concept of *Swadeshi*. *Swadeshi*, the "home manufacture" economic movement, connected to anticolonial nationalism, advocated for a thorough transformation of the colonial political economy by outlawing foreign economic exploitation in favor of autonomous economic development.[23] Phalke's own self-promotion as the patriarch of the Indian film industry aligned neatly with these commitments—he claimed that "my films are *Swadeshi* in the sense that the capital, ownership, employees and stories are all *Swadeshi*."[24]

Despite these historical tensions, the fiction of common origin has endured to the extent that 2013 is being touted as a dual centenary. If Bombay cinema and Hollywood were not exactly separated at birth—like the iconic twin brothers of Hindi film melodrama—industry celebrations of the apocryphal Indo-American film century continue to thematize the restoration of an estranged kinship (see fig. 1.3).

Figure 1.3. Hollywood and Bombay cinema, reunited—one
lone wolf above a pack of wolves. Billboards at a South
Delhi movie theater, January 2014.

While the idea of a common origin might be more fiction than fact,
it nevertheless suffuses much Indo-American film industry interaction.
Take for example the keynote speech at the 2012 Frames conference, the
long-running industry confab hosted in Mumbai by the Federation of
Indian Chambers of Commerce and Industry (FICCI). The Frames 2012
keynote speaker was MPAA Chairman Chris Dodd, who remarked in
his opening comments, "I am honored to be here to celebrate with all
of you something else that unites our two countries—Movies."[25] Similar acknowledgments of bilateral unity were on the program for Frames
2013, with keynotes delivered by film and television executives from
Disney, Viacom, and Sony, as well as the dean of the UCLA School of
Theater, Film, and Television.

Of course, foundational myths invoking an Indo-American film
century are convenient and retrospective mappings, allowing industry
folk to validate negotiations and comparisons. Nevertheless, origin stories are useful ways of tracing long-standing itineraries of connection.

Indeed, if we look back to 1913, we can see how India figured prominently in Hollywood's self-conception both on- and off-screen. In its
very earliest imagination of global expansion, Hollywood instantiated
the tropes of transcultural encounter with India, particularly through
popular actuality, travelogue, and ethnographic genres.

Despite the political, legal, and economic disenfranchisement of
workers of Indian origin in turn-of-the-century Southern California,
India before Hollywood primarily resonated as a lifestyle: the public's
fascination with Theosophy, "bungalows" dotting the Pacific Coast
(named for the Indian thatched roof houses), and hand-woven Indian
"dhurrie" rugs that decorated Southern California homes. While Indian
furnishings complemented the eclecticism of California's local aesthetic,
early short films at the dawn of Hollywood were designed to demonstrate the lengths to which American film companies would travel to
secure more exotic entertainments. These included Edison's *Dramatic
Scenes in Delhi* (1912), *Views in Calcutta* (1912), and *Curious Scenes in
India* (1913), Powers's travels films like *Views of Bangkok, India* (1912),
and Mutual's *Life in India* (1913). Such "descriptive" or "scenic" films featured banyan trees and royal palms, landmarks and ruined remnants
of past conflict, and natives at play and at work in the hustle-bustle of
colonial urban life.

In the Dorsey Expedition pictures, like Reliance's *Up from the Primitive* (1912), which used animal life from the Ganges to demonstrate
evolutionary principles, Western cameramen were depicted as intrepid
"film explorers" bearing the marks of their encounters with the East's
savagery. In showcasing India as a setting for imperial grandeur, Edison's
Durbar films competed with heavily promoted films from Gaumont
and Pathé that showcased George V's coronation as emperor of India.
Edison's films also screened against Kinemacolor exhibitions of Durbar
footage in New York in 1912.

"Educationals" like Éclair's *Life in India* (1913) showed industrious
natives plying a variety of trades, and were paired together with films
like Essanay's *China and the Chinese* (1913) to form a compendium of
oriental behavior. Extending beyond racialized pedagogy, longer two-
reel films, shot on location and in the studio, elaborated on India as a
signifier of danger and, at the same time, a safe safari destination. For
example, Zukor's Arab Amusement Company released an animal series

called *Wild Life and Big Game in the Jungles of India and Africa* (1913). Typically hyperbolic advertising from Zukor promised that "the soul of India has stolen into the film . . . !"[26] and the film was endorsed by Teddy Roosevelt, well-known for his love of big-game hunting. There were other popular pictures in a similar vein. Solax's *Beasts of the Jungle* (1913), where an American engineer loses his daughter to the wild tropics, was full of wild animals and an Indian "atmosphere" that helped to popularize the animal picture. Selig's *A Wise Old Elephant* (1913) was also set in India, but was filmed on the Selig wild animal farm in Los Angeles. To decorate his films, Selig hired a naturalist to tour India (as well as Australia, Japan, South America, and Africa) for plants, vegetation, and animals for the farm. By 1915, the Selig Zoo was one of the best furnished in the United States, with two dozen Bengal tigers and a number of "sacred monkeys."

In addition to these stories, early cinema also popularized dramas of anticolonial uprising, including Francis Ford's *The Campbells Are Coming* (1915), which featured murderous sepoys and native princes that attack "an English town" in India full of women and children. Such was the popularity of these "sepoy stories" in the teens that American film studios planned to construct permanent "India" sets in California to streamline their production.[27]

Early on, the American industry went on location to India to film short travel films that required geographical validity. However, as the industry moved toward longer features, "animal films" could be shot in the studio (as described above, some had their own zoos) and "India" could be suggested by a tree, a tiger, and a well-placed turban. Producers often used recycled stock scenic footage to buttress films shot in the studio.

It is clear that these representations of India allowed Hollywood to imagine a nascent global enterprise where white supremacy was confounded and thrilled by Asian mystery. Reflecting on the conventions of adventure and astonishment, we can see how India served to "orient" Hollywood as a spatial and symbolic practice. What were the permutations and implications of this orientation?

India played a key role in the representation of Otherness in early Hollywood, providing what Edward Said calls an "imaginative geography" that symbolized Hollywood's sense of its boundaries as well as the "kinds of suppositions, associations, and fictions" that populated the "unfamiliar space" outside its own.[28] Of course, Hollywood produced "India" in its own studios as well as by traveling to South Asia, and the fabrication of scenarist attraction was as critical to the representation of alterity as the travelogue footage filmed "on location."

For Hollywood, then, India functioned as real and diegetic space. In furnishing the requisite tropes of Otherness to orient Hollywood's modernity, these permutations of site and scene constructed India as a "contact zone," Mary Louise Pratt's term for those social spaces "where disparate cultures meet, clash, and grapple with each other, often in highly asymmetrical relations of domination and subordination."[29] Interactions within this contact zone served to anchor Hollywood transculturalism, although the mysterious danger of Asia signified what Homay King calls an "enigmatic indecipherability" that threatened the limits of Hollywood modernity.[30] Hollywood's early Indological fascination was part of a broader representational logic through which American "envisioned" Asia.[31]

At its inception, Hollywood invested in strategies of meaning-making that constructed India as a mysterious backdrop to exoticism and a place of mystery (see fig. 1.4). Representations of India helped propagate an iconography of exoticism that oriented Hollywood in particular directions. As Sara Ahmed notes, the question of orientation is always "a matter of residing in space," a desiring directionality that locates a body in space as well as the possibilities of its extension to other spaces.[32] Following this idea, it is clear that at the same time that India represented the power of Hollywood to bring a distant and exotic land close to home, it also framed the spatial limits to Hollywood's ambition. This spatialization—the ways that industries "take place" in spatial configurations—informs my second usage of the term "orienting."

India played multiple roles in this spatial orientation of Hollywood. For as central as India was to signifying Hollywood orientalism, South Asia marked the edge of American cinema's material circulation, as used film prints entered South Asia marked by the passage of transit through more lucrative international markets in Europe. In addition, India emerged as a kind of translation point between Orient and Occident. As early American film companies sent cameramen on globetrotting tours to gather footage for the popular scenic shorts of the time, India featured prominently as a stopover between China and the Middle East.

What the flashlight revealed.

Figure 1.4. "What the flashlight revealed"—American cinema casts a light on Indian debauchery. Here, Roscoe Harding photographs the Indian prince's harem, revealing the abducted, plaintive English girl in the background. Still and caption from *Motography*'s review of Selig's two-reel *The Flashlight*, released in 1915. John C. Garret, "The Flashlight," *Motography*, November 6, 1915, 970.

Since it was neither Near- nor Far-, and somewhat distinct from the Middle-, India was ideally positioned as entry point into the East. This bolstered Hollywood's own sense of spatial self-imagination. Decades before the Institute of Pacific Relations declared Hollywood "as close to Asia as it is to Europe,"[33] the American film industry thought of itself as the Archimedean point between East and West. In its capacity to represent the distant at home, Hollywood's imagination of India helped to coordinate this fictional centrality. Yet India's role in spatializing American cinema reflected not only Hollywood's journey eastward—from the beginning of Hollywood, in fact, India served as a way to orient the Orient.

Historically, India named a kind of limit to Hollywood. On the one hand, Hollywood's early popularity in the subcontinent confirmed its universality. On the other hand, the challenges Hollywood faced after the introduction of sound cinema in India illustrated its linguistic provinciality. Beginning in late 1910s, India shifted from subject and style to a possibly lucrative market for the American industry. India was critical to the orientation of Hollywood at the dawn of a cinematic century marked by the successes and failures of inter-industry encounter.

While global Hollywood's domination is often likened to an imperial regime, it is clear that Hollywood's dominion in India was precarious after the 1920s. There is little sense to the notion of a "Hollywood raj" in India. Indeed, if economic domination is one of the key measures of global Hollywood, then India has been something of a sticking point in Hollywood's hegemony. In other words, while global Hollywood is commonly seen as the epitome of cultural imperialism, its historically lackluster market impact in India is proof—as many accounts show— that the empire can indeed strike back. This rhetoric of insurgency is exemplified by a number of contemporary comparisons and is another way to "orient" Hollywood. For example, Kaushik Bhaumik notes that, "from very early times, the crucial factor connecting Bombay and Los Angeles is a contested relationship between subaltern and hegemon."[34] Similarly, Heather Tyrell claims that "the reasons for Bollywood's resistance to colonization by Hollywood are aesthetic and cultural as well as political."[35] Lalitha Gopalan observes that the playful jabs taken at *Jurassic Park* (1993) and *Titanic* (1997) in recent Hindi and Tamil cinema "confidently acknowledge that Indian cinema audiences belong to the same virtual global economy where films from different production sites exist at the *same level*—a democratization of global cinephilia."[36] Echoing this logic, the editors of a recent Indian media anthology claim that "if Hollywood represents the homogenizing effect of American capitalism in global cultures, a study of Bollywood allows a unique opportunity to map the contrasting move of globalization in popular culture."[37] Assessing the international impact of India media poses the opposite argument, evidenced by *Newsweek*'s claims that "globalization isn't merely another word for Americanization—and the recent expansion of the Indian entertainment and film industry proves it."[38] However, while inverting its directionality, these assessments retain domination as a characteristic theme in Hollywood–Bombay relations.[39]

As I noted above, Hollywood has also been energized by more contemporary reorientation—the Indian economic "miracle" of the past twenty years. The global economic expansion of the 1990s was fueled, in part, by the rise of "emerging markets" in Brazil, Russia, India, China, and South Africa. The economic growth of these BRICS nations represented twenty years of liberalization and privatization. India, in particular, was thought to have shrugged off the derisory label of the "Hindu rate of growth." While world media routinely ignored significant deprivation and crisis, particularly in the agricultural sector, Indian corporate growth was lauded as second only to China. State support and sanction for Bombay media's corporatization initiatives attempted to capitalize on the information sector's explosive growth in the period following liberalization.[40] Celebrations of this success enabled the global projection of India in events like Delhi's hosting of the 2010 Commonwealth Games, which, like the Olympics in Tokyo in 1964, Seoul's 1988 Olympics, and the 2008 Beijing Olympics, was designed to showcase Asian modernity on a world stage. Exemplifying India's prominence at an address to the Indian parliament, Barack Obama recently called the U.S.–India strategic and economic relationship "one of a defining partnerships of the 21st century."[41] India served as a fulcrum in America's "pivoting" toward Asia in global political and economic relations.

As we now know, Obama was speaking during a global recession. Initially, the global financial community thought that the Indian economy would survive the brunt of the downturn. However, international confidence in the Indian economy clearly eroded as direct foreign direct investment (FDI) fell by more than 30 percent in 2010, to US$24 billion.

The FDI crisis is just the tip of the iceberg. Coming to a consensus, the world press has replaced once-breathless stories of India "shining" with the view that India is sinking. The international investment community cites a litany of Indian financial woes: uncertainty about tax laws; overly complex licensing procedures; rising inflation; higher lending rates; intractable corruption; protectionism; insecurity about intellectual property protection (particularly patents, but also copyright); weak infrastructure; a slowdown in industrial production; plummeting currency rates; a real estate downturn; and an expanding trade deficit.[42] International skepticism about India's economic future continued to grow through 2011, though India eased foreign ownership rules on international retailers, opening the door to a greater Wal-Mart presence in India (later reversed when members of the governing coalition threatened to revolt). Nevertheless, once common bullish long-term forecasts of double-digit growth now claim a more modest 6 percent. Any idea that India might be the new Europe is now a prognostication of economic gloom rather than a signal of booming times ahead. The steady depletion of confidence in what Gurcharan Das once called "the India story" has created confusion about what direction the state and capital should take.[43] Indian finance authorities vacillate between continued liberalization that might foster international investment or increasing protectionist measures to help raise revenues and nibble away at the deficit. While the troubling election of a new right-wing government in 2014 has generated renewed international faith in Indian macroeconomic conditions, there is still the prevailing sense that the boom times may be a thing of the past.

However, the exhausted narrative of the Indian economic "miracle" presents another opportunity for a reorientation of media industry relations. While economic interdependency is critical to the proximity between industries, can't we consider what *other* forms of contact are available? If contemporary events have exposed the endemic nature of economic precarity, perhaps we can reject the monopoly of financially driven comparison and look instead at multiple frames of relationality between media industries. One benefit of the economic crash is that scholars can take a breather from accounts of economic magnitude, but this means changing entrenched conventions of industry comparison.

Developing economic alignments dominates industry talk about finance, but it also suffuses academic methodologies. After all, despite the rhetoric and texture of media encounter, straightforward economic magnitude is central to descriptions of screen transit, with legitimacy granted to those accounts that demonstrate definitive, measurable, and spectacular market impact. For example, in his study of the international development of film industries before World War II, Gerben Bakker excludes Japanese, Indian, and Hong Kong industries on the grounds that "since 1945 they have become quite successful relative to Europe, but before that they were internationally insignificant."[44] Similarly, Manuel Castells suggests that the Indian film industries have "evolved largely independently from the global network of media networks," and only now, because of state and market subsidy, are more enumerated "structures of collaboration" between Indian and American media industries proliferating.[45] To follow Bakker's rationalization, we needn't be interested in Hollywood in India, which, in the mid-1990s, made about as much money as it did in Israel and less than it did in Poland. To follow Castells, we needn't look at Hollywood in India outside the high-profile corporatization of Bollywood made possible by the economic liberalization of the early 1990s. For all their analytical clarity, such approaches run the risk of missing the more ephemeral, less enumerated points of contact that seep into and slip beyond official histories and formal political economies.

Orienting Hollywood proposes to disrupt the conventional geometry of media industry comparison, constructing epistemologies of relation that recognize but also challenge the conventions of economic interaction. In calling for a more textured type of media comparison, I want to look across geographic zones of media circulation, but I also want to excavate the forms of contrast invoked in histories of encounter. This dynamic comparativism has methodological and conceptual consequences. A spatiotemporal approach recognizes that comparison not only maps the encounters between industries, but also frames how "industry" is defined. A critical approach that attempts to deepen and broaden logics of connection must recognize that comparisons have complex legacies and politics. Retaining the efficacy of comparison as a critical force requires the appreciation of its analytical, figurative, and historical nature. Such a critical approach also requires an acknowledgment of the limits of comparison as method and practice.

To Affinity (and Beyond!): Media Industries in Comparison

Central to both empirical and interpretive work, comparison is a widely used type of scholarly analysis, informing methodology, theory, and practice in the humanities and social sciences. As a gauge of measurement in both quantitative and qualitative methods, comparison regularizes difference within standard frameworks—in other words, comparison is a form of framing. This suggests stasis, but comparative methods are also dynamic because they organize claims and engage contrasts. At the same time, comparison tends toward objectification by formalizing phenomena in the process of analysis, creating trajectories of proximity and distance, networks of affinity and dissimilarity, and taxonomies of features both shared and exceptional. But comparison is also a tremendously broad enterprise. Susan Friedman has usefully described a number of imperatives to comparison, from the cognitive (comparison is integral to analogical and figural thinking) to the sociocultural (comparison is a way of organizing human behavior and social relations) and the ethicopolitical (comparison can either revivify or reject the "romance" of the universal and the singular).[46]

Interdisciplinary work means thinking critically about comparison, engaging the multiple dimensions of comparativity produced across disciplinary cultures. This means understanding comparison as a kind of "traveling concept," Mieke Bal's term for the movement of meanings between disciplines, scholars, and histories, with "processes of differing assessed before, during, and after each 'trip.'"[47] Thinking archeologically about media, for example, Katherine Hayles suggests that a comparative media studies can provide a "rubric" for the study of print and digital productions in a way that is historical, formal, procedural, and material. Multiplying approaches to and theories about media transition can help ward off teleologies of technological development.[48] In a more sociological vein, Daniel Hallin and Paulo Mancini suggest that a comparative approach to media demystifies assumptions about the universality of media practices while making possible certain structural similarities that link media systems to one another.[49] The focus here is on the generation of concepts and theories through "ideal types," those necessarily abstract "concepts and generalized uniformities of empirical process."[50] Both the genealogical and sociological approaches to comparative media represented by Hayles, Hallin, and Mancini are united by a project of clarification, yet they preserve Bal's possibilities for more experimental and speculative forms of comparison. Capturing the contradictions of comparison with a focus on media structures, Sonia Livingstone declares that the comparative study of cross-national media industries is both an "apparent impossibility and an urgent necessity."[51]

Yet, comparison, like familiarity, can also breed contempt, especially when you consider its history of institutionalization. Postwar intellectual formations like area studies used comparison to justify Cold War mentalities, focusing on the regional and the national as a geopolitical unit.[52] The institutionalization of comparison in modernization theory forged a policy alignment between university and state interests. Comparison's role in this disciplinary history was to frame the national as an index of psychological, social, and cultural disposition. In this way, the national was a "modular" form, capable of registering difference through a common discourse.[53] Modernization theory activated such national distinctions to organize media industries in hierarchies according to their development. Even in oppositional disciplinary cultures like political economy, which seek to address structural inequality and the management and redistribution of resources, the national serves as a site to amass data and situate power. Approaching media industries in terms of national aggregation can lead to accounts of straightforward economic magnitude that overshadow the complexities of screen transit described above.

Yet the national remains an important force for engaging with the spatial and temporal practices that organize media industries. Sanctioned by state and market bureaucracies, media industries are implicated in the processes of national legitimation in the domain of law (through intellectual property, authorship, and domicile), in the routines of cultural work (through labor laws and censorship), and by enacting exclusivity in the field of cultural policy (through quotas, import restrictions, spectrum allocation, and communications infrastructures). Intersecting these institutional itineraries is a more experimental dimension or sense of culture, where the national delimits an archive of vernacular forms linked by custom, habitation, and language that can transcend territorial limitations and create new forms of collectivity and practice. Taken together, the notional concepts of the national as a common frame of reference for cultural belief/action and the notational concepts of nation as a marker of attribution and circulation have created a powerful incentive for media industries to continue to "think nationally" even in a globally dispersed field of cultural production.[54]

In media industries scholarship, the national is a dynamic frame of comparison that assembles and focuses modes of coherence and dispersion. On the one hand, the national in media industries discourse refers to a set of representational practices produced under a centripetal logic of "local" coherence—in terms of authorship, location, audience, narrative, genre, and style—and a set of institutional practices through which the state exercises a mandate of preservation against the tide of the foreign—in terms of subsidies for film production, quotas, and other import restrictions. On the other hand, national media refers to a set of relationships produced through a centrifugal logic that prioritizes dispersion over cohesion, whereby movements like Mexican cinema and New German cinema are validated as national expressions not because of their exclusivity but through their international circulation and relations with other industries.[55]

These complex modes of inclusion and exclusion are assembled under the sign of national distinction in the media industries, and not always according to the same logic. For example, for decades the Indian government engaged with the film industry as a revenue source (via taxes) or a source of moral decay (via censorship). Hollywood played a critical role in the imagination of national transformation, as Indian economic liberalization encouraged the proliferation of institutional contact between Bombay cinema and Hollywood. The government's desire to more fully recognize the industrial legitimacy of the film sector can be seen in the economic "reforms" of the late 1980s, part of a wave of broader global transformations between the state, capital, and media. For example, in the 1980s, the South Korean government implemented economic reforms to position media production as a national strategic resource in the global market.[56] Unlike in India, this strategy was a deliberate response to Hollywood's dominance in Korea, enabled by the direct distribution of Hollywood films to local theaters in Korea beginning in the late 1980s.

In another example of the complex deployments of the national, anthropologist William Mazzarella details the rise of mass consumerism in India since the mid-1980s. As Mazzarella argues, this consumer shift marks a fundamental transformation of the older logic of developmentalist self-sufficiency, represented most strongly in India's import-substitution initiatives during the 1970s. Mazzarella notes that the liberalization of Indian consumer markets and the influx of foreign brands in the past three decades have completely reorganized the infrastructure of Indian marketing. One of the most unexpected outcomes of the post-developmental aspirational allure of a "consumption-led path to national prosperity," Mazzarella insists, is the connection of Indian self-sufficiency *with* the recruitment of foreign investment.[57] In other words, within the logic of globalization, the *foreign* can function as a signifier of the national where it once might have functioned as its antithesis.

Clearly, the national is a complex register of comparison, requiring careful deployment as an analytic. It can serve as a vital and energetic way to study media industries in global and local contexts, but not at the expense of other frames of reference. Tracing the material itineraries of commodity transit does not always map onto preexisting national configurations—there are many places where, as Eric Cazdyn puts it, "film and the nation fly away from their fixed borders."[58] For those of us interested in working on media industries, our task is not simply to refuse the national as a ready index of comparison, but to compare differently: to figure a politics and practice of relation that is transformative as well as taxonomic.

In *Asia as Method*, the critical scholar of East Asian history and cultural studies Kuan-Hsing Chen calls for a form of scholarship that refuses a central, ideal reference point around which to structure comparison. He suggests an "inter-referencing strategy" as a response to classic foundational strategies of comparison, one that multiplies frames of reference. His framing of the "West" is especially useful:

> Rather than continuing to fear reproducing the West as the Other, and hence avoiding the question all together, an alternative discursive strategy posits the West as bits and fragments that intervene in local social formations in a systematic, but never totalizing way. The local formulation of modernity carries important elements of the West, but it is not full enveloped by it. Once recognizing the West as fragments internal to the local, we no longer consider it as an opposing entity but rather as one cultural resource among many others. Such a position avoids either a resentful or triumphalist relation with the West because it is not bound by an obsessive antagonism.[59]

In this way, we might gesture beyond comparison to what Rey Chow calls "entanglement," an analysis of encounters figured "through disparity rather than equivalence." By disrupting tidy classifications, entanglements signal a "derangement in the organization of knowledge caused by unprecedented adjacency and comparability or parity."[60] Entanglement may be a form of comparison appropriate to the task of demonstrating that Bombay and Hollywood media histories are disjunct, adjacent, and intertwined.[61]

These entanglements are scattered across inter-industry relations over the last century of encounter between Hollywood and India. For example, as early as the 1930s, Hollywood's local agents worked with regional and central film industry organizations in India to lobby the British colonial government to reduce import duties on film stock and equipment and to decrease entertainment taxes. Three decades later, the Commissioner of Entertainment Tax in Uttar Pradesh put forward a plan to establish a "raw film" stock industry in UP, with investment from Kodak and Hollywood distributors in Bombay.[62] Also in the 1960s, at a time when Indian revenue was minimal for global Hollywood, the Motion Picture Export Association claimed that American cinema performed "an invaluable service in supplying entertainment to professional men and their families and civil servants." American cinema was deemed critical in India, especially "to the large body of high school and college students, who [relied] on English language films to sharpen their conversational skills in that tongue."[63] And in the early 1970s, the Indian government linked American imports to a reciprocal arrangement sponsoring the commercial exhibition of Indian films in the United States. Two decades later, in the 1990s, reciprocity framed American and Indian cinema working together to secure common copyright interests.

The challenge for a comparative study is to systematize these encounters yet stay attuned to the particularity of interaction. Any narrative of inter-industry engagement must account for ruptures and breaks as well as continuities across a shared history. We must also avoid flattening encounter into symmetrical engagements, as if relations are always configured according to equal stakes. This means paying attention to the different cultural forms that organize media industries in distinct ways.[64] At the same time, we must understand industry interactions in terms of the "occasions" for which they are oriented and intended.[65] In addition to this "occasionality," we might also—to follow Rita Felski and Susan Friedman's formulation—engage media industries as "*agents* as well as *objects* of comparison."[66]

Of course, both Bombay cinema and Hollywood have rich and widely documented histories. As yet, however, there has not been a full-length work that looks at how these histories are entangled, considering the partial and strategic alignments between industries as well as minor alignments and fleeting moments of mutual interest. In highlighting industries in transit and in contact, *Orienting Hollywood* elucidates how media artifacts are distributed across multiple trajectories, territories, and histories of exchange. At the heart of this inquiry is a central question—what were the close encounters that drew Hollywood into

Bombay media ecologies, establishing mutually contaminating points of contact?

Encounter is the primary theme of this study and comparison its primary method. *Orienting Hollywood* deploys archival research, interviews, political economy, discourse, and textual analysis not only to document encounter but also to show how it was staged and imagined. Evidence is taken from a wide array of materials ranging from the archive to the screen: policy documents, industry sources, interviews, reports, memos, and other ephemera, fan letters, the trade press and popular journalism, and of course the films themselves. In terms of methodology, this book works toward disarticulating the classic text–industry–audience triad that has structured much media studies inquiry. Along with its privileged objects, this analytic prescribes countervailing disciplinary priorities: textual analysis is suited to the task of exegesis; political economy articulates industry to the national and global; and ethnography opens up diverse occasions of viewing and forms of belonging. *Orienting Hollywood* insinuates itself in the fissures between these disciplinary approaches.

The chapters in *Orienting Hollywood* are somewhat loosely organized, but they cohere around the theme of Hollywood–Bombay relations. Such a "thematic orbit" of rather loosely interconnected chapters makes possible a number of forms of inquiry:[67] to document the history of influence, to trace the nature of interoperability, and to thematize the character of interaction. Employing a comparative framework, and proceeding in thematic rather than chronological fashion, each chapter in this book is organized around three or four case studies. This itinerary follows a historiography that Kent Ono has called *retracing*, "an attempt to read the historical as part of the contemporary, next to the contemporary, within the contemporary, and by the contemporary."[68]

Chapter 1, "Framing the Copy: Media Industries and the Poetics of Resemblance," shows how the dynamic of copying framed relations between the two media industries. In this chapter, I argue that the historical relations between Hollywood and Bombay cinema can be traced through the problematic of the copy. Moving through a variety of examples across a hundred years of industrial interconnection, I show how the copy institutes the work of analogy between Bombay and Hollywood, creating frameworks of comprehension and comparison between them. This chapter's critical, analytical, and historical imperative is motivated by the idea that the copy not only produces similarity between the industries—that seems obvious—but that the copy is capable of signifying difference and distinction as well.

Although the copy frames the comparison of media industries, it does not flatten out asymmetries between them. In fact, the copy attests to the fundamental inequalities of comparison, the political and cultural struggles over the meaning of innovation and influence in the global media. Mapping a trajectory that is both historical and spatial, this chapter frames copying by investigating the economic, cultural, and institutional arenas in which the work of analogy takes place. I begin with those rules of geopolitical transformation that try to institutionalize imitation in ways that preserve structural domination between the West and the Rest. I then focus on intellectual property as a specific manifestation of this institutional logic of imitation to show how copy practice in the historical formation of Bombay cinema became a problem for Hollywood. I end with a close analysis of contemporary Bollywood remake culture, demonstrating how the copy is evoked as a way to draw distinctions between the global media industries. Throughout this chapter, I try to complicate the easy historicism that places one industry as "less developed" than another, as if there was a singular trajectory of/called "progress" along which industries are thought to develop from the cottage to the globe.

Chapter 2, "Managing Exchange: Geographies of Finance in the Media Industries," examines the spatial distribution of filmmaking regimes between Bombay and Hollywood, focusing on the ways in which money and investment possibilities manage the exchange between the film industries. This chapter takes on a number of interrelated case studies in the transnational geography of finance: repatriation, coproduction, and outsourcing. Focusing on key moments in the history of Indo-American media relations from the 1920s to the present, these case studies form a triptych around the figure of exchange. After I describing the Indian conglomerate Reliance's investment in American studio DreamWorks, demonstrating how Hollywood has moved from creditor to debtor in a century of inter-industry encounter, I shift away from the high-profile, slick rhetoric of global media investment toward the granularity of financial exchange. This first section focuses on the 1950s and 1960s, as Hollywood profits were "blocked" in India and American studios looked for ways to first repatriate, then expend their money. Complicating the smooth, invisible exchange presumed by statistics and industry data, this section shifts the rational discourse of numbers toward the messy materiality of exchange between media industries, "reembodying" money as an actual transaction. The second section looks at the history of Hollywood's Hindi productions in India. I begin with an appraisal of Hollywood's early engagement with Indian locations as a geographic index. This engagement combined fiction with reality, with screen representations of India produced through travelogues and the fabrication of American scenarists. The imagination of India played a critical role in the worlding of Hollywood space and place.

The shift to India as an actual production location, after some fitful attempts in previous decades, took off in earnest in the mid-2000s, with a number of Hollywood studios committing to "local language" production. In this section, I trace the production and reception of two failed Hollywood coproductions—*Saawariya* (Sony, 2007) and *Chandni Chowk to China* (Warner Brothers, 2009)—to indicate the limits of crossover productions. The cultural anxieties of coproduction are most clearly exemplified in the national and ethnic attribution of labor in contemporary outsourcing discourse and practice, which serves as the subject of my third case study. The structural transformation of cultural labor and new technologies of remote management, both made possible by a neoliberal alignment of government and industry, institutionalize older labor prejudices even as they disaggregate discrete spheres of cultural production. This section traces the cultural politics engaged by India's location as Hollywood's virtual workshop.

My third chapter, "The Theater of Influence: Reimagining Indian Film Exhibition," focuses on the rise of the multiplex theater in India over the past fifteen years, as it transformed the economies of scale in film production and distribution. The multiplex is the primary point of entry not only for new film genres and foreign cinema, but also for the new economic cultures of corporatization and multinational investment in the Indian film industries. This chapter analyzes the cultural politics of the new Indian movie theater and its iconic display of modular forms of consumer mobility. Designed to offer a premium service built around the coordinated release of high-budget domestic and foreign features in major urban centers, multiplex theater construction in India arose alongside the reconsideration of urban space in the national imaginary. Yet, as I show in this chapter, the multiplex is a relatively recent manifestation of theatrical innovation in India, a transformation in which Hollywood has played a critical role.

In the first section of this chapter, I trace the history of American influence on the reorganization of the built environment and in the architectural imaginary of exhibition. Hollywood has long been interested in establishing Indian theater chains as a way to enhance the distribution of American cinema. This history of American influence on India's exhibition infrastructure is bookended by two key failures: first, Universal's unsuccessful bid for Madan Theatres in the 1920s; and then, seventy years later, the failed attempt of Warner Brothers to build a multiplex chain in Maharashtra in the mid-1990s. The second section of this chapter places the Indian multiplex within a broader retail imaginary in India. The Indian government once gave relatively low priority to cinema construction, focusing sparse steel and concrete resources to projects more amenable to developmental modernity like dams, roads, bridges, and other material infrastructures. Now, however, nationwide investment in the retail sector places the multiplex alongside the shopping mall in a new disciplining of the consumer. In this section, I locate the Indian multiplex within a network of public amusements that produces forms of elite urban sociability. Collapsing the space of the mall and the multiplex marks a certain entry point "into" the West; defined by the architectonics of consumer mobility, these places are also gateways into the globalization of Indian life. In the third section of this chapter, I focus on the capital city Delhi's Chanakya movie hall, a modernist landmark and iconic theater for Hollywood in India that was recently razed to make way for a new multiplex theater. That a beacon of architectural modernism was itself subject to the logic of modernization attests to the rapaciousness of urban development in the postcolonial city. Chanakya's demolition and the protests that surrounded it engage the ironies of progress that suffuse the multiplex era.

Chapter 4, "Economies of Devotion: Affective Engagement and the Subject(s) of Labor," focuses on the routes and routines of working bodies in transnational screen culture. Drawing the historical into contemporary practice, I attend to the question of how subjectivity and labor—marked by racial, religious, class, and national difference—become implicated in various itineraries of contact between Bombay and Hollywood. My interest here is in both the formalized trajectories through which labor travels and the more extemporaneous processes that distribute the activity of real and represented bodies in the social worlds of work. In this chapter, I show how the production of cross-cultural intimacy is inscribed in industry exchange, creating forms of affinity tied to the circulation of laboring bodies between Hollywood and Bombay. Engaging these bodies—across different histories and scales of movement—can illuminate they ways in which media work is materially, socially, and culturally organized. Here I focus on the cultural politics of "traveling" bodies, detailing how categories of difference are inscribed within an "affect economy" of transnational media industries.[69] The connections made by stars, fans, and industry representatives between Hollywood and Bombay cinema maps the distribution of emotional engagement across media worlds. In this way, laboring subjectivities become a key site of transcultural media encounter.

In print stories, festivals, and correspondence, expressions of devotion and religious affiliation become part of an industrial configuration in which attachment emerges as a symbolic resource. Reading the journalistic, corporate, and fan archive, this chapter considers "geographies of intimacy" across three case studies in the history of Bombay and Hollywood encounter.[70] The first two case studies show how interpersonal encounters signify industry relations through different travel narratives. The first case study addresses the promotional discourse of celebrity tourism that construes labor as leisure, garnering starstruck press and popular devotion. I show how the common discourse of Hollywood star travelogues depends on tropes of comparison, particularly those predicated on a kind of racialized Otherness. My second case study looks at letters and other forms of correspondence that cast American and Indian media relations in more informal and personal terms. As a frame for inter-industry relations, epistolary communication capitalizes on the "affective economies" of attachment.[71] The third and most extensive case study engages devotion in a more historical register, focusing on the popular characterization of Indian film work as "Hindu" at the same time that religious caste was used to characterize tensions between labor and management in interwar Hollywood. This parallel trajectory of appropriation enables a historical comparison between the social worlds of Indian and American labor, even as anti-Asian nativist anxieties came to the fore before and after the formation of Hollywood. Taken together, these case studies highlight the affective charge of interaction, showing how intersubjective intensities of contact are mobilized in the intimacy of encounter between media industries.

In the concluding chapter, "Close Encounters of the Industrial Kind," I offer a final engagement with Hollywood–Bombay cinema relations in order to illustrate the historical complexity of circulation. I show how a single film distributes a plurality of objects, agents, meanings, sites of reception and distribution, and point out those places where media industries are made and engaged in historical and contemporary contexts. In showing how Hollywood and Bombay cinema drift and are taken up in different places and times, my intention is to frame media industries not only as preexisting administrative systems but as textual, institutional, and creative arrangements. This more textured, nuanced understanding of industry allows for the thickening of connections between Hollywood and Bombay within the transit of historical encounter—and that, in short, is what this book is all about.

1

Framing the Copy

Media Industries and the Poetics of Resemblance

An Indian approach to filmmaking, which by the very fact
of its being Indian acquires a universal significance, is what
is required. Imitation may be our sincerest form of flatter-
ing Hollywood, but it is no key to unlock any of the non-
traditional markets for our films. We have long suffered
India through Hollywood's eyes; let us at least use our own.
A camera is nothing without a conscience.
"Market in America?" *Filmfare*, November 27, 1964

As I noted in the introduction, contemporary media discourse imagines
Hollywood and Bombay cinema in a dance of difference and similarity: in one moment, facing each other as opposites; in another, joined
in partnership. Bombay cinema is often described in terms of excess,
chaos, prolixity, and national particularity, while Hollywood is defined
by efficiency, transparency, economy, and global universality.

In this chapter, I engage these dynamics of contrast and identity
to reimagine the historical relations between Hollywood and Bombay cinema. My focus here is the copy, which I understand as ideology, analytic, practice, and artifact. As an extended meditation on the
copy—conceived traditionally as forgery—this chapter troubles the
master narrative of originality as the conventional standard of cultural
value. Addressing the problematic of the copy highlights the persistence
of the structuring binaries—original/counterfeit, reality/mimesis, truth/
artifice—that inform the comparative evaluation of film industries.

Beyond simple imitation, copying signifies that which is transformative, dynamic, and emergent. Moving through a series of case studies
across a century of industrial interconnection, I show how the copy
conceptualizes the work of analogy between Bombay and Hollywood,

creating frameworks of comprehension and comparison between them. Not only does the copy produce similarity between the industries—that seems obvious—but the figurative analogue also signifies distinctiveness.

Copying is often associated with Bombay cinema, whose common reference as "Bollywood" seems inevitable. With Bollywood linked to imitation, inspiration, and translation, Hollywood appears in relief as the standard bearer of originality. Piracy kills Hollywood yet makes Bollywood possible, or so the script of innumerable headlines goes. Hollywood is innovative and authentic, while Bollywood is derivative and fake. Moreover, with the legislative prominence of "intellectual property," piracy now saturates the discourse of the copy. The overwhelming statutory focus on piracy sensationalizes its market impact, demonizes media practitioners as thieves and terrorists, and instrumentalizes what Lawrence Liang calls the "porous legality" of commodity life in the Indian mediaspace.[1]

This chapter insists that we venture beyond the legal justification of copyright not simply to mount a defense of media piracy as has been done elsewhere,[2] but to pluralize the copy across a broader domain. Despite its dominance as metaphor, piracy does not encapsulate the array of practices and meanings associated with copying. The copy resonates far beyond the register of media piracy.

Appreciating how the copy "frames" the interactions between Bombay cinema and Hollywood means paying attention to the boundaries of constraint and possibility mobilized through media industry practice. My use of "framing" performs multiple functions here. Framing refers to the structuring yet largely unseen ways through which the copy enacts the relationship of one media industry to another.[3] Framing also refers to how the copy has been indicted by the spectacularly criminalized discourses of piracy.[4]

Although the copy frames comparison between media industries, it does not flatten out the asymmetries between them. In fact, the copy attests to the fundamental inequalities of comparison and the struggles over the meaning of influence in the global media. Mapping a trajectory that is both historical and spatial, this chapter investigates a number of arenas in which the work of analogy takes place. I begin by outlining the geopolitical transformations that institutionalized imitation in order to preserve structural domination between the West and "the Rest." I then focus on intellectual property as a specific manifestation of this institutional logic of imitation to show how copying in the historical formation of Bombay cinema became a problem for Hollywood. I end with a close analysis of contemporary Bollywood remake culture, which demonstrates how the copy is evoked as a way to draw distinctions between the global media industries.

While it is often cast as the underside of industrial relations, the copy is critical to transformation in cultural practice. In investigating the material, symbolic, and discursive flows between Hollywood and Bombay, this chapter offers ways to interpret the copy as well as account for its emergence as a key paradigm of comparison in the media industries.

Imitation, Development, and the National

In a 1941 polemic against wartime isolationism, publisher Henry Luce argued for the United States to become "the powerhouse from which ideals spread throughout the world and do their mysterious work of lifting the life of mankind from the level of the beasts."[5] The agencies charged with exercising this mysterious progressive force were to be assembled in the decades to come. The doctrine of "development" served as the ideological core of Luce's upgraded vision of manifest destiny.

Development was the outcome of economic trajectories beginning in the fifteenth century, as European territorial expansion created networks of center–periphery relationships to be fully exploited as colonialism advanced.[6] Five centuries later, colonialism was recast with a more benevolent face. Twentieth-century development promised the alleviation of poverty, the promotion of literacy, and the betterment of public health, all implemented through the state's massive investment in infrastructure. Development came to embody the very essence of social transformation, exiling imaginations of other possible futures to the periphery.[7] From dream to partial reality to nightmare, the itinerary of modern development was enabled by a catastrophic alignment between militarist geopolitics, trade liberalization, and the rapacious extraction of human and nonhuman resources.

Development is driven by two core beliefs: first, that there are predictable paths to and through the modern; and second, that the national is a sufficiently modular form of difference to serve as a placeholder in modernity's evolutionary queue. These beliefs also enabled modernization theory and the other functionalist orthodoxies that formed the dominant intellectual justification for area studies beginning in the 1940s. These intellectual movements, holding sway over decades of economic and social policy, understood the national as a distinctive organic totality, where "modern" nations were simply more advanced than "traditional" ones. This conception of the national was central to the missions of American foundations like Ford, Rockefeller, and others. These agencies offered Western support for nationalist elites to implement state media monopolies in the Global South.

In this way, development helped to secure the geopolitical alignment between intellectual movements, foundations, markets, and governments. What could serve as the motive energy of development, propelling Henry Luce's mysterious force of progress? The answer, according to some American theorists of media development, was to institutionalize copying in the broadest possible way. In the Indian case, the developmental role of imitation was best exemplified in Daniel Lerner's speech at the new Indian Institute for Mass Communications (IIMC) in 1968, which insisted that modernization could be achieved if the newly developing nations imitated the West.

The IIMC's infrastructure had been put in place some years before, in consultation with the Ford Foundation and the communications theorist Wilbur Schramm, both key figures in the institutionalization of socioeconomic development through the media. In his 1968 speech celebrating the opening of the IIMC, Lerner encapsulated the affirmative spirit of developmental imitation, noting that the Western professional communicator conveys to "a large audience of people . . . a picture of their own future."[8] This mimetic formulation was represented on the small and the big screen alike.

By the time that the National Aeronautics and Space Administration and other American agencies were helping to advance Indian electronic technology in the early 1970s, particularly the creation of a satellite television network, Hollywood had long embodied the developmental standard for the Indian media industries.[9] "What Hollywood does today, the world does tomorrow," noted E. P. Menon in 1938, on the occasion of the twenty-fifth anniversary of the "founding" of the Indian film industry.[10]

As Hollywood closes in on its first hundred years in India, this aspirational function has evolved. Hollywood functions "as a crucial marker of film form" and "the locus of both envy and resentment" in setting the Indian film industries' standards for technical and promotional sophistication.[11] In addition, Hollywood often serves as the benchmark, with India getting the short end of the comparison. For example, in the 1930s one commentator noted that "India has four hundred movie houses only, compared with 20,500 of U.S.A., with one-third the population."[12] After independence, the Indian film industry's underdevelopment in comparison with Hollywood was seen as a consequence of its emergent status. As William Allen put it in 1950, India's geographically disparate film institutions and looser labor obligations were "an obviously unsound but natural state of affairs in a new and rapidly changing civilization."[13] These developmental frameworks demonstrate that Hollywood has furnished the imagination of media modernity, defining the path along which all other cinemas must necessarily travel. For India, Hollywood historically represented both a culture of aspiration and one of anticipation. The imitative logic of development situates Bombay cinema somewhere between a *not-quite* and a *not-yet* Hollywood.[14]

Relatively marginal support from Indian state and market institutions undermined the relationship between cinema and indigenous development. After independence in 1947, the Indian state's commitment to rapid modernization focused on nationalizing banking, transportation, postal, telecommunication, and electronic sectors.[15] Cinema was not included among the key projects of Indian developmental modernity. However, it did serve as a vehicle for social reformers who understood it as indecent, akin to gambling and prostitution, in need of regulation through taxation and censorship.[16] Beginning in the 1950s, the alignment between the regulation of screen consumption and the management of civic virtue underscored the creation of import/export councils, development corporations, and inquiry committees that allowed the state to function as both "patron and disciplinarian" for the Indian film industries.[17]

During this national transition, Hollywood served a critical role in marshaling arguments for greater Indian film industry subsidy.[18] These arguments hinged on Hollywood's centrality to American economic power and insisted on following a similar model in India. For example, a 1939 pamphlet titled *The Place of Film in National Planning*, written by K. S. Hirlekar, a key figure in the early institutional organization of Indian film industries, argued that film "is playing an important role in the progress of all advanced nations of the world," and that the neglect of cinema by central and provincial Indian governments demonstrates that they have "not fully realized the tremendous latent power . . . of film in educating the masses, especially the illiterates, for individual and national advancement."[19] A few years later, as secretary to an Indian delegation on a study tour of American and British studios in 1945, Hirlekar noted the importance of the film industries to domestic economies, claiming that "it is urgently necessary that an organized and centralized effort must be made to put the film industry in this country . . . on a stable and progressive foundation," and that "it is the State, and the State alone which can take the lead in supplying the finance for its organized and well-thought-out development."[20]

On the other hand, K. A. Abbas's long experience with political progressivism allowed for a recognition of the animating contradictions of an imitation-led development. Speaking at a symposium on development and cinema organized by the IIMC, the famed writer and director rejected the need for the Indian film industries to "improve" by investing in imported technology. Rather than place Indian cinema in a position of inferiority to Hollywood—the classic position of the developmental paradigm—Abbas activated the strategic possibilities of an indigenous cultural sovereignty, resignifying the "primitivism" vilified by development as a form of cultural value.

Echoing Julio García Espinosa's call for a revolutionary "imperfect cinema," Abbas saw material and technological scarcity as a cultural resource.[21] "'Resources'—hardware like studios, cameras, lighting equipment, sound-recording apparatus," argued Abbas, "may be imported (if not indigenously produced) . . . but 'Creativity' which is much more important, indeed it is the *sine qua non* of film production—cannot be imported or taken on loan."[22] Abbas's suggestion that indigenous artistic development was directly linked to industrial deprivation inverts the logic of development without completely rejecting it. Reiterating *Swadeshi* (national self-sufficiency) as well as import-substitution industrialization's claims on national aesthetic innovation, Abbas continued: "Many countries of the world, big and small, which went through revolutions, had to start (or resume) the activity of cinema production almost from scratch . . . embargoes and political boycott, and sometimes economic consideration of saving on foreign exchange, made it difficult, if not impossible, to import foreign equipment and raw stock. But they made world classics with old and repaired cameras, scraps of film stock, and developed revolutionary technique."[23] From institutional imitation to a politics of deprivation, the shift in tone from Hirlekar to Abbas exemplifies Hollywood's changing role in India. Once, Hollywood may have served as an idealized model of industrial rationalization, but now Hollywood was incompatible with an aesthetic sovereignty predicated on the national. This move from epitome to antithesis shows how development and the copy stage Indian media innovation in complex ways. As a discursive arrangement, development is predicated on forms of institutional imitation that reproduce global media asymmetries. At the same time, the "emergent" economies of the Global South, whose ever-developing status is internalized as permanent subordination, become the chief drivers of innovation in a global capitalism where "the new" is both a barrier to overcome and a form of crisis intrinsic to the media industries themselves.

Intellectual property has become central to distributing imitation and innovation in these new global media formations. Releasing the emerging economy's "pent-up" entrepreneurial energy—supposedly held back by government and regulation—is the fundamental charge of neoliberal intellectual property regimes today. It is to the copy's contradictory role in the history of these regimes that we turn to next.

Hollywood and Intellectual Property in India

K. A. Abbas's rejection of aesthetic conventions in the late 1970s, detailed above, is in keeping with the mood of the times, prioritizing national self-reliance over technological fealty as a way to grow the communications industries.[24] However, in the 1980s new forms of technological imitation associated with video piracy reinvigorated the models of classic development. In this section, I examine what happens when the moral geopolitics of development, which manage social transformation through imitation, encounter the material and technological realities of the copy. While I focus on the last few decades, I also draw on a longer historical legacy of copying in the founding of First World economies. How does an ideology predicated on imitation reconcile itself with everyday practices of duplication? More to the point, how did India emerge as a central front in Hollywood's war on media piracy?

Increasingly, global Hollywood finds itself embroiled in a kind of asymmetric warfare, where the most powerful media industry in the world is stymied by micro-practices of distribution and reception. Hollywood sees piracy as an existential threat tied to the explosive alignment of new technology, home taping, and downloading, and worries that such everyday consumption practices sound the death knell of industries.[25] Entertainment firms estimate that six hundred million pirated DVDs are sold in India every year, compared with only two million legal copies.[26] Indian media also considers piracy a problem, especially since high-speed Internet penetration rates in India are growing, escalating the potential of illegal downloading.

In response to the threat of media piracy, the Motion Picture Association of America (MPAA), the trade and lobbying organization that represents the export interests of the major Hollywood studios, coordinates antipiracy operations in over eighty countries. These operations strengthen existing national copyright protections, synchronize efforts among local governments and agencies, and provide logistical, technical, and legislative support during and after litigation. International piracy, counterfeiting, and other "unauthorized expropriations" of U.S. intellectual property (IP) came to the forefront of U.S. trade policy concerns in the early 1980s once it became conventional wisdom that the future of U.S.-led global entertainment was predicated on the production, ownership, and marketing of IP-based goods and services. Hollywood's legal apparatus began to take special interest in India at this time.

A UNESCO report estimated that, by 1980, there were one million VCRs in use in India with thirty million cassettes in circulation, enabling an entire economy of pirate distribution.[27] The relaxation of VCR imports during the India-hosted 1982 Asian Games contributed to the proliferation of VCR hardware, even though various media industries threatened a boycott. B. K. Karanjia, the editor of the trade magazine *Screen*, called for the Indian government to recognize piracy as "an evil of immense magnitude" that actually threatened state and federal coffers because of taxes lost due to lower box-office earnings.[28]

In the meantime, the dirigiste economy instituted by the Nehru government after Indian independence had begun to slip. The new Rajiv
Gandhi government, ushered in by a vision of India secured by commodity consumption, presided over the final phases of the state-to-
market transition in the mid-1980s. The Indian mediasphere exploded
in an economy of signs and images, facilitated by television and video
technologies.

By the end of the 1980s, Hollywood claimed that it had lost
US$10–US$15 million in annual revenue to Indian video piracy.[29] This
represented a small share of revenues lost to the estimated fifteen thousand video libraries and five thousand illegal video parlors, in addition
to the innumerable hotel, restaurant, and community cable hookups that
were thought to cost the Indian film industry an estimated US$300 mil-
lion per year.[30]

American commerce saw great opportunity in the strengthening Indian market economy, but remained concerned with India's failure to
tighten intellectual property regimes. The United States placed India on
its priority watch list in the early 1990s, in no small part due to Hollywood lobbying.[31] The Office of the U.S. Trade Representative (USTR)
supported the Indian Copyright Act's 1994 amendment, designed to har-
monize Indian intellectual property policy with the World Trade Organization's enforcement protocols.[32] The same year, the MPAA set up a
Delhi-based office and coordinated seventy-five antipiracy operations
in eighteen months, raiding storage units and duplicating centers with
the aid of municipal police across India. Publicizing the new enforcement initiatives, the confiscated cassettes were showcased in print and
television reports. These raids were exercises in local intimidation and
police power, designed to promote institutional alignments rather than
to systematically scour piracy from the mediasphere.[33]

Despite relatively minor funding commitments, collaboration among
Indian and American organizations has raised the profile of antipiracy
initiatives to coordinated international initiatives. For example, the
MPAA contributed US$2,000 to the Indian Media Protection against
Copyright Theft organization in the early 1990s, asking the Indian gov-
ernment to start staging "show trials" to go after the piracy business.[34]
In another instance from the mid-1990s, the Film Makers Combine,
the Film Federation of India, and the MPAA entered into a policy and

enforcement compact, while the Modi Group joined Walt Disney in a co-venture called the Disney Consumer Products in order to track character licensing in India.[35] The objective of these initiatives, as the MPAA's director of Asia/Pacific antipiracy operations noted, was "not to pursue every violator, because we don't have that kind of clout or resources in a country as vast as India; [rather] we must strengthen the forces against piracy and educate viewers and cable operators to insist on the visual quality of the genuine product."[36] Meanwhile, consumers had already made their choice, as video compact discs replaced video-cassettes as the preferred media of piracy, offering greater mobility and ease of replication, alongside a characteristic—and by now somewhat affirming and comfortable—degradation in picture quality.[37]

As regional Indian industries staged demonstrations and theater shutdowns to protest videodisc piracy in the late 1990s, Indian film production houses like Yash Raj Films worked with police in the United States and Britain to raid grocery stores for pirated discs in Chicago and London. However, confiscations and raids became even less of a deterrent in the years to come. Part of a neighborhood, black- and gray-ware markets were also extensions of diffuse transnational networks of production and distribution. Pirate media circuits connected local entrepreneurial communities with dense translocal economies of distribution enabled by long-standing smuggling routes. As piracy technology morphed from analog to digital, state hysteria ratcheted up, associating piracy not only with criminality but with terrorism as well.

In the last fifteen years, the Indian government has strengthened national laws in line with global trade initiatives, especially those designed to protect domestic and export revenue for software and biotechnology industries. A number of acts covering designs, patents, and semiconductors have been signed into law, while the main copyright law was amended in 2000 to reflect India's expanding treaty obligations.[38] Supporting these policy changes, the tabulation of piracy losses grew to a full-blown multinational enterprise at the turn of the twenty-first century. In state and market reports, piracy emerged as a verifiable fact, substantiated by the production of statistics and big numbers.[39] Indeed, counting revenues lost to global film piracy remains a growth industry. Tabulated by the very enforcement agencies set to gain from their maximization, these figures inform a statistical imaginary that legitimates criminalization and tighter intellectual property restrictions.[40] The enumeration of piracy losses has aligned Indian and American state and market interests, serving as a crucial "center of calculation" for the media industries.[41]

Every year, the USTR issues an annual "Special 301 Report" that surveys the global intellectual property landscape, listing those countries that the United States deems the greatest threat to the security of American intellectual property.[42] Part of a series of initiatives designed to strengthen bilateral intellectual property agreements,[43] the 2010 report listed India on the "Priority Watchlist," reserved for those nations deemed the most notorious infringers of U.S.-owned intellectual property rights. In addition to "Internet Markets," the 2010 report locates the best-known Indian pirate "physical markets" at Nehru Place and Palika Bazaar in Delhi, Richie Street and Burma Bazaar in Chennai, and Manish Market, Heera Panna, Lamington Road, and the Fort District in Mumbai. Piracy's pervasive threat is reinforced by the overlap between the real and virtual reality of the market.

Legal harmonization between state regulatory structures is predicated on the technocratic assumption that emerging markets can strengthen their national economies by committing to stronger intellectual property regimes. Indeed, both the USTR and Hollywood have argued that India must strengthen its IP regimes in order to protect the burgeoning fortunes of Indian film exports. Conversely, developing nations have recognized the strategic importance of deferring IP regimes in order to spur innovation and break technological dependency, as India did with patents after independence. Many governments diagnose Western initiatives on copyright internationalization as a thinly veiled recapitulation of traditional dependency.[44] There is, after all, a relationship between stronger IP protection and the recruitment of foreign direct investment from more developed nations, which is why the MPAA's major tactic in the 1990s was to lobby the Indian government for stronger copyright protection.[45] However, as Peter Avery notes, "no unified theory of economic growth takes the aspect of counterfeiting and piracy into account."[46] Perhaps history can offer some instruction where economic theory has failed.

While it is now considered antithetical to the self-interests of the Third World, piracy was essential to the founding of the First. Prior to the chartering of the East India Company in the early seventeenth century, merchant adventurers otherwise known as pirates, sanctioned by the Elizabethan crown, forged the burgeoning interrelationship between colonialism and capitalism, collapsing the distinction between trade and plunder.[47] Nineteenth-century industrialization in Europe and the United States was made possible by the smuggling of technology and the sharing of trade secrets, often with the full knowledge and encouragement of governments that were in the process of writing their first copyright and patent laws.[48] Even as piracy was crucial to developing national industries and cultural patrimonies, it made possible the diffusion of technology and know-how that rejected artificial political boundaries. Media industries now claiming the moral high ground on originality were built with the brick and mortar of intellectual property theft. For example, Jane Gaines details a "heyday of copying" in early cinema that fueled anxiety about ownership and control yet also facilitated the consolidation of media industries engaged in unauthorized duplication of a competitor's material.[49]

Piracy can accelerate, skip, or "leapfrog" nations over the predetermined stages of development, creating unpredictable shifts in global economic power. Nowadays, the idea of leapfrogging is associated with emerging markets where the acquisition and transformation of modern technologies has created media infrastructures in "lesser-developed countries." Media technologies in leapfrogging markets can be instituted with lower capital investment, more proliferate distribution, and a more potent ethos of innovation. Even contemporary discourses of development have begun to account for piracy, from characterizing Asian commodity piracy as a form of technology transfer and West-to-East economic aid, to acknowledging that a too-stringent intellectual property scheme holds back economic development and innovation.[50]

Although the production and distribution of media piracy seems to confound national borders, piracy is embedded in locality just like traditional forms of cultural labor. After all, national differences still define distinctions between what counts as piracy and what does not, just as large-scale pirate reproduction is concentrated in certain areas. Yet, piracy's mobility, its uncanny everywhereness, undermines Hollywood's reliance on discrete national territories and predictable exhibition platforms from the movie theater to the TV. Piracy confounds the space/time of development and "gestures toward leveling the difference between developed and developing countries."[51]

Media piracy, more fully and flexibly than perhaps any other forms of commodity manufacture, takes full advantage of the reproducibility of information. Copyright law's imperative to propertize the intangible and monetize the radically transferable has profound effects on the temporality of the copy as well. Like the art forgery, a shortcut that translates and updates "the original" for contemporary purposes, the phenomenology of the copy disrupts and leapfrogs the teleological time of development.[52] Piracy's uncanniness is rooted in this ubiquitous spatiality and temporal immediacy: "everything gets pirated within 24 hours of launch," notes Komal Nahta, the publisher of the Indian trade journal *Film Information*.[53]

The ubiquitous immediacy of media piracy is bolstered by a discourse of monstrosity that thematizes the industry's insistence on more stable forms of commodity life. The rapacity of piracy preoccupies—one might say that it haunts—the media industries more than any other form of consumption. At the same time, piracy folds the teleology of development back on itself, creating noisy discontinuities that reverberate through the space and time of industry. Because piracy is ubiquitous, it resists enumeration—that is what accounts for its grotesqueness—yet piracy nevertheless remains a social fact. Piracy is slippery, ephemeral, and it seems to escape the corroboration of evidence, yet entire industries are hopelessly committed to counting its occurrences and tabulating its effects.

Hollywood supports such empirical investigation with some creative scripting. Hence the longstanding Hollywood strategy of associating piracy with a savage, gendered violation—"I say to you that the VCR is to the American producer and the American public as the Boston strangler is to the woman home alone," claimed the president of the MPAA, Jack Valenti, in congressional testimony in 1982.[54] The ensuing legal battles around the VCR, which confirmed the legality of time-shifting in home video recording, imbued the copy with a kind of ghostly presence, out of joint with the original, living in a parallel space and time. The numerous Indian "remakes" of American film in the midst of a U.S. industry crisis in the mid-1970s inspired narratives of monstrous reanimation, with one reporter noting that "Hollywood isn't really dead . . . it's alive and living well in Bombay."[55]

Contemporary linkages between media piracy and terrorism have reconfirmed the diabolical alterity of piracy, as intellectual property was enveloped within broader U.S. security policy after September 11, 2001.[56] Rooted in the colonial history of mimesis, development's monsters of improper imitation—the zombie, the parasite, the doppelganger, the copycat, and the terrorist—are spectral presences that have returned to haunt the global modern.

Despite such horror-show assertions, piracy is not, as Ziauddin Sardar maintains, another economy "behind the façade of the real economy."[57] Piracy is the real economy. Only in technocratic antipiracy discourse has media distribution and consumption been rendered strange and monstrous, disconnected from everyday life. The practitioners of piracy in the Global South—consumers, cablewallahs, street peddlers, and hawkers—are fundamental to the circulation and vitality of commodity culture, part of everyday urban experience. Monstrosity and spectacle must be recognized as part of a media industries campaign to exoticize the copy.

Mapping the political economy of terrorism onto piracy helps to articulate the copy's monstrous threat, but what does it tell us about the everyday forms of "participative illegality" that characterize commodity engagement in India and the Global South? How are we to account for circuits or forms of exchange that undermine the narrative of development by doing "justice to the creative instincts of survival?"[58]

As Ravi Sundaram argues, piracy creates low-cost media infrastructures that outstrip the normative barriers of legality and illegality, producing forms of urban engagement with the market and commodity culture. Departing from the predictable discourses of intellectual property predicated on spectacle, ownership and criminality, Sundaram's conception of "pirate modernity" speaks to the constitutive experience of piracy in the Indian mediascape.[59]

Furthermore, material commodity circuits disaggregate the alleged fidelity of the original. In the 1910s, India was the last stop on Hollywood's global tour. After American cinema had recouped its investments in the domestic market and made big profits dumping its product on Europe, India would receive used and worn Hollywood prints. The original Indian experience of Hollywood was therefore always one of degradation, with prints marked by the passage of global transit. Brian Larkin's concept of "infrastructure" captures the functionality of this corrupted media detritus within global circulation.[60] Like Sundaram, Larkin breaks from a purely negative portrayal of piracy, paying attention to provisional and informal networks whose "messy discontinuities" are immanent to media technology, while threatening their stability and reproduction. Piracy challenges the smooth efficiencies reflected in the mirror of media development and attests to the reality of breakdown in the experience of modernity.

Piracy both constitutes and disturbs the straightforward narrative of European modernity. In the alternative modernities of the Global South, constituted by the functional experiences of collapse, development's disavowal of piracy is stripped of its political transcendence. Or, to borrow another of Ziauddin Sardar's felicitous renderings, "Development, as many have learned, can be a real fake."[61]

The "Hollywood of India": Orienting Bombay Cinema

In previous sections, I showed how the imitative logic of development and its pirate inversion drew analogies between Hollywood and Bombay cinema. It is equally important, however, that we pay attention to how Bombay and Hollywood have been conceived of as opposites throughout their history of interaction. Going back to the formation of the film industries, for example, the U.S. Consul General in Calcutta noted in 1922 that "there are two distinct communities to be considered in this market, the Indian and the European, each with its separate taste and demanding a different kind of film."[62] And as early as 1925, newspaper accounts were suggesting that "Bombay is the latest competitor to Hollywood."[63] Import practices that differentiated elite audience taste reproduced East–West distinctions, sustained by the distinctive promotional strategies of Hollywood and Indian films across different sections of newspapers like the *Hindustan Times* in the early 1940s.[64]

With India at the threshold of independence and its allegiances in the coming Cold War unclear to an increasingly nervous West, the notion of Bombay as Other to Hollywood gained traction. During World War II, as the stage for the Cold War was being set, some in the Indian film industry insisted that members of the U.S. army in India were sending films back to Hollywood with advice on how to crack the Indian market. Anticipating this early Cold War tenor in the 1930s and 1940s, Bombay's film studios were seen as "a menace to British commercialism in India, an avowed enemy to Hollywood, and the special object of increasing Russian interest."[65]

The emergence of "Bollywood" as a shorthand for Indian media production has only strengthened the perception of Bombay as Hollywood's antithesis, able, as Rajinder Dudrah claims, to "serve alternative cultural and social representations away from dominant white ethnocentric audio-visual possibilities."[66] In a more explicit reference to the national as an oppositional possibility, Stephen Teo notes that Bollywood signifies a "different kind of Hollywood": "a system of production and cinematic representation that is based on the idea of national cinema but which replicates the Hollywood model to produce films. Whereas Hollywood is global, "Bollywood" is a national mode of cinematic representation, and the films that are produced from this latter mode are significantly marked by national characteristics."[67] For Teo, "Bollywood" represents a transformative principle where the national is opposed to Hollywood's global universalism. Of course, the claim that national cinema is a kind of protective barrier against Hollywood imports has been played out in the domain of twentieth-century cultural policy, particularly in the elaboration of protectionism and subsidy. Here, "national cinema" maps a set of textual practices produced under the logic of "local" coherency, most often in terms of authorship, location, audience, genre, narrative, style, or industry.

There are number of problems with this idea of national cinema. First, the analytic of exceptionalism fails to consider the international encounters that produced the ideal of national cinema itself. For example, the Mexican studio system after World War II was buttressed by state subsidy and explicitly framed as an imitation of the classical Hollywood system, yet nonetheless distinctive from it. This system, argues Charles Ramírez Berg, "filtered the Hollywood paradigm through the cultural lens of Mexican cinema to produce films that were at once derivative and distinctively Mexican."[68] Evoking a set of relations between film texts and the sociocultural contexts of their production, national cinema is actually constituted in and through its relation with other industries.[69] Extending this idea in his discussion of Malaysian film culture, William van der Heide argues against the essentialism and homogeneity of national cinema, accentuating instead the intertextual and cross-cultural forces that distribute and name forms of film production across various spaces of practice.[70]

The exceptionalism of national cinema fails to account for how resemblances facilitate contact between the different film industries. For example, on a 1940 visit to Hollywood, part of a world tour to promote Indian independence, the Gandhian activist Kamaladevi Chattopadhyay assured her American audience that "we always think of our movies in terms of yours."[71] Similarly, in a speech welcoming an Indian film industry delegation to Hollywood during the early Cold War, the U.S. director Frank Capra would claim that "between the largest free nations, one the youngest, the other the oldest, there is a kinship of the spirit—a kinship that can mean only good for all mankind."[72] More than fifty years later, as media exchanges and investment between India and the United States proliferated, *Time* magazine claimed that "Bombay is shaping India's future—and our own."[73] Commenting on the wave of Indian corporate interest in acquiring beleaguered Hollywood properties, Reliance BIG Entertainment chairman Amit Khanna reframed Capra's optimism by suggesting a "natural synergy between the film industries in India and the U.S."[74]

In addition to these affinities, driven by the exigencies of geopolitical and corporate convergence, the clearest analogical link between Indian and American media industries has been the historical rendering of Bombay as the "Hollywood of India." However, Bombay's career as the Indian equivalent of Western industry predates Hollywood. Before the decimation of its textile industries, in the nineteenth and twentieth centuries Bombay was popularly referred to as the "Manchester of India," joining cities like Dacca, Mirzapur, Ahmedabad, Ludhiana, Kanpur, and Coimbatore in holding the Northwest English appellation for industrialized urbanism.

Bombay's Hollywood moniker is inextricably linked to the perception of the city's imagined malleability. On an 1890 visit, the celebrated American Orientalist Edwin Lord Weeks found Bombay to be "the proper and fitting threshold of India, an index, or rather an illustrated catalogue of all the Eastern races."[75] This idea rehearsed a common perception of Bombay as India's gateway and microcosm. As Gyan Prakash notes, "Bombay developed by intertwining and interweaving different histories. Strategies of survival fashioned it into a place of porosity and hybridity, a swirl of intensities and movements that brought different agents into relationships and fashioned the city as a social space."[76] In terms of economic history, Bombay enabled *both* imperial expansion and the possibilities for domestic Indian industry.[77]

Historically, it took some time for Bombay to lay a singular claim as the "Hollywood of India."[78] Dadar's Kohinoor studios, with their stars and numerous productions scheduled in a factorylike system, were "flatteringly" referred to as "the Hollywood of India" in the 1920s.[79] By the mid-1940s, Bombay's Hollywood appellation circulated quite freely in press and industry discourse, and beyond.[80] For example, a 1946 Indian economics textbook notes that "Bombay accounts for two-thirds of the total number of films produced in the country and is, therefore, entitled to be called 'India's Hollywood.'"[81]

Despite the predominance of Bombay's association with American industry, other Indian cities like Bangalore, Madras, and Calcutta were often linked with Hollywood. For example, in 1930 Michael Pym wrote in *The Power of India* that Bangalore "bids fair to become India's Hollywood."[82] In a 1952 article on the Indian film industries, Jack Howard claimed that Madras film operations like Gemini Studios, because of their commitment to "scientific organization, planning, efficiency and adherence to schedules," were "more conspicuously patterned after Hollywood methods" than Bombay.[83] For decades, there was little consensus on an Indian equivalent for Hollywood. As late as 1951, *The Reporter* would claim that "India's Hollywood is scattered over the nation's three largest cities—Calcutta, Bombay, and Madras."[84]

While the "Hollywood of India" sobriquet changed hands before settling (sort of) on Bombay, "Hollywood" itself always referenced an unstable spatial identity. Even as Hollywood became associated with the center of American film production in the early 1920s, its spatial significance was already unmoored. In 1920, for example, Harrison Rhodes claimed that Hollywood "may be considered as symbolic, since there are activities elsewhere," and Katherine F. Gerould wrote about Hollywood as a text, a state of mind, an attitude and temper, and "a national point of view."[85] In Rachel Field's 1937 novel *To See Ourselves*, one character claims that "you can't explain Hollywood to anybody beforehand. There isn't any such place, really. It's just the dream suburb of Los Angeles."[86] The journalist and noted California historian Carey McWilliams explained these portraits of symbolic and fantastical displacement in terms of Hollywood's "distillation of a pure essence" necessary to the circulation of commodity culture.[87] Over the next few decades, the literal and symbolic sign of Hollywood came to preside over the production of film in the United States even as its physical referent came to denote what McWilliams called "the abandoned center of the industry."[88] The director John Ford, who did more than anyone to locate the Western in the global film imaginary, summed it up best when he claimed that "Hollywood is a place you can't geographically define. We don't really know where it is."[89]

This spatial mutability has facilitated generic reference to *any* film industry as "Hollywood." Hollywood's modularity is exemplified in a Golden Harvest advertisement from the early 1990s (see fig. 1.1), which reads, "Golden Harvest welcomes delegates to the Asia Pacific Film & Cinema Conference. Hollywood. Hollywood East." By referencing the size and productivity of Hong Kong's industry in relation to America's, and by restaging the iconic Hollywood sign, Golden Harvest reinscribes the power of the Hollywood as a standard of equivalency.

The fictional singularity of Hollywood film production, along with its alliterative adaptability, has created a industry currency where a number of national, regional, and local film industries are coined in its name, from Nolly-, Lolly-, Kolly-, to the most famous, Bollywood. The "-wood" suffix aggregates disparate media practices under the sign of a single film industry as opposed to multiple ones, lending a notably unstable set of industrial practices the fictional stability of singularity. After all, "industry" refers less to an actually existing object or social practice than to a conceptual construct that does the work of drawing and illustrating connections between diverse ways of knowing and doing.

The "-wood" suffix soothes the anxieties of spatial displacement that structure the media industries, drawing together practices that are in fact defined by various degrees and forms of instability. The suffix names a particular localization of cultural production *alongside* a more generic marker of national attribution. This spatialization of innovation, linking culture and economy under the sign of a single industry, preserves the fiction of territoriality in an increasingly distributed economic geography of production. This spatial ontology connects localized practices to more distributed global networks. The "-wood" suffix therefore names a more formalized industry rather than an informal aggregation of production practices. To become a "-wood" is a media industry rite of passage, signifying sufficiently established and sustainable industries.[90] Taken together, the various -woods are a common frame of reference between industries, a mode of translating between one and the other through a common metric of conversion.

How might we historicize the geography that reiterates Hollywood as the generic location of media production, capable of referencing both distinction and resemblance? The origins and circulations of "Bollywood" offer answers to these questions while engaging imitation in complex ways.

In 2001, the *Oxford English Dictionary* (*OED*) online edition listed an entry for "Bollywood" for the first time. When the new *OED* illustrated print edition was published two years later, Bollywood joined "Botox" and "Viagra" as new terms of English-language general circulation, with a list of 112 citations testifying to the rapid proliferation of Bollywood as shorthand for the "Indian film industry, based in Bombay." While journalistic convention suggested that Bollywood was named by a *Cineblitz* writer in the 1980s, the *OED* located the origins of the term in the British writer H. R. F. Keating's 1976 novel *Filmi, Filmi, Inspector Ghote*.

The *OED*'s reference to Bollywood's "origin" in Keating's novel invokes a term implicated in a palimpsest of translations, copies, and remakes.[91] In Keating's story, detective Ganesh Ghote investigates a murder on the set of *Khoon ka Gaddi*. In the course of his investigation, Ghote vows to learn everything about the *filmi duniya*, the world of the Bombay film "set-up called Bollywood."[92] Remarkably *Filmi Filmi*, the novel that purportedly mentions Bollywood for the first time, concerns a Hindi film production of *Macbeth*, and references another cinematic transposition of the Shakespeare play, Akira Kurosawa's 1957 film *Kumonosu-jô* (*Spider Web Castle*), released in the United States as *Throne of Blood*.

Bollywood's convoluted mimeticism is borne out by Madhav Prasad's etymology of the term.[93] In 1932, Wilford Deming, an American engineer who briefly worked with Ardeshir M. Irani on the production of the first Indian sound film, sent greetings to *American Cinematographer*

Hollywood East

Hong Kong makes more movies per head of population than anywhere in the world. One for every 42,000 people. The USA makes one for every 573,000.

Hong Kong is the fourth biggest producer of motion picture entertainment in the world. Only the USA, India and Japan make more movies of which only the USA exports more.

Two words capture the essence of Hong Kong's dynamic motion picture industry: Golden Harvest.

In Hong Kong last year Golden Harvest productions accounted for nearly twenty-five percent of local box office. Golden Harvest is also a leader in distribution. UIP chose Golden Harvest to handle their Hong Kong distribution. And the longest running film in Hong Kong's history (*The Yen Family, 569 days*) was a Golden Harvest release.

Elsewhere in Asia Golden Harvest is a leading partner. The largest cinema chain in Malaysia and Asia's most modern and luxurious 10-screen multiplex in Singapore are just two examples.

Golden Harvest welcomes delegates to the Asia Pacific Film & Cinema Conference.

Welcome to Hollywood, Hollywood East.

Golden Harvest

Figure 1.1. Hollywood as modular form. *Screen International*, April 23, 1993, 11.

magazine from "Tollywood"—a reference to Tollygunge, the Calcutta suburb that housed a number of film studios.[94] Thus, notes Prasad, "it was Hollywood itself, in a manner of speaking, that, with the confidence that comes from global supremacy, renamed a concentration of production facilities" in its own image.[95] From Tollywood, it was just a matter of time before the clever portmanteau "Bollywood" struck the Bombay-centered Hindi film industry. Many critics have inveighed against the term, suggesting that Bollywood is "weighed with misnomers about Hindi film as a mere Hollywood mimic."[96] After all, popular legitimacy and critical success is often conferred through the patrimony of originality. This is precisely why so many critics and practitioners are contemptuous of the term "Bollywood."

Yet, the contemporary emergence of "Bollywood" as a vernacular reference to Indian media production is another example of how the copy constitutes the relation between American and Indian media. A "cheeky and parodic echo" of Hollywood, "a mimicry that is both a response and a dismissal,"[97] Bollywood signifies the practices of derivation as Hollywood's Indian equivalent. As Ashish Rajadhyaksha notes, Bollywood can be understood as a relatively new culture industry designed to integrate the packaging of big-budget Hindi films across an array of international promotional sites from shopping malls and multiplexes, TV game shows, fashion runways, and dance extravaganzas, to soft-drink and fast-food advertising, sports marketing, music videos, and cell-phone ringtones.[98] "Bollywood" is now part of an industrial and conceptual apparatus that facilitates the transnational mobility of Indian media more generally.

Taken this way, Bollywood can be understood less as a coherent industry and more as the expression of a relation, with the copy at its root. Bollywood's primary claim toward the multiple histories and directions of cultural flow is therefore contained within "Bollywood" itself, a heteroglossic term that connotes a complex set of material and discursive links between Bombay and Hollywood. At the same time, a deliberately "frictional" term like Bollywood resonates with the grindings of space against place in the location and naming of media industries.[99] Inscribing the copy within broader social and historical processes of commodity transformation, "Bollywood" accesses autonomy and influence in the global media industries. But what of its manifestations in material practice? The next section shifts attention from the copy as concept to copy as artifact in the production of the Bollywood "remake."

A Thorn in Hollywood's Side: Considering the Remake

In a Los Angeles jail cell, six Indian men chat in Hindi, contemplating their future. Their plotting is reminiscent of *The Usual Suspects* (1995), the slow-motion parade into the LA haze upon their release parallels the title sequence to *Reservoir Dogs* (1992), and the final shoot-out recalls *Heat* (1995). These and many other quotations from Hollywood film suffuse the robbery and betrayal narrative of *Kaante* (*Thorns*, 2002) (see figs. 1.2 and 1.3). Ironically, *Kaante* is a Hindi heist film that many criticized as a theft of a different order.[100] Given that director Sanjay Gupta shot most of the film in Los Angeles with an American crew, Hollywood was never far from the making of *Kaante*.[101]

In the previous section, I argued for the productivity of resemblance embodied in the term "Bollywood," despite the fact that the film industries have historically conceived of the copy solely in terms of piracy. In this section, I read a specific production history in order to trace the ma-

Figures 1.2 and 1.3. *Reservoir Dogs* and *Kaante* introduce their main cast.

terial and conceptual itineraries traced by the copy as it moves between Bombay and Hollywood.

In 2000, Sanjay Gupta and actor Sanjay Dutt met with Hollywood technicians at the first International Indian Film Academy Awards at London's Millennium Dome, an event designed to promote Bollywood for a global audience. According to Gupta, the two Sanjays were "so impressed with the technical finesse that was used to amplify the creative expression that [they] thought of making a film which would embody the same philosophy."[102] *Kaante* was originally planned for a New York shoot, said Gupta, with a car chase in the visual style of films like *The Rock* (1996) and *Gone in Sixty Seconds* (2000) coordinated by Hollywood action director Spiro Razatos.[103]

Gupta's interest in genre as a kind of transnational aesthetic intersected with the ongoing global popularity of the action film. Initially planned as a lower-budget film, *Kaante* morphed into a male multi-star crime thriller and, unlike most Bollywood releases, relatively few song-and-dance sequences. One of the most hyped films of the year, *Kaante* was also supposed to inspire Bombay filmmakers toward bigger budgets and more overseas coproduction. It also followed a series of high-profile successes for Bombay cinema, including *Lagaan*'s nomination at the 2002 Academy Awards in the Foreign Language Film category, and the global success of films like *Kabhi Khushi Kabhi Gham* (2000), *Asoka* (2001), and *Dil Chahta Hai* (2001). These films pushed Bollywood to the front of global media consciousness.

Kaante was completed at a cost of Rs.400 million (over US$8 million), a third over budget, with a thirty-five-day shoot on location in Los Angeles (the song sequences were filmed in India). Many of the 130 Hollywood technicians employed for the film lowered their normal salaries, eager for the chance to work on a major Bollywood production. The same team that used two hundred still-cameras to film the opera of gunfire in *Swordfish* (2001) coordinated *Kaante*'s "bullet-time" special effects, originally popularized by *The Matrix* (1999). Hollywood hairdresser Barbara Cantu and makeup artist Myke Michaels were hired to "get the look right."[104]

Kaante was set for release in 2002, a moribund year for commercial Hindi cinema—"definitely the worst year for Bollywood in a decade," as one trade expert noted.[105] *Kaante*'s release was postponed in July, and then delayed again to avoid being released during Ramadan, when Muslim audiences traditionally decline. In this domestic exhibition lull, Indian distributors turned to an "unprecedented" slate of Hollywood films like *Bloodwork* (2002) and *Insomnia* (2002). One exhibition programmer noted that "never in Hollywood's history in India has such a large number of English (language) films been released within a month."[106] Given Hollywood's predominance, especially during November 2002, Bombay filmmakers were hopeful that the still-unreleased *Kaante* would set the possibilities of remaking as a production strategy, with further Hindi-dubbed Hollywood releases and Hollywood-inspired films providing additional box-office relief. After all, Hollywood remakes had become more popular as American films played across proliferating Indian cable television channels. Some in the industry imagined a future for Bollywood as a kind of repackaging machine for Indian releases of world cinema, and *Kaante* seemed to fit the bill.[107]

Kaante took advantage of visual style in big-budget Hindi cinema, driven by advertising aesthetics and new technologies like sync sound, sophisticated cameras and cranes, digital editing suites, and color correction. The use of new production technology, enabled by a lowering of import duties, also aligned with a consolidating corporate culture in Bombay film production, prioritizing scheduling, completion guarantees, film insurance, early scripts, written contracts, and payment by check instead of cash. These new priorities of big-budget production demonstrated that cinema in India could be a business worthy of investment, shifting away from the older, more chaotic practices associated with "black" money finance.[108] Furthermore, publicity, branding, cross-promotion, and corporate synergies were becoming increasingly important. *Kaante* was produced by Pritish Nandy Communications (PNC) as part of its ongoing shift from television to feature film. In 2002, after the film's principal shooting was completed, PNC signed a deal with 20th Century Fox to produce English-language films in India.

Kaante's key innovation may have been in the marketing and promotional sector. Even as American and European firms remained distressed by media piracy in the subcontinent, Indian licensing emerged as an area of major international interest. For instance, Leo Entertainment opened for business in February 2001 as the Indian film-marketing arm of Leo Burnett, the venerable American advertising firm that was now part of the French multinational advertising conglomerate Publicis. *Kaante* was one of the first film projects for Leo, which was also trying to boost the Indian image of its client Coca-Cola. Coca-Cola's presence was seen in a number of Bombay productions in the year of *Kaante*'s production, providing a thematic backdrop in *Mohabbatein* (2001) and funding 20 percent of the budget of *Yaadein* (2001), signaling what brand theorists call "an adaptive global marking strategy" by linking an international brand to nation-specific media.[109]

For *Kaante*'s marketing, Leo turned to the Indian brand Thums Up, a Coca-Cola subsidiary. According to the manager of Leo in Bombay, Thums Up "has a more macho, rugged image—it's a stronger cola than Coke or Pepsi."[110] A number of placements featured the indigenized cola: Leo produced a Thums Up promotional tie-in with the film; the Thums Up logo appears briefly on-screen; the thieves shoot the thumbs up gesture associated with the drink; and the film's closing credits indicate that the "*Kaante* team [is] refreshed by 'Thums Up'—a quality product of Coca Cola." This heavy product placement is part of the growth of transnational branding in India. Nowadays, big budget in-film sponsorship is coordinated with event promotions as well as specifically designed campaign strategies that take the brand from pre-release to post-release. The role of the strategic campaign has become even more important as pre-release music sales—the traditional buzz-builder for Bombay cinema—have diminished as a stand-alone part of film marketing. As Aswin Punathambekar points out in his reading of *Kaante*'s marketing, these new campaigns live uneasily alongside older practices of film publicity built on social ties and events like the *mahurat*, a ritual used to announce a new project.[111] The history of branding and publicity is also invoked by long-standing Western brands, which are using the contemporary marketing interest to reinvent themselves in a newly liberalized Indian economy.

One of *Kaante*'s primary branding partners, Coca-Cola, has had an interesting time in India. It was widely available until 1977, when rarely employed provisions of the Foreign Exchange Regulation Act obligated Coke to cut its stake in its Indian operations to 40 percent and reveal its "secret formula." Rather than comply with the Indian government's import-substitution policies, famously promoted by the firebrand Union

Minister for Industries George Fernandes, Coke closed its Indian operations. In the meantime, a number of Indian brands were launched under the support first of Pure Drinks' Campa Cola, which repurposed Coke's distinctive cursive logo, and then Parle's Thums Up, with more carbonation and its distinctive slightly bitter flavor, described as reminiscent of betel nut.

Thums Up became India's most popular cola, and Parle, with the success of its other sodas like Gold Spot and Limca, gained a majority market share. This declined with the entry of Pepsi in 1988 under an Indian joint venture that bought out former Coke franchisees.[112] By the time Coke returned in 1993, after the market was deregulated in the wave of early 1990s market liberalization, a newly independent Pepsi was already established as the key foreign soft-drink brand in India. Coke acquired Parle, and with it Thums Up as well as other local brands. Coke focused on marketing its flagship drink as a global brand and neglected marketing for Thums Up, until it was clear that, bolstered by sales in semi-urban markets, the Indian drink was outselling Coke by 400 percent. In 2001, Coke began to shift its marketing campaign to a more specifically Indian market, using Hindi film superstar Aamir Khan in its 2002 "Thanda Matlab Coca-Cola" campaign ("Cold Means Coca-Cola") and continuing to promote its rival subsidiary Thums Up's masculine image. This history shows how Coke has used a native cola to recapture a global brand's majority share of a domestic market, appropriating what began as a well-timed imitation.[113] Ashis Nandy captures the spirit of this strange commodity mimesis, noting that Coca-Cola's "philosophy is phagocytic; it eats up other adjacent philosophies and turns them into ornamental dissents within its universe."[114]

Kaante's marketing dovetails with the indigenous remaking of a global cola brand, and the histories of mimesis are refigured by the film's status as a Hollywood remake. In reviews of *Kaante*, a few critics were willing to concede that the film's style and narrative helped imagine copying and influence in interesting ways. Neelam Wright claimed that the empty LA streets, caricatured American stock-types portrayed in the film, and stylistic exaggerations created a kind of pastiche of American action cinema that critiques Hollywood aesthetics.[115] In the *New York Times*, Dave Kehr described *Kaante* as a "delirious Bollywood reimagining," adding that "Bollywood embodies a tradition of excessive generosity."[116] Of course, *Kaante*'s alleged referent, *Reservoir Dogs*, was generous in its own reimaginings, taking elements from *The Big Combo* (1955), *The Killing* (1956), *The Taking of Pelham One Two Three* (1974), *City on Fire* (1987), and others.

Reservoir Dogs director Quentin Tarantino's many appropriations are integral to his avowedly public cinephilia. While Tarantino's rise from video-store clerk to film auteur is seen as confirming an enduring myth of Hollywood—that talent inevitably rises to the surface—Sanjay Gupta's self-acknowledged "homage" exemplified for many the sad state of entrepreneurship in the Indian innovation economy. Gupta's appropriations were seen as evidence that Bollywood really had nothing new to offer by rehashing Hollywood. Such accusations of Hollywood plagiarism have long compromised the critical appraisal of Hindi cinema. Reference texts like *The Encyclopedia of Hindi Cinema* note that "a large majority of Hindi films ape Hollywood in a manner singularly devoid of inspiration."[117] Furthermore, Ravi Vasudevan and Rosie Thomas claim that the historical lack of academic attention paid to Hindi cinema comes from the popular perception that it copies Hollywood—either "Hindi cinema is derivative of the sensational aspects of the U.S. cinema," or it is dismissed as "second-rate copies of Hollywood trash."[118] Given the critical dismissal that copying seems to invoke, some critics have attempted to recover an indigenous authenticity either by restoring the legitimacy of popular cinema in focusing on its recasting of Indian literary tradition, or by foregrounding cinema's foundations in the epic texts of pan-Indian mythology.[119]

These critical appraisals have been echoed in industry discourse and practice. Early on, the lack of a rationalized Indian film industry was blamed for the preponderance of remakes. The secretary of the Indian Motion Picture Producers Association, Y. A Fazalboy, noted in 1938, "The criticism that ideas are being copied will no longer exist if a number of studios join together."[120] The notion that Hollywood stood in for an absent institutional structure of Hindi cinema extends to contemporary complaints about the relative lack of formalized screenwriting training in India. Mahesh Bhatt, who directed a Hindi remake of *It Happened One Night* in 1991, claims that Hollywood films were "the classrooms where I learnt the ABCs of story telling through sounds and pictures."[121] Here, the ordinary translations of the copy redress institutional deficiencies in film instruction, with Hollywood serving as an archive and pedagogy: a repository of styles, narratives, and techniques for generations of Indian filmmakers. The film director Farah Khan calls these and other forms of pastiche—including Hindi cinema's increasing capacity for self-citation—the creation "of something new with the help of references."[122]

Despite *Kaante*'s place in a long history of film remakes in India, the film garnered special attention in Hollywood, which was just becoming comfortable seeking monetary redress for "unauthorized" remakes in India. One Hollywood studio lawyer noted that, "until now it has not been worth our time tangling with filmmakers in a Mumbai court. But if this *Reservoir Dogs* rehash starts making serious money in the East, then we shall have to start investigating how closely such movies are copying the originals."[123] This concern with *Kaante* echoes Hollywood's already well-established cynicism about film production culture in India. As far back as 1953, one commentator would note that "Hollywood supplies a great deal of the Indian movie industry's raw material in plots and ideas, without having anything to say about it. Local producers watch imported features with an eagle eye and frankly plagiarize the more popular productions scene by scene. One producer explained that he saw nothing ethically wrong with this, as otherwise the Indian masses who do not understand English, and have few chances to see foreign films anyway, would be denied these masterpieces."[124] By the 1980s heyday of video piracy in India, Hollywood turned its ire on remakes as well, estimating that U.S. majors lost over US$1 billion in royalties and remake fees in India, given rights set at about US$100,000 per film. *Coming to America* (1988) made little impact at the box-office when it arrived in India in 1989, but its Tamil-language remake was very successful, as was *Appu Raja* (1989), the Indian remake of *Twins* (1988). In the early 1990s, multiple versions of *Pretty Woman* (1990) and *Ghost* (1990) were remade in a number of Indian languages.[125] By the 2000s, the Bombay-based *Trade Guide* called remake-happy Indian screenwriters "mere translators."[126]

In September 2008, Warner Brothers unsuccessfully sued to block the release of *Hari Puttar: A Comedy of Terrors*, but in a landmark development the following year, the producers of *Banda Yeh Bindass Hai* (2010), reportedly paid US$200,000 to 20th Century Fox for straying too close to the script of *My Cousin Vinny* (1992). However, as collaborations with Hollywood increase, Bombay producers seem less willing to threaten potential partnerships. This has given rise to the "official adaptation" like the Hindi film *We Are Family* (2010), where producer Karan Johar bought the remake rights to *Stepmom* (1998).[127]

Mirroring the sanctioned Indian copies of Hollywood are Hollywood copies of Hindi cinema. As part of a larger development deal with Reliance BIG Pictures, Brett Ratner's reedited English version of the Hindi film *Kites* (2010) was released simultaneously with the "original" in May 2010, with twenty-eight minutes of cuts—"things that just wouldn't translate"—and the majority of non-lead actors dubbed in American dialects. "For me," says the star of the film Hrithik Roshan, "it's about breaking barriers. The larger goal, the big dream, is to have an Indian film watched by a world market."[128]

As with other forms of the copy, reducing the remake to intellectual property piracy obscures the dynamic forms of interoperability in the global media industries. Hollywood is one of the many ingredients in the spicy mixture of the "masala" film, and as Madhav Prasad notes, the very idea of "Bollywood" destabilizes the hegemony of Hollywood by attesting to the play of difference and repetition at the heart of cultural production. In other words, Bollywood signals the possibility of variation that is inherent in the manifestation of Hollywood as a "dominant idiom."[129] Remakes signal the fundamental recursion that animates the biography of the commodity. The remake can also function, as Patricia Aufderheide notes, to express both "resistance to and fascination with dominant cinema and culture."[130]

"Indianization" refers to precisely this phenomenon, where Hollywood is remade for domestic audiences. While Sumita Chakravarty describes Indianization as the "selective assimilation of technical codes and values" used as "a tactics of survival adopted by beleaguered or berated film industries,"[131] it is clear that remakes are one of the better-articulated forms of creative development within the Indian industry. In her ethnography of the Indian film industry, Tejaswini Ganti describes the complex processes through which Hindi film producers evaluate the suitability of particular Hollywood scripts, scenes, and plots for adaptation, focusing on how "the process of Indianization becomes an arena for Hindi filmmakers to construct difference at the level of the nation."[132] Sheila Nayar argues that remakes are more like "extracted skeletons," plot repositories that are molded and shaped for a more sufficient and efficient cultural refilling."[133]

Ganti and Nayar link Hindi adaptations of Hollywood film to a national cultural consciousness, but remakes in principle challenge any immutable link between texts and the spaces of their production and reception. Remakes prioritize a dynamic of circulation rather than stasis as the driver of cultural production. Embodying the tropicality of translation, remakes are texts whose circulation extends the film commodity's space and time of relevance. In its dispersion through the trade and traffic of image culture, the remake breaks free of the forms of spatial restraint presupposed by the national.

Yet *Kaante* specifically evokes the national in its difference from a purported Hollywood original, adding a theme of national identity absent in *Reservoir Dogs*. In *Kaante*, the Army major (Ambitah Bachchan), a distinguished veteran of an unnamed foreign conflict, attempts to rouse the national pride of his fellow conspirators by claiming that while the Italians and Chinese have their own criminal organizations, "What do we Indians have? Nothing." Meanwhile, a bigoted detective who wants to "get those damn Indians" pursues the gang, who buy weapons from an arms dealer so boastful of funding Kashmiri separatism that they throw him off a building for "attacking India." *Kaante* exploits the jingoism that emerged in some Hindi war films following the 1999 Kargil conflict in Kashmir. However, its production history belies a simple exploitation of India–Pakistan tensions. Upon their arrival in Los Angeles just after September 11, 2001, *Kaante*'s stars were worried about being mistaken for terrorists. For example, though he is one of the most famous stars in the world, Amitabh Bachchan carried newspaper clippings proving his celebrity, just in case the ugly looks he sometimes received in LA escalated to confrontation. Meanwhile, Sunil Shetty was "taken for a dubious Asian" and frisked in his LA hotel after he forgot his room key.[134]

Nationalist resonance and mistaken identities aside, ironically it was Quentin Tarantino who recognized *Kaante*'s other significant departure from *Reservoir Dogs*. In a 2007 interview at the Indian Film Festival in Los Angeles, Tarantino professed admiration for the film:

I started watching it and I knew it was *Reservoir Dogs*. But then the film is longer. You guys are crazy because you like long movies. And that's what I like too. But we have a studio system here. But yeah, coming to the point, here I am watching a film that I've directed, and then it goes into each character's background. And I am like WHOA: that's something. Because I always write the backgrounds and stuff in my scripts but it always gets chopped off during the edit. And so I was like this isn't *RD*. But then it goes into the warehouse scene and I am like, "WOW—it's back to *RD*." Isn't it amazing? Wow.[135]

Kaante uses other Hollywood films—especially *The Usual Suspects* and *Heat*—to construct a narrative of motivation absent in *Reservoir Dogs*. While *Kaante*'s gang is implicated in the business of death, their crimes are justified through a set of familial obligations, including the restoration of family unity and the fulfillment of a wife's dying wish. In the lead-up to the robbery itself, the criminals have multiple opportunities to lament their former lives and consider future choices. The affective attachment between the characters and their male camaraderie produces the characteristic audience sympathy common to the "Indianized" Hollywood remake. In this way, *Kaante* fleshes out the skeletal narrative economy of *Reservoir Dogs*, just as the copy directs the original toward new forms of signification.

In both *Kaante* and *Reservoir Dogs*—twinned stories of impostors, cops playing villains and vice versa—the law must hide a copy of itself inside the criminal world in order to expose it from within. This collapse between the inside and the outside of legality tells us something about the trajectory of the Bollywood copy. *Kaante*'s extensive quotations of Hollywood serve as a reminder of the historical disparagement of the Hindi remake as inauthentic and unoriginal. At the same time, the remake engages an international division of cultural labor that supports the invigoration of new markets and commodity forms. Staging the drama of translation, *Kaante* engages the work of the copy in the age of Hollywood reproduction (see figs. 1.4 and 1.5).

Figures 1.4 and 1.5. *Reservoir Dogs* and *Kaante*'s mirroring credits

After Development: Refiguring the Discourse of Copying

Regimes of copying, as Celia Lury notes, are juridically determined, but are "the outcome of economic, political, and cultural struggles between participants in cycles of cultural reproduction."[136] In this chapter, I have traced the morphology of the copy through a number of iterations. Engaging the copy critically, analytically, and historically demonstrates that imitation is a complex industrial dynamic, evoking asymmetries in the exercise of cultural power while relativizing what is considered unique. In this way, the copy frames Bombay–Hollywood comparison in the fields of commodity transit, textual economy, and industrial practice.

As we have seen, the copy rewrites the historical interactions between the Bombay and Hollywood industries. The copy enacts and makes legible the social, economic, and political conflicts that take place when one film industry crosses into the domain of another. While this chapter spans economic development, the naming and location of media industries, and challenges to ownership regimes, it rests on the constitutive role of the copy as a way of comparing, evaluating, and calibrating media industries and markets.

In this chapter, I have deliberately avoided a standard chronological history in order to more effectively demonstrate how the copy exemplifies connections across spatiotemporal formations. Yet, in fine-grained accounts and broader geopolitical shifts, across the many manifestations of industrial autonomy and influence, I have tried to keep a central target in mind. That target is the pernicious paradigm of "development," which attempts to arrange in neat evolutionary periods the fundamental differences in the experience of media across the Global North and South. My intention is to find cracks in the smooth surface of similarity—thereby exposing the hypocrisy of self-fulfilling prophecies of transformation— while showing how the copy has insinuated itself into the conventional agenda of development. Although the politics of the copy has not replaced development as a new form of transcendence, the copy impels the contradictions and instabilities of media modernity.

This idea runs counter to our common perceptions, as the copy is vilified as fraudulent, a rote manifestation of the remarkable original. This view of the copy as inherently inauthentic helps to draw contemporary transnational contrasts, where the "newly" industrializing countries of the East are thought to have built and secured their economic power by copying the West. The cultural politics implicated in this work of comparison have dominated media industry hierarchies for a century or more. This chapter challenges this conventional wisdom by approaching the copy in a much more expansive way, paying attention to its actual manifestations in media industry practice. Of course, industries depend on replication in the material and symbolic production of cultural commodities. However, the copy can also transform, innovate, and energize media practice. In order to grasp this fully, however, we need to depart from some common characterizations of the copy.

Although the copy is considered the illegitimate remainder of modern commoditization, it is in fact constitutive of it. The discourse of development, predicated on institutionalized imitation and determinedly oblivious to the everyday functionality of media piracy in the Global South, has relegated the copy to an exoticized form of criminality. Intellectual property legislation has emerged as a critical tool in the corporate management of screen culture, but it has failed to instantiate a normative distinction between inspiration and impersonation as a means of securing the prospect of stable markets. History is clear that such distinctions have been selectively evoked, largely in retrospect.

Yet the copy frames a politics of East–West encounter fundamental to the experience of media modernity, where, to follow Naoki Sakai, "contact is capable of transforming both parties worked in the transaction."[137] The copy has drawn Hollywood into the Bombay media ecology, catalyzing mutual forms of contamination. Throughout its hundred years in India, the copy has propelled Hollywood's drift across the trajectories of consolidation, competition, and collaboration.

2

Managing Exchange

Geographies of Finance in the Media Industries

It is almost impossible to compare Bollywood to Hollywood. Instead of being two sides of the same coin, they
are separate currencies all together, with a wildly fluctuating exchange rate
Stephen Alter, *Fantasies of a Bollywood Love Thief*

Described as a "Mahabharata in polyester," the long-standing feud
between the Ambani brothers remains India's best-known corporate
soap opera.[1] Mukesh and Anil are the sons of Dhirubhai Ambani, a one-
time textile magnate who transformed Reliance Industries into India's
largest company and helped launch widespread retail stock investment
in India. After Dhirubhai died in 2002, simmering family disagreements
boiled over into the public arena and Reliance was split, with elder
brother Mukesh taking over the company's massive energy, chemical,
textile, and retail market interests. Operating through the new Reliance
Anil Dhirubhai Ambani (ADA) Group, the younger brother took charge
of telecommunication, energy infrastructure, health, and entertainment
interests.

Reliance ADA is now valued at over US$40 billion and the telege-
nic Anil Ambani has emerged as the face of global Indian media. It
doesn't hurt that he is married to the Hindi film actress Tina Munim
and maintains close personal ties to many of the biggest celebrities in
Indian media. Reliance BIG Entertainment (RBE), the media and entertainment subsidiary of Reliance ADA, relentlessly pursues mergers
and acquisitions at a local, national, and international level. Ambani's
media ambitions helped to coin the term "bollygarch," suggesting, as
Suketu Mehta claims, that in scale Bollywood "easily out hollywoods
Hollywood."[2]

RBE's big investments in existing media businesses took off in 2005, when it acquired a controlling interest in Adlabs, one of India's biggest film companies. RBE now has interests in film, broadcast, and new media services in English, Hindi, Marathi, and other languages. RBE subsidiary BIG Cinemas is now India's biggest movie theater chain, with over five hundred screens in India, Malaysia, and the United States. However, RBE has made much larger inroads into overseas corporate media acquisition.

Reliance's joint-venture investment in the Hollywood studio Dream-Works in 2008 remains its highest-profile acquisition. DreamWorks was founded with much fanfare in 1994 by director/producer Steven Spielberg, former Disney studio head Jeffrey Katzenberg, and music industry executive David Geffen. Ten years later, DreamWorks had become a cautionary tale for studio production in the "new," heavily consolidated Hollywood, and was sold to Paramount Pictures in 2006. By 2008, Spielberg was looking for a way to split from Paramount at the expiration of the current DreamWorks contract. In June 2008, an attempt by DreamWorks to resuscitate independent film production was buoyed with the announcement of a US$1.4 billion financing deal, including a US$500 million contribution from Reliance. The Indian conglomerate had already begun pursuing a "Hollywood strategy," signing production contracts with LA-based independent production studios run by A-list Hollywood actors.[3] Reliance also hoped to further leverage Hollywood's existing stakes in Indian outsourcing. This hope represents the emergence of a Möbius-like geography of cultural production, where an India-based conglomerate with an ownership stake in a Hollywood studio takes advantage of the cost savings of Indian labor.

Some in Hollywood, recalling Sony's purchase of Columbia Pictures and Matsushita's purchase of MCA and Universal Studios, predicted a new wave of Indian media acquisition just as Japanese electronics firms had taken over American studios in the past. However, the global economic crisis of late 2008 slashed Reliance's market value to the point that it was now unable to provide the promised US$500 million toward financing the new launch of DreamWorks. A proposed distribution agreement with Universal also fell through, prompting DreamWorks to turn to Disney. Eventually, in July 2009, Reliance, DreamWorks, a syndicate of banks led by JPMorgan Chase, and Disney (as the late-entering distribution partner) announced a US$825 million development deal to finance new production projects over the next three years. Reliance contributed US$325 million toward the new partnership.[4]

Reliance's many forays into Hollywood illustrate the complex connections between the Indian and American screen industries. Reliance's initiatives, predicated on buying up Hollywood debt, represent a possible realignment of power in the global media industries. In the early twentieth century, Hollywood's relationship with other national cinemas was as a competitor but also a creditor, navigating overseas protectionism and quotas with the promise of coproduction and subsidization of local industry. In the aftermath of global military conflict, Hollywood invested overseas to take advantage of production and exhibition infrastructures decimated by two World Wars.

Now, we are seeing an accelerating process of reversal that began in the 1970s, with Asian investment capital buying up Hollywood debt. The twentieth-century maps a dramatic shift in the historiography of finance for Hollywood, which has served as microcosm for American economic power, with the United States moving from a creditor to a debtor nation in less than a hundred years.

This chapter pays examines the ways in which money and investment flows manage the exchange between Hollywood and Bombay industries. How are these flows imbricated in media industries, and how does industry make visible and intelligible certain forms of exchange? This chapter takes on three interrelated case studies in the transnational geography of finance: repatriation, coproduction, and outsourcing. Focusing on key moments in the history of Indo-American media relations from the 1920s to the present, these three case studies compose a triptych around the figure of exchange.

From Hollywood's blocked profits in India, to American studio efforts at Hindi-language production, and special effects postproduction work sent to India, each case study poses a challenge to Hollywood's global distribution of risk. After all, repatriation is basically a problem of how to bring profits back home and how to expend them when and where you can. Coproduction also addresses the question of how to spread money around. Finally, outsourcing engages the respatialization of labor as a way to take advantage of local distinctions in talent and wages.

While the movements of big money have dominated our imagination of media industries, this chapter is also about money as transactional, as both mechanism and medium of exchange between Hollywood and Bombay. These varied currencies of exchange engage India as a solid geographic reality as well as a fictive location to manage the movement of profits, production, and personnel. "India" emerges as both space and place between these logics of institution and image-making in the film sector.

Settling Accounts: Hollywood and Blocked Money in India

Big numbers drive commercial media industries. But media industry ledgers are not the only places where box-office tallies are counted and various accounting logics enumerated. Numbers also suffuse the representation of media industries.[5] Yet, the massification of numbers and statistics in the media industries belies the underlying granularity of exchange. Big numbers are one thing—what about the *actual* circulation of money? Complicating the smooth, invisible exchange presumed by statistics and industry data, this section shifts the rational discourse of numbers toward the messy materiality of exchange between media industries.

Here, I focus on the practical problem of remittances and blocked funds. I look at the movement of foreign exchange between India and the United States in the late 1950s and 1960s as it framed national capital crisis and film culture. Hollywood may be defined by efficiency and global circulation—the very emblem of commodity mobility—but with its profits "blocked" and unrepatriable back to the United States during this time, Hollywood was somewhat immobilized in India. This section engages the following question: what forms of exchange were facilitated by this blockage of money?

Currency is a financial instrument that circulates through international markets, and "foreign exchange" refers to foreign currency reserves held by state actors like the United States and India. Foreign exchange was essential to Indian film culture in the 1950s and 1960s because Indian dollar reserves facilitated the international purchase of film stock and other production equipment during a time of domestic shortage. Reserves also paid for overseas location shooting and funded Bombay cinema's postproduction processing and dubbing work in foreign studios. Furthermore, the promise of earning valuable foreign exchange expanded Indian cinema's globalization into the U.K. and the Untied States in the 1960s.

The Indian film industry's interest in earning and expending foreign currency was part of a wider national crisis that had been exacerbated by depleted foreign exchange reserves. The late 1950s and 1960s were a period of intense economic and political instability in India that some historians have referred to as a "shaking of the center."[6] This prolonged and intense political instability was brought on by famine, drought, and war, jeopardizing the very idea of the national. The massive international obligations incurred by India for food, arms, and imported consumer goods in the 1960s precipitated a foreign exchange crisis, exacerbated by drastic devaluations of the rupee enacted to increase global interests in Indian exports. Weakened by a fracturing and fragile national imaginary, the Indian state became very nervous about the balance of payments and exchange reserves. In short, foreign exchange was not just a financial instrument during this crisis; it served as a form of political currency between India and the rest of the world, particularly the United States.

At this critical juncture, film was recruited to the cause of national economic security. The Indian government turned to restricting the repatriation of exhibition and distribution profits, in a sense, "blocking" Hollywood's money in India as a way to prevent the flight of precious foreign exchange back to the United States. In the early 1960s, Hollywood had less than a 5 percent share of the Indian screen, earning a total profit of over US$1 million in India on revenues of over US$3 million, still just 1 percent of overall worldwide revenue for Hollywood. However, Hollywood's earnings were symbolic of the larger debt that India owed the United States at the time, underlying the bickering between the Indian government and the Motion Picture Export Association of America (MPEA), the international counterpart to the Motion Picture Association of America. One trade crisis followed another and MPEA contracts in India came and went, accompanied by Hollywood protestations and embargoes. At the same time, the Indian government looked for international help to promote Indian cinema overseas, with the hope that it might dramatically increase the foreign exchange that Indian producers could earn and add to the national exchequer.[7]

The Indo-American film crisis that began in the 1950s was part of a global rise in protectionist measures against Hollywood and coincided with the rise of labor agitation within the American film industry.[8] Facing the accumulation of "blocked" funds, Hollywood companies operating in foreign countries turned to investing in coproductions and funding location shoots for Hollywood films; for example, Paramount used blocked funds to film *The Ten Commandments* (1956) in Egypt.[9] In the early days of blocked fund spending, Hollywood turned toward creative bookkeeping, investing in shipbuilding and buying whiskey and furniture to sell in American dollars.[10]

In 1956, the Hollywood studios combined for over Rs.11 million in gross India billings, of which just over Rs.4 million was spent on local overhead, and close to Rs.5 million (US$1 million at the official exchange rate) was transferred in cash out of the country, with the remainder spent on things like duty. Remarkably, Hollywood repatriated almost the same amount that it spent in overhead in its local Indian offices. In 1957, concerned over shortages in foreign exchange, the Indian government slashed the import quota of films to 10 percent of 1947 import figures. Hollywood negotiated an agreement whereby the quota could be raised to 75 percent, as long as remittances were restricted to 12.5 percent, with the remaining funds to held in a blocked account.[11] Under the terms of a March 1957 agreement, the MPEA agreed to a fixed number of imported films per year and repatriation restrictions. Under continued pressure from an Indian administration concerned over shortages in foreign exchange, the next fifteen years saw dramatic changes in the import duty charged to Hollywood imports into India (increasing the cost of importing a single print into India by as much as US$1,500). There were also new restrictions on the amount of money that Hollywood was allowed to take out of India in dollars. Under the new agreement, U.S. distributors could convert only US$400,000 worth of rupees to foreign exchange, leading to an increasing stockpile of unrepatriable or "blocked funds." U.S. distributors imposed an embargo, despite paying the increased duty on a few films like *The Birds* (1963), playing them in leased theaters in major Indian cities.[12]

Extensive correspondence between studio offices in Hollywood and local Bombay branches, as well as India-related memos and minutes of meetings from the MPEA and the Kinematograph Renters Society (which represented Hollywood's exhibition interests in India), show that remittance restrictions were at the forefront of American film concerns in India beginning in the late 1950s. There were, of course, other matters of business to be discussed, from tabulating the specific cuts mandated by Indian censor boards for Hollywood films, to requesting film prints for Indian government and American embassy screenings, as well as procuring hospitality and gifts for Indian producers and distributors visiting the United States. The great volume of studio correspondence dealing with remittance interests dwarfed these concerns.

Two central questions animate this correspondence: first, how can Hollywood repatriate its profits out of India in dollars, and later, how can Hollywood spend more of its rupee profits in India? These questions map a shift as Hollywood moved away from focusing on repatriation toward expending blocked funds within India. The Indian government supported this shift and the MPEA recognized the government's interest in Hollywood doing "the maximum possible to help the Indian motion picture industry."[13] Clearly, blocked funds expenditure was related to a broader project of industrial reciprocity in the 1950s, as Hollywood offices around the world were "advised" on "the importance of maintaining face and good public relations with all foreign countries."[14] Furthermore, Hollywood's use of blocked funds to subsidize Indian production and exhibition in the 1950s and 1960s was part of a wider discourse of friendship at a moment when the West desperately sought Indian cooperation in the Cold War.

A 1959 MPEA proposal set before the Ministries of Commerce, Finance, Information, and Broadcasting, and the Export Trade Promotion Board, addressed a number of possible uses for the expenditure of blocked funds:

(1) Financing location shoots in India with the eventual agreement that 50 percent could be used from blocked funds, and the remaining 50 percent to be paid for in foreign exchange (Hollywood could use 100 percent of blocked funds for production, but then India would have a claim on an foreign exchange earned by the film's exhibition around the world);

(2) Blocked funds could also be used, "in cooperation with Indian capital where possible, in the building, purchase, leasing and renovation

of motion picture theatres in India" (although air-conditioning equipment would have to be purchased in the United States with dollars and then imported—import permits would be automatic);

(3) Blocked funds might be used for the outright sale or leasing of Indian pictures for foreign territories other than India (likely the Caribbean and the Middle East, but the Indian government especially prized U.S. distribution);

(4) Blocked funds could also be used for travel expenses for Hollywood executives traveling to or within India (a common practice in other countries where Hollywood accrued blocked money);

(5) Funds could be used to pay for the international airfreight of Hollywood prints around the world with an international airline that has expansion interests in India (this included Air India);

(6) Funds could be used to offset income taxes of Hollywood technicians and artists working in India;

(7) Funds could be directed toward processing films (as long as the Indian processing was publicized in return (this might prevent overseas flight by Indian producers).[15]

In addition, in the early 1960s, the Foreign Finance Committee of the MPEA considered a number of initiatives to expend blocked funds in India. For example, the MPEA discussed selling US$3 million worth of blocked rupees to an Indo-Norwegian shipping company to operate a liner services between India and the U.S. East Coast and/or the Gulf. Hollywood also planned an initiative to help fund an American mining company's efforts to export manganese ore out of India. There were curious one-off initiatives as well. For example, proceeds of a screening of *The Millionairess* (1960), released at the New Empire theater in June 1961, helped support a workingwomen's hostel in Bombay. Hollywood was the scene for a most unusual auction in 1963, as forty thousand items of Indian jewelry were presented in Los Angeles in order to both raise money for the National Defense Fund and to bring in foreign exchange to India.[16] A confidential 1964 memo asked whether Hollywood's blocked rupees could be used to pay for Air India freight for Hong Kong–based Shaw Brothers' studio prints into India. In this way, blocked rupees could be used to facilitate Hong Kong cinema distribution in India, but it also wrangled a way for the Shaws to use Hollywood blocked rupees to pay for airfreight anywhere that Air India flew—most critically for them, between Hong Kong and Tokyo.[17] While scattered and isolated, these assorted creative initiatives were united by the common goal of expending Hollywood's blocked funds in India.

One of the major ways in which Hollywood spent blocked funds was to lease theaters in Bombay, establishing links to iconic movie palaces. MGM linked to the Strand and Metro, Fox leased Sterling and got access to Regal to show *Cleopatra*, Paramount and Universal had ties to the New Empire and the New Excelsior, and Warner Brothers, looking for a Bombay theater to showcase *My Fair Lady*, leased the Strand, which also had an arrangement with Fox and United Artists.

While the Indian government insisted on Indian participation in theater ownership, refusing dollars to buy theaters outright, Hollywood used its blocked funds to renovate and refurbish Indian movie theaters.[18] In exchange for exclusive screenings of Hollywood films like *The Birds* and *Cleopatra*, members of the MPEA sometimes offered interest-free loans from its blocked funds to theater owners interested in renovation. As we shall see in the next chapter, given the long-standing restrictions on theater construction in India, these theaters became iconic in the exhibition imaginary in India. Indian producers complained about the money spent on refurbishing these elite theaters, especially given the restrictions placed on theater construction in India over the preceding twenty years.[19]

The film industry crisis of foreign exchange was also linked to changes in the representation of Hollywood in the Bombay industry. In order to sketch out this shift, let's review the structural conditions in the Indian industry at the time. In India, cinema was largely excluded from state-subsidized industrialization after independence. The production sector suffered from import duties on equipment and film stock, while the exhibition sector was hobbled by a ban on new theater construction. Policy initiatives aimed at regularizing film finance in the early 1950s were not taken up until the late 1960s. With the postwar collapse of the studios, independent star–producers entered into the film trade with an entrepreneurial mind-set. The popularity of melodrama and other genres in Hindi cinema's "Golden Age" obscured a somewhat precarious Bombay industry fragmented by sectorial conflict. National networks were not a priority and disparate local regimes and priorities fractured large-scale domestic investment.[20] Even though domestic revenues had risen by the 1960s, the Bombay film industry faced difficult financial times as tensions between the production, distribution, and exhibition sectors increased.[21] High entertainment taxes, rising percentages for distributors and exhibitors, and government surveillance of tax-evading film stars hobbled the production sector. Furthermore, interest on private loans to the industry ranged from 50 to 80 percent annually, and as production costs rose, more independent producers joined the film trade. With inflation on the rise and currency devaluation on the horizon, the industry increasingly looked overseas for new sources of revenue.[22]

The Indian government begrudgingly recognized the film industry's international imperatives. From the mid-1960s on, the Indian government granted the expenditure of valuable foreign exchange to film producers wanting to shoot overseas, under the assumption that the expenditure of foreign exchange would promote Indian cinema overseas and encourage exports. However, while 1960s Hindi cinema depicted a colorful world of global travel and leisure,[23] the industry was stymied by the difficulty in making money flow freely. With film export to Africa, the Middle East, Southeast Asia, and the U.K., the Indian industry earned Rs.22 million worth of foreign exchange, but spent Rs.30 million mostly on importing raw film and on financing the "export promotion" of location shooting abroad. The deficit created a backlash in the editorial pages of *Filmfare*, which noted, "By what strange logic can government allow exchange earned from certain fixed territories to be squandered in totally different territories without even a ghost of a chance of the films concerned finding release there? When foreign exchange is so scarce, when millions in the country miss a meal, cannot the film industry itself in its own larger interests call upon producer members to miss a foreign location or two, unless vital to the plot, which such locations rarely are."[24]

Hollywood remained at the center of the broader Indian foreign exchange crisis throughout the 1960s as film publications documented a shift in the representation and reputation of Hollywood in India. Shifting from a fascination with the foreign exchange possibilities of Indian cinema's cooperation with Hollywood overseas, the tone quickly darkened to one of deep suspicion with Hollywood emerging as the enemy. This divergent discourse on foreign exchange is clear in the pages of the trade newspaper *Blitz*, in headlines separated by only three years. On June 24, 1967, the paper advised film producers to "go West" and earn foreign exchange, while on January 3, 1970, they advised the industry to "End Hollywood Monopoly" in India, stay home where it belonged, and to stop wasting foreign exchange on shooting globetrotting Hindi films like *Sangam* and *Love in Tokyo*.

The January 1970 comments from A. M. Tariq, chairman of the Indian Motion Picture Export Corporation, illustrate the severe deterioration of Bombay cinema's relationship with Hollywood over the issue of foreign exchange. Writing in *Blitz*, Tariq claimed that "we must end the stranglehold of Hollywood in India, and the sooner we do it the better it will be not only for the Indian film industry but for Indian filmgoers too . . . For too long, we have been exploited by Hollywood and, over the years, crores [tens of millions] of rupees have been taken out of India." He also insisted on the end to "Hollywood's monopoly over prestige theaters in India," and demanded that Hollywood distribute Indian films on a reciprocal basis. "But they will not do this," he added, noting that "it has always been a one way street with them." *Blitz* "fully endorsed" what it called Tariq's "brilliant suggestions."[25] Tariq's comments make clear that some in Bombay resented the power Hollywood exerted over the Indian industry. At the same time, in calling for Hollywood distribution of Hindi cinema, Tariq's statements also exemplified Bombay's continued hope for greater reciprocity between American and Indian industries.

Into the 1970s, "blocked funds" discourse and practice continued to feature reciprocal measures, although trade embargoes still limited Hollywood export to India. As a result, Hollywood found some creative ways to spend its unrepatriated profits in India. For example, in 1975 MPAA president Jack Valenti used blocked funds to pay for a party at the U.S. embassy during the International Film Festival in India, where he lobbied the U.S. ambassadorial core to plead Hollywood's cause to the attending Indian government officials. By this time, Hollywood had amassed almost Rs.60 million in blocked funds that were funneled into more location shoots. Most famously, Columbia spent over US$300,000 worth of blocked funds to shoot a sequence in *Close Encounters of the Third Kind*. These scattered incidents were part of a larger blocked fund logic emerging in the 1970s, where U.S. companies agreed to direct 20 percent of India earnings into U.S.–Indian coproductions and give 20 percent toward providing interest-free loans to Indian corporations. In 1978, the Kinematograph Renters Society offered the Indian Film Finance Corporation an interest-free loan of Rs.10 million, culled from the vast store of blocked funds in India, on the condition that the money be used for the construction of new theaters. Foreshadowing its interest in multiplex theater construction in the 1990s, discussed in the next chapter, Hollywood was convinced that investment in the Indian theatrical sector would allow greater exhibition venues for American features. By the early 1980s, 40 percent of Hollywood's gross earnings in India were dispersed toward operating and maintenance costs for local distribution offices, while an additional 30 percent was used to fund interest-free loans used by the National Film Development Corporation to finance theater construction and aid domestic filmmakers. Of the remaining earnings, less than 10 percent was distributed toward repatriation to the United States, with the last 20 percent added to the pool of blocked funds.

Hard currency repatriation limits were liberalized in the 1990s, and contemporary limits on direct investment and foreign exchange are now much looser than they were in the 1970s. Hollywood is still trying to find ways to both profit from and collaborate with Bombay cinema. Despite its unpredictability, "blocked funds" actually facilitated a form of inter-industry exchange, as one form of circulation was enabled by the arrest of another. As we shall see in the next section, Hollywood's Hindi coproductions represent a different "token" of exchange between the United States and India.

At Home, in the World: Hollywood's Hindi Productions

From the beginning, Hollywood's engagement with India combined fiction and reality, with the screen representation of India produced through travelogue and fabrication by American scenarists. As I noted in the introduction, India was both a physical place to "orient" early Hollywood and an imagined space of the fantastic, an otherworldly realm. While early Hollywood used India-based production to demonstrate its global reach and legitimacy, "India" was also a transnational production, with many scenes filmed in New Jersey, Connecticut, and right at home on the West Coast. The imagination of India played a critical role in the "worlding" of Hollywood space and place.

For example, Mutual's *The Toast of Death* (1915) was set in India but filmed in California. For reviewers, knowledge of this physical displacement actually added to the film's veracity. One reviewer noted that it was "notwithstanding the fact that California was the locale of the production, a real Oriental atmosphere pervades the film, and it seems doubtful if Director Ince could have staged a more convincing picture in Bombay itself." The reviewer then listed the crucial details that made the picture a convincing account of Indian life: "Elephants, camels, long retinues of servants, Indian princes and potentates, English officers and troops of every color and variety, tropical vegetation, servants, thatched huts and regal palaces, are all there in profusion, each lending its bit toward the whole effect."[26]

This piecemeal fabrication of India was common to Hollywood's production apparatus in the early years. For example, *The Lucky Charm* (1918) featured a Hindu temple and an Indian village built in Miami. This trend continued in many of the India scenes in Hollywood's landmark "empire films" of the 1930s, like *Gunga Din* and *The Rains Came*, which were filmed in Utah. A 1935 article in *Popular Mechanics* assessed the ways in which the Indian location was composed:

> Sometimes the movie-made scenery is even better than the real thing, and now and then, when a company is sent half way around the world to film parts of a picture, the results may be thrown away because lighting and technical problems cannot be controlled as well as nearer the studio. Three years ago, one studio spent months in shooting atmosphere scenes in India for backgrounds but after 70,000 feet of expensive, authentic film had been brought back most of it was discarded because a sharp-eyed location hunter had found identical scenery within a day's drive where the same scenes could be photographed to better advantage.[27]

In other words, Hollywood's local fabrications of Indian location could realize cost advantages while preserving the requisite alterity to transport viewers to exotic realms. By the 1970s, however, Hollywood's conventional wisdom suggested that actual travel to India could create on-screen realism and more directly cement a connection to the Indian audience. As I argued in the previous section, Hollywood's blocked funds subsidized some, but not all, of these "Indian" productions.

In the late 1970s, American film interest in India peaked with the production of *Shalimar* (fig. 2.1). Ranveer Singh and Krishna Shah's New York–based Judson Productions collaborated with Bombay's Laxmi Productions, using private Indian and American financing rather than the estimated US$17 million worth of blocked funds in India. A former stage director, Shah was a well-known American television screenwriter. He visited the film and television institute in Pune to see hundreds of Hindi films to familiarize himself with the idiom. *Shalimar*'s intent, as Shah described it, was to "show that viable films can be made by America or Britain in cooperation with India."[28] *Shalimar* was filmed mainly in Bangalore, and staffed with British rather than senior Indian film technicians. The film starred Rex Harrison as a jewel thief along with John Saxon, Sylvia Miles, and Hindi film stars Zeenat Aman and Dharmendra.

Occasional collaborations like *Shalimar* aside, there have been relatively few Indo-American productions in the past few decades. In the early 2000s, however, there was a marked interest in Indo-American productions as a way of breaking through Hollywood's market ceiling in India. Faced with an intransigent Indian market, Hollywood committed itself to "local" language film production in India. While Hollywood's interest acknowledged the increasing global investment in the Indian media sector, it also recognized that American cinema remained stuck at a 5–8 percent market share in India. Hoping to take comparative advantage of preexisting global distribution chains and with deep pockets for the capitalization of production, Hollywood entered into Hindi film production in a very public way.

A large majority of these films have been commercial and critical failures, illustrating the cultural complexity of producing narratives that combine an avowedly international agenda with more local theatrical traditions and audience preferences. In this section, I trace the emergence of contemporary Indo-American coproductions and assess the difficulties that Sony, Disney, Warner Brothers, Fox, and other studios have had in making Hindi films for a domestic and international audience.

There have been over two dozen such Indo-American collaborations, involving production and distribution co-ventures in India and abroad

Figure 2.1 Poster for *Shalimar*.

for films like *Marigold* (2007), *Roadside Romeo* (2008), *Saas Bahu Aur Sensex* (2008), *Do Dooni Chaar* (2010), *Dus Tola* (2010), *Zokkomon* (2011), and *Dum Maaro Dum* (2011). Hollywood's Hindi productions are designed both as "crossover cinema" to appeal to a broad international audience *and* as an indistinguishable part of Bollywood itself. Part of the reason that most of these films have been critical and commercial box-office failures is that, in its efforts to employ "localization" strategies in an acknowledgment of cultural difference, Hollywood has homogenized this difference into a *market*, naturalizing formulaic stereotypes of audience.[29] However, these films do represent a remarkable shift in Hollywood's India strategy. Through stand-alone and coproduction arrangements, these films cement Hollywood–Bollywood industry ties, integrate production and distribution, and popularize Hollywood in India. Hollywood studio's traditional Mumbai offices—some in existence for seventy-five years—are themselves insufficiently "local" partners for American studios. Hollywood is now looking for new ways to situate itself within the Indian mediascape.

Spearheading a push into Hindi production, Sony Pictures Entertainment (SPE) released its first Indian film, *Saawariya* (*Beloved*), in November 2007. *Saawariya*'s director, Sanjay Leela Bhansali, had directed the 2002 Hindi hit, *Devdas*, India's submission for Best Foreign Language Film at the 2003 Oscars. Based on a Dostoevsky short story, *Saawariya* was planned as the first Hindi film release for a major Hollywood outfit.

By the time of *Saawariya*'s production, Sony had already committed to Asian film production. One of Sony's subsidiaries, Columbia Pictures Film Production Asia, coproduced *Crouching Tiger, Hidden Dragon*, while Sony's independent film division, Sony Pictures Classics, distributed the film in the United States. Released in 2000, *Crouching Tiger* became the highest-grossing foreign-language film shown in the United States and was touted for proving the benefits of local production and global distribution. Sony was also involved in international Indian film distribution. In 2001, Sony Pictures Classics helped to distribute the Oscar-nominated Hindi film *Lagaan* in the English-speaking world.

Sony recognized that the economic value of Indian production and distribution extended beyond the big screen. In the 1990s, Indian cable television combined domestic programming with British and American soap operas, talk shows, news channels, and "generation oriented" music television, which engaged urban youth cultures and the industries that supported them (especially fast-food, soft-drink, music, and apparel sales). Threatened by the stark reality of empty cinema halls, the film industry geared itself to become a major television content provider. Themed TV channels exclusively designed to showcase cinema took off in the mid-1990s, with Hollywood supplying a good deal of content. In addition, with the proliferation of cable and satellite television in the 1990s, Hollywood studios struck lucrative Indian syndication deals for American television series. While Hollywood had dubbed India "the market of the future," in 1992 the U.S. majors received only US$70,000 a year for Indian television programming. However, with the government unblocking the rupee under new liberalization "reforms," program deals were soon struck in U.S. dollars and the average price for a syndicated U.S. television series went up from US$800 an hour to US$1,800.[30]

By the mid-1990s, transnational media companies involved in Indian television found that regional-language programming was more cost effective than syndication. In early 1994, Rupert Murdoch's STAR network acquired Indian programmer Zee Television and announced plans to set up a twenty-four-hour Hindi channel. Sony didn't want to miss the boat. In 1995, Sony Entertainment Television (SET) launched as a Hindi-language television channel focusing on family fare. Part of SET's interest in India was the possibility of leveraging its corporate parent's extensive film catalog. Repurposing Hollywood film content and syndicating American television hits alongside the production of Hindi-language television programming, Sony's initiatives illustrated what Melissa Butcher calls "the bi-directionality of transnational flows."[31] In 1997, Sony launched the AXN network, "built with Asian viewers in mind," and routinely featured American television hits like *CSI* for Indian audiences.[32]

Other networks followed suit. HBO launched in India in September 2000, with licensing agreements with Paramount, Universal, Warner Brothers, and Sony, and distribution through Turner International. HBO then joined Sony Entertainment's bundle of services in 2003 before returning to a Zee–Turner collaboration in 2005. Zee Network launched Zee Movies in March 2000, acquiring over seven hundred titles from U.K. and U.S. companies including Warner Brothers International Television and MGM. At the same time that American cable companies were able to leverage Hollywood films on their Indian networks (often in dubbed versions), production of local-language television clearly presented new possibilities for collaboration. Sony hoped to build a television presence associated with their production and distribution of locally produced films in India, which had been cleared by the Indian government in 1998. Fox and Universal quickly followed up on Sony's local initiates and secured the requisite permissions as well.

In the lead-up to the production of *Saawariya*, Sony Picture Entertainment CEO Michael Lynton said that Sony "recognize[s] the potential and importance of the Indian market and welcomes the opportunity to team up with the film industry in India. This is a defining moment for us as a company, and for filmmakers, artists and audiences in India as well."[33] Sony was getting more interested in India as its traditionally robust foreign markets were slowing, particularly in Western Europe, where theatrical attendance continued to decline. India, along with Russia, seemed like lucrative entry points for Sony. Both countries had strong domestic film industries with projected positive attendance growth. In Russia, already among the top ten foreign markets for Hollywood, movie attendance had increased by more than 30 percent in 2005. Sony had recently announced a Russian production and distribution venture in partnership with the Russia-based Patton Media Group. Moving beyond distribution, Sony was hoping to build on local-language production success elsewhere, and it already had production interests in China, Brazil, and Mexico. In addition to its television interests in India, Sony dubbed releases into Hindi, Bhojpuri, Telegu, and other languages. In 2007, Sony's *Spider-Man 3* became Hollywood's highest-grossing film in India, with six hundred English and regionally dubbed prints earning US$17 million. *Harry Potter and the Order of the Phoenix* and *Pirates of the Caribbean: At World's End* were also Indian successes . However, as Uday Singh, managing director of Sony in India, noted, a Hollywood film in English might attract five million viewers. Dubbing would only extend that audience to thirty million, which was still a mere fraction of the overall theatrical audience in India.[34] Hollywood clearly needed a bigger multiplier.

Sony was also looking to enhance its brand identity in India as its Hollywood competitors were eating into one another's distribution profits. In 2005, Warner Brothers started distributing Fox's pictures in India, after Fox shut down its Indian distribution arm, active since the 1930s. Universal and Paramount were planning to dissolve an international distribution partnership in 2007, working on developing distinctive distribution networks in key foreign markets.

Sony also wanted to jump ahead of Hollywood's long-anticipated Hindi production slate. In 2002, Fox planned to produce three of director Ram Gopal Verma's films, but the deal fell through. In early 2006, Disney announced a move into local-language production in India, partnering with Yash Raj Films to make animated films. Viacom's subsidiary Paramount also announced a Hindi production schedule, building on its experience in successfully localizing MTV for an Indian audience. With incentives for foreign investment in production, shifts in censorial policy, and a relaxing of the script-approval process and local hiring preconditions—which had curtailed Hollywood production in places like China—Hollywood's interest in Indian production was at an all-time high.

No wonder, then, that anticipation for *Saawariya* was intense. Sony opened a TV licensing office in India in 2007, just before the release of the film and partnered with Eros International, the India-based media group, on a Hindi production and distribution deal designed to release six to eight films per year. The deal was an unusual arrangement: Sony would handle U.S. distribution, while Eros would manage global distribution outside India and the United States. The two companies would share distribution in India.

Saawariya was released during the Hindu festival of Diwali in November 2007, across one thousand screens worldwide (over 750 in India). Combining the usual Bollywood love story with highly artificial art design, matte paintings, and unusual theatrical framings, *Saawariya* clearly attempted to navigate multiple film cultures. Most of the film takes place in a red-light district, where the protagonist, Ranbir Raj (played by Ranbir Kapoor), dances and romances against the background of recognizably Western imagery (figs. 2.2–2.4). In line with the producer's crossover intentions, *Saawariya* imagines the West as a backdrop to Bombay cinema action. The film's hodgepodge of iconography imagines European modernity as pastiche, surface, and special effect.

Figures 2.2, 2.3, and 2.4. In *Saawariya*, the protagonist, Ranbir Raj (played by Ranbir Kapoor), dances and romances against the background of recognizably Western imagery.

Saawariya was an almost immediate commercial and critical failure. While Sony had Sony offered Bhansali another picture even before the film's release, the Rs.350 million film was seen as an expensive, formulaic Bollywood romance suffering from sky-high expectations. The *Hindustan Times* noted that "as soon as the *Saawariya* premiere was over at around 1:30 am at Mumbai's IMAX multiplex, the word was out that it would find the going tough at the national box-office."[35] The editor of *Film Street Journal* and longtime Indian industry watcher Komal Nahata called *Saawariya* a "debacle, a bomb, a disaster."[36] Remarking on the film's production design, which drew inspiration from the Venetian Resort in Las Vegas, one Canadian reviewer claimed that we were "witnessing an Indian variation on an American cartoon based on one of Europe's great cities."[37]

Set in the colonial summer capital of Simla during the British Raj, the film stars Ranbir Kapoor, a fourth-generation scion of the famed Kapoor acting dynasty. However, *Saawariya* lacked other major A-list stars in leading roles and offered a weak mix of a dozen songs packed into a film that ran thirty minutes shorter than the usual Bollywood fare. *Saawariya* was quickly swamped by the release of *Om Shanti Om*, a raring, cheeky tribute to seventies Hindi cinema starring Shah Rukh Khan and featuring cameos from over thirty other Indian film stars. Budgeted at Rs.200 million, and released on over 1,400 screens worldwide, *Om* also had chart-topping songs released months before to generate buzz for the film. Responding to competition from *Saawariya*, *Om*'s star Khan said, "I wish Sony all the best, as they have taken a big chance fighting with me," adding, "I am India's giant."[38] Both films' directors also got into a spat, reported in the Indian media gossip pages, over a reported slight against Bhansali's mother. However, the real bone of contention was the concurrent release date, with Bhansali claiming priority because of an earlier announcement.

Sony had spent a massive Rs.50 million on a promotional "visibility" package for *Saawariya*, but it was no match for Khan's overwhelming public profile, which kept *Om Shanti Om* in the news for months before its release. After its opening weekend, *Om* had taken in US$19 million in India and *Saawariya* just over US$13 million. International audiences were kinder to the Sony picture than domestic ones, but the damage was done. In a sharp rebuke to the Indo-American coproduction slate, producer Mahesh Bhatt added to the consistent criticism of *Saawariya* in the press: "I hope that this will function as a wake-up call to investors in Hollywood. You may have your marketing network, you may have your inexhaustible financial network, but you need to get a sense of the palate of the Bollywood consumer."[39] In the wake of *Saawariya*'s difficulties, many Indian media executives expressed public concern about Hollywood financing. Ronnie Screwvala, chairman of media company UTV, said that Hollywood financing for Hindi productions "does not make sense for us."[40]

Nevertheless, Hollywood studios remained interested in Hindi acquisitions. A new Disney–Yash Raj partnership announced the production of animated films, including *Roadside Romeo*, and Viacom announced a fifty-fifty partnership with India's TV18 Group to produce multimedia programming.

In 2007, the same year as Sony's *Saawariya* disappointment, Warner Brothers announced the development of two Hindi film projects, part of a proposed annual slate of three to six Hindi releases. Its inaugural project, announced in August 2007, was an action–comedy tentatively titled *Made in China*, to be directed by Nikhil Advani, whose debut film, *Kal Ho Na Ho*, had been a box-office and critical success in 2003. In addition to its directorial credentials, *Made in China* was to star Akshay Kumar and Deepika Padukone, who was now hugely popular after her critical and commercial success as the female lead in *Om Shanti Om*.

Warner's new film was also going to be the first Hindi film shot in China, where Hollywood had shown increased interest. In 2005, press reports suggested that Hollywood studios planned to invest over US$150 million in the Chinese film industry. While exhibition quotas kept Hollywood releases to a minimum, Sony and Warner Brothers developed production and financing interests in China. Excited by explosive economic growth, cheap location shooting, and the tradition of vibrant martial arts genres and generations of film-school trained talent, Hollywood was more and more interested in producing Chinese-language films for the domestic and international market. CineAsia, the annual film industry conference, held its yearly meeting in China for the first time in 2005, with a keynote address from MPAA CEO Dan Glickman, who had lobbied for China's entry to the World Trade Organization as Bill Clinton's agriculture secretary in 2001.

Warner Brothers had already invested heavily in the Chinese multiplex sector after pulling back from Indian theatrical expansion plans in the early 1990s (see chap. 3).[41] Warner's Indian deal helped publicize its broader localization commitment. In 2007, WB had thirty-five "local language" films on its worldwide production slate, but Warner's Hindi film venture was seen as way to activate Hollywood's dual interest in China and India, a purpose clearly visualized on the front page of *Variety* on February 12–18, 2007, with the headline "H'Wood Quest: Rupee vs. Yuan."

Warner's new Hindi project, renamed *Chandni Chowk to China*, was initially budgeted at US$12 million and planned for worldwide release following the Beijing Olympics in the late summer of 2008. The Indian production houses, Ramesh Sippy Productions and Orion Pictures, would come on to produce the film, with Warner Brothers holding worldwide distribution rights. Ramesh Sippy, who directed *Sholay* (1975), perhaps the most famous Hindi film in history, noted that "what we hope to achieve at the minimum is a greater knowledge and understanding of the workings and systems of Hollywood and the Indian film industry. I am sure we both stand to gain a lot from each other."[42] Hindi cinema's reigning action star, with over one hundred films to his credit, Akshay Kumar was to play a cook who is mistaken for a martial arts master. Curiously, the film story mirrors Kumar's own experience working as a cook in Bangkok before coming back to India in the early 1990s. To prepare for his new role, Kumar trained with Huan-Chiu "Dee Dee" Ku, a Hong Kong–based martial arts coordinator who worked on Quentin Tarantino's *Kill Bill: Vol. 1* (2003).

Chandni Chowk was set to begin filming in January 2008, with a planned six-month China shoot. Set up as an "assisted production" rather than a Chinese coproduction, the film was seen as a step toward a long-awaited Indo-Chinese coproduction agreement, as the Indian industry looked for wider commercial distribution in China and an exchange of actors and technicians between the Beijing Film Academy and the Film and Television Institute of India. While some sequences were eventually shot in Shanghai and near the Great Wall, the China shoot had to be shortened because Olympics organizers found that the film production distracted from preparations for the upcoming Games. China filming shifted to Bangkok as part of a larger project to bring location shooting to Thailand. Commenting on the shift, director Advani noted, "Bangkok's topography is quite similar to China. Also, it's a very Bollywood-friendly country. So we just had to let go of the real country because the action scenes required Olympian skills and infrastructure."[43] Cheaper than European location shooting, Thailand was emerging as a popular shooting location for Bollywood, with Bangkok a particularly favored backdrop for gritty crime dramas and action shoots. Like *Saawariya* before it, *Chandni Chowk* used identifiable foreign footage to serve as the backdrop of the main story (see figs. 2.5 and 2.6).

Figures 2.5 and 2.6. *Chandni Chowk*'s foreign signifiers.

Chandni Chowk was just Warner's initial foray into Indian production. In February 2008, WB announced a second Bollywood coproduction deal, *Saas Bahu Aur Sensex*. In April, after signing a postproduction and film restoration deal with the Chennai-based Prasad Corporation in December 2007, Warner Brothers Pictures India signed a four-picture production and distribution deal with the Chennai-based Ocher Studios, hoping to build a South Indian audience. In May 2008, Warner Brothers announced a Hindi remake of its 2005 comedy *Wedding Crashers*. This was to be the first "authorized" Hindi remake of a Hollywood film. In December, Warner announced a three-picture deal with *Chowk* director Advani's People Tree Films.

The Bombay terrorist attacks in late November 2008 delayed the release of *Chandni Chowk to China*. Eventually released in India, the U.K., Australia, and Germany on January 16, 2009, *Chandni Chowk* was described by a senior Warner executive as "a fusion of two rich cultures. These are the two nations that Hollywood is most excited about."[44] While *Chandni Chowk* used China as a kind of window dressing for song sequences, in the style of *Saawariya*'s Euro-pastiche, the constant refrain of bilateral friendship and camaraderie in the film spoke to Warner's commitment to China and India (see figs. 2.7–2.10).

Figures 2.7–2.10. Warner's commitment to China and India was represented by a constant refrain of friendship and camaraderie in the film *Chandni Chowk to China*.

The film's protagonist, Sidhu (Akshay Kumar), travels to China to fight a master criminal that has oppressed a Chinese village for years. Sidhu's victory joins India and China together in a kind of social realist fantasy that reiterates the mutual national admiration initiatives of the 1950s before the two nations went to war in 1962.

However, like *Saawariya* before it, *Chandni Chowk* opened to scathing reviews and was declared a box-office flop. After average opening billings, theater attendance declined precipitously. With budget and release costs approaching Rs.1 billion, *Chowk's* failure was a costly one and Hollywood began to question its coproduction strategy in India, especially as distribution-oriented ventures, like Fox STAR's fifteen to eighteen picture deal in India (including *Slumdog Millionaire*), were less risky and more profitable. When it came to organizing coproductions, Fox was more careful than its Hollywood brethren. In 2010, Fox entered into a two-picture Tamil production deal with A. R. Murugadoss, who had directed the Hindi remake of *Ghajini* (2008), an enormous box-office success (the "original" Tamil *Ghajini* [2005] was inspired by the American film *Memento* [2000]).

Other American studios looked for more ambitious measures and decided that Hollywood-branded Hindi productions were not the best strategy in India. In 2012, a few years after Disney failed to acquire a majority stake in the production house Yash Raj Films for over US$800 million, Disney acquired a 93 percent stake in the India media conglomerate UTV Software Communications. With interests in film and television production, postproduction, and distribution, UTV was a significant player in the Indian mediasphere. Disney had initially acquired a 15 percent stake in 2006 and doubled its stake two years later for US$190 million. Disney's investment, inked the same year that Reliance announced its DreamWorks partnership, marked an upswing in acquisition activity between American and Indian media. Disney's almost-full purchase in early 2012 represented a new trajectory for Hollywood in India. The deepening alignment between American and Indian media conglomerates paid almost immediate dividends as Disney–UTV distributed *The Avengers* later the same year. The film went on to become one of Hollywood's highest-grossing successes in India.

The coproduction and acquisition initiatives described in this section demonstrate Hollywood's interests in India as part of a global production enterprise. Of course, these are high-profile, large-scale initiatives between integrated media companies. Given the clear financial imperatives, what are the cultural politics implicated in these forms of co-location? The next section takes up this question by examining contemporary transformations in the management of offshore labor or "outsourcing" as a way of gauging the relationship between the Indian and American media industries. Focusing on a number of practices—from location shooting to postproduction and new technologies of labor integration—the next section looks at how the laboring body is entangled within geographies of cultural production. The Indian worker, employed through the displacement of American labor, has emerged as the key figure in a discourse of racialized anxieties and has disrupted corporate narratives of outsourcing's efficiency.

The Cultural Politics of Media Outsourcing

Contemporary outsourcing practices reflect a thirty-year trajectory in the transformation of American labor, from the rise of container shipping technologies that facilitated the transport of low-cost overseas commodities, to wage stagnation, and the decline of American manufacturing. A new international division of labor (NIDL) rose out of numerous crises in Western industrialized economies in the 1970s, including widespread unemployment, capital flight, poor investment in domestic industries, and increasing poverty in the newly industrializing countries (NIC) of the East. As multinational companies began to redistribute production activities from the West to lower-wage areas in the East, the labor power of the NICs became part of their export-oriented infrastructure.[45] The shift in electronics manufacture—particularly semiconductors—to Asian centers since the mid-1960s created an international assembly line system where labor intensive and repetitive tasks were assigned to a female workforce that bears the brunt of gender harassment, health hazards, low pay, a lack of benefits, and limited options for upward job mobility.[46]

The NIDL's impact on the screen industries, Toby Miller suggests, has been to shift cultural production around the world as media industries take advantage of local currencies, labor laws, foreign investment incentives, and new technologies of connectivity. Miller notes that the "flexible specialization" of work in Hollywood has moved toward a system of contracting creative processes to independent companies around the world, with revenue, distribution, and joint-production arrangements tying together the studios with a dispersed array of international players.[47] The NIDL consolidates seventy-five years of Hollywood internationalism, from the importation of directorial talent from Germany in the 1920s, international location shooting in the 1950s, foreign direct investment, runaway production, and a kind of "peripheral Taylorism" from the 1960s onward.[48] As a group of us claimed in *Global Hollywood*, Hollywood's engagement with the NIDL, accompanied by the inevitable disenfranchisement of below-the-line workers, spreads risk and investment around the world, creating complex networks of exchange by relying on "cultural consanguinity, favorable rates of exchange, supine governments, minimal worker internationalism, and high levels of skill equivalency."[49] The critical location of international labor exploitation at the intersection of national industrial development and global integration is part of the post–World War II trade policy consensus, where, as Saskia Sassen notes, "national boundaries do not act as barriers so much as mechanisms reproducing the system."[50]

Hollywood's labor management demonstrates the continued role of the national in the creation and extraction of value in the global economy. The NIDL heightens the ability of multinational companies to extract labor power from different locations. Local economies, currencies and conversion rates, labor laws and union representation, training centers and management philosophies play a crucial role in instituting economic variation across the world. Even when such variations only partially correspond to national contiguities, they are legitimated through ties and affiliations with existing state governmentalities. The national does not only map onto activities concretized in a particular geographic enclosure, however. Understood outside the domains of sovereign exclusivity, the national is a type of *spatial performance* that produces and reproduces the territorial through forms of social practice.[51] Outsourcing demonstrates that the national is an enumerating center and command metaphor for industrial, institutional, and cultural difference, spread across an array of social practices from informal codes of etiquette to regularizations of identity and domicile.[52]

While the classical international division of labor was rooted in man-ufacturing, new technologies have spurred the shift toward information outsourcing, a move aided by the heavily deregulated and privatized service sectors of newly industrialized economies. Successive U.S. ad-ministrations, interested in lowering costs in labor-intensive commod-ity production, have promoted American workforce management and technical expertise while encouraging foreign direct investment. What began as lower-cost alternatives to commodity manufacturing shifted to the remote management of services as an information technology (IT) revolution was enabled by a highly interconnected telecommunica-tions infrastructure, massive server capacity, and high-bandwidth data transfers.

In 2001, the U.S. Department of Commerce (DoC) released a report acknowledging the productivity gains associated with the film industry's new technologies of labor. "Runaway production"—the displacement of film and television shooting from the United States to foreign locations, incentivized by cost savings through tax and labor subsidy—increased from 14 to 27 percent of the total percentage of U.S. film and television production in 1998, raising the question: how American was Hollywood anyway? The DoC recognized that foreign governments were now ac-tively recruiting Hollywood production and postproduction activities in order to build an infrastructure for their own film industries:

A technological revolution in the industry has changed the nature of film production to such an extent that physical proximity is no longer a requirement for the many persons and sub-industries involved in the film production chain . . . Long distances and geographical borders are simply not as important as they once were. This phenomenon holds true for many other specialists involved in film production, particularly those involved in the post-production phase. The ease of transmitting data over long distances and in short periods, combined with the addition of tech-nical infrastructure and a skilled labor force, has enabled film makers to take advantage of lower labor and production costs in other countries [that] have developed appropriate infrastructure and skilled labor.[53]

Of course, outsourcing in the film sector was just a small part of a much wider global phenomenon, and by the mid-1990s India was well on its way to gaining a competitive advantage in the international reorganization of IT work.

Indian IT competency came to the forefront of American managerial consciousness in the 1990s, where Indian firms like Infosys, Tata Consultancy Services, and Wipro handled coding work for Western firms worried by the Y2K software glitch. American companies were interested in India's English-language skills among the educated middle class and low labor costs that facilitated the construction of massive labor centers designed for service tasks. In addition, India's night/day time difference with the United States enabled global IT work to take place around the clock, demonstrating the ways in which spatial disintegration can be coordinated by the management of new "geographies of temporality."[54] The Indian call-center phenomenon has receded in recent years, with rising labor costs, lower-cost competition from Southeast Asia, and what some in the Indian industry see as a "lack of empathy" with the American customer service and end-consumer base. Furthermore, outsourcing has become a thorny electoral issue in the United States, occupying a featured place in debates about citizenship and labor.[55]

Despite political tensions, a diverse array of "back-office" labor tasks is now outsourced to India. Outsourcing has not been limited to media technology—India has also emerged as a hub for medical tourism and child surrogacy. In recent years, American medical laboratories began outsourcing to India for blood test diagnosis, CT/MRI scans and x-ray analysis, and medical transcription. "Business process outsourcing" is commonly routed to India for data crunching, legal and financial research, and other document work for management consultancies and law firms.[56] Under an encroaching bottom line, American newspapers have outsourced local reporting, copyediting, and layout design. The Indian outsourcing model has been so successful that Indian firms like Wipro are building "outsourcing campuses" in China, Vietnam, and Romania.

Recently, India has emerged as a significant site for Hollywood's "media content outsourcing" tasks. A number of initiatives speak to the overall trend. In 2007, Sony Pictures Imageworks acquired a majority stake in the Indian effects studio FrameFlow. The following year, Warner Brothers Motion Picture Imaging allied with the Indian firm Prasad Corp to provide postproduction services to Indian, American, and international clients. Also in 2008, NBC Universal acquired a 26 percent stake in NDTV Networks, while Disney increased its share in UTV Software Communications from 15 to 32 percent (on its way to an even larger share) and signed a ten-year deal to lease space at ND Studios near Bombay. In 2009, Adlabs Films, founded as a film-processing unit and now a subsidiary of the giant Indian conglomerate Reliance ADA Group, announced plans to expand into analog-to-digital content conversion. Adlabs's announcement was part of a larger international strategy, including digital content distribution to fiber-optic technology, linking movie theaters in the United States and India, and digitally restoring films in Indian archives. Adlabs's interest in monetizing India's cinema's degrading back catalog through digital restoration, in addition to providing processing services compliant with U.S. Motion Picture Association standards, is a "spillover" effect of IT outsourcing.

Hollywood has long known about the cost savings of film production in India. On a visit to Hollywood in 1928, A. Narayanan, of the Exhibitors Film Service of Bombay, claimed that cheaper labor (including lower wages for stars), inexpensive materials, and natural scenery accounted for the proliferate production of Indian cinema.[57] Nevertheless, for decades, India stood largely on the sidelines of the international division of labor. This was primarily the result of perceived inadequacies in the technical infrastructure of its domestic film industry. The distributor J. P Jhalani noted in 1947, while on a trip to the United States with producer/director Mehboob Khan, that "if a reciprocal agreement could be made with some large American company to help us build up our studios and equip them with the best American facilities, it would be of material benefit to both our countries."[58] Yet, despite calls to upgrade facilities, in 1965 it was common knowledge that between the major Indian film production centers of Bombay, Calcutta, and Madras, only five to seven studio facilities could handle the demands of foreign producers. Given the relative lack of local production facilities, Hollywood studios interested in Indian coproduction were obliged to edit locally shot Indian footage in the United States and add postproduction effects in London FX studios. All of this changed, however, along with the shifting constellation of cultural, industrial, and institutional alignments in the 1990s. Economic liberalization, television advertising, the emergence of digital graphics studios, corporate accountability, and the rise of the personal computer set a course for the future of Indian labor outsourcing in the media industry.

While Western European and Japanese film industries considered outsourcing work to India in recent years, the Indian commercial digital graphics sector has become a fairly prominent provider of editing and other postproduction work (including digital animation and computer-generated imagery, compositing, color correction, and digital sound) for big-budget, effects-intensive, American feature films. Since the late 1990s, graphics studios in Bombay and Madras, and IT labs in the high-tech centers of Bangalore and Hyderabad, have done postproduction work for a number of Hollywood films, including *Gladiator*, *Spider-Man*, *Nutty Professor II: The Klumps*, *Titanic*, *Independence Day*, *Swordfish*, and *Men in Black*. Cost savings are a major factor: entry-level salaries for Indian visual effects artists are less than a tenth of Hollywood starting salaries of $40,000–$50,000.

Many Indian digital media companies consolidated their position within the domestic market by riding the wave of computer-led graphics design in the 1990s, producing commercials for Indian cable television channels and slick marketing portfolios for the fashion industry. Designing thirty-second spots for multinational clients keen to tap the discretionary income of the Indian consumer, Indian graphics firms built relationships with hardware manufacturers like Silicon Graphics to drive the technology of promotion for their brand portfolios. In addition, the computer-aided flair of the 1990s Indian television commercial pushed the envelope on visual sophistication in Indian corporate design. A number of prominent cinematographers and production designers cut their teeth working at these graphics companies, bringing digital postproduction and nonlinear editing techniques with them when they crossed over to the film industry. The intersection between television advertising and brand design philosophies, based largely on the functional possibilities of computer-generated graphics, greatly influenced the rise of the "aesthetics of global display" in mid-1990s Indian media.[59]

As digital postproduction technologies integrated into larger commercial film industries worldwide, and as special effects broadened from being a generic visual marker of science-fiction film, the demand for Indian animation and postproduction services took off in the mid-2000s.

While Hollywood's reliance on special effects outsourcing dipped after the September 11, 2001, attacks, Indian firms with more open production schedules focused on domestic film and television. By the time Hollywood returned a few months after 9/11, Indian firms like Crest Animation, UTV Toonz, JadooWorks, and Maya Entertainment were ready to compete for business.

Many of these firms, originally founded as outsourcing partners, moved into original programming for Indian and international audiences. LA-based Hollywood contract houses also opened Bombay affiliates. For example, Visual Computing Labs, which created two hundred computer-generated shots for the Hindi film *Jodha Akbar* at the same time its corporate parent Tata Elxsi was working on *xXx: State of the Union*, *Into the Blue*, and *Spider-Man 3*, opened up a new facility in Santa Monica in 2009.[60] Rhythm & Hues was a high-profile visual effects outfit founded in Los Angeles in the late 1980s that opened studios in Mumbai, Hyderabad, and Cyberjaya in Malaysia, in order to facilitate a twenty-four-hour production schedule.[61] Dozens of Mumbai-based Rhythm & Hues technicians worked on *The Chronicles of Narnia*, which became the first American film with a significant Indian collaboration to be nominated for an Oscar for best visual effects (VFX). These companies are also able to capitalize on the rise of special effects in Indian cinema. Recently, Indian films like *Enthiran* and *Ra.One* have ratcheted up expectations for the visual and effects industry. *Love Story 2050* (2008) had 1,300 VFX shots, paving the way for the prodigious use of VFX in big-budget Hindi cinema but also boosting confidence in Indian effects houses. However, the bankruptcy filing of Rhythm & Hues in 2013, on the heels of its widely admired work on *Life of Pi* (2012), demonstrates the endemic precariousness of the VFX sector. Michael Curtin and John Vanderhoef suggest that this instability is due to the subcontracting process that drives the industry in a "race to the bottom."[62] Prana Studios, an India-based firm with strong Bombay cinema connections, acquired Rhythm & Hues in 2013.

Recently, there has been a spike in 3D conversion, sparked by the global success of films like *Avatar* (2009), which created new Indian postproduction contracts. Following the popularity of *Avatar* in India, Reliance MediaWorks announced a tie-in with In-Three, a California-based 2D–3D conversion company to convert both new and back-catalog Hollywood films in a process called "dimensionalization." In addition, the Indian postproduction and camera rental company Prime Focus rebranded its North American facilities in 2009, premiering a 2D–3D conversion service called View-D. The work of Indian studios adding a third dimension to Hollywood films is projected to cut 50 percent off the usual costs of 3D conversion. This move toward 3D also justifies upgrading existing multiplex screens and has the benefit of curtailing piracy because of the specialized technologies of reception required for 3D films. In March 2011, Lucasfilm announced a partnership with Prime Focus to produce the 3D conversion for *Star Wars: Episode I—The Phantom Menace*. Furthermore, in July 2011, MediaWorks announced a partnership with the California-based visual effects company Digital Domain to open media outsourcing studios in Mumbai and London. Launched in 1993 by director James Cameron and other investors, Digital Domain has worked on special effects on films from *Titanic* to *TRON: Legacy*. Reliance's MediaWorks partnership is significant because it offers the Indian firm an entry into the elite budgetary echelon of Hollywood film production.

With the volume of American postproduction work being outsourced to South Asia—along with music composition, poster design, web marketing, and other promotional tasks—the global film press wondered whether Hollywood was becoming more and more Indian. However, we should be wary of industry utopianism that mythologizes the collapse of spatial distance in the remote management of cultural labor.[63] After all, there are intense cultural and intersubjective pressures exerted by the fiction of co-terminality in the commodity industries that contract labor overseas. As the call-center phenomenon has made clear, outsourcing creates tremendous fault lines between citizenship and labor, sparking anxieties about workers losing jobs to overseas competitors.

Responding to the consistent presence of alterity in labor outsourcing, the commodity industries broker what I call "symbolic forms of proximity" to dampen the anxieties of consumers and managers alike (workers don't seem to count), while facilitating the coordination of specific tasks. These symbolic forms of proximity encompass a number of practices facilitated by new technologies of near-instantaneous connectivity. Primary among these is the idea of co-presence, which approximates the forms of interaction deemed crucial to maintaining the intimate sociality of modernity.[64] The comfortable familiarity of "live" contact via telephone, satellite link, or the Internet soothes worries about managing dispersed local labor cultures. Another form of proximity is brokered through English-language public culture, which becomes important for managerial control and authorizes networks of familiarity between American industries and their laboring Others.[65]

Despite the management of intercultural difference, the lingering effects of developmental inferiority remain. Shortly after its founding, Indian animation company Toonz invited Rob Coleman from the visual effects giant Industrial Light and Magic (ILM) to deliver the keynote speech at an international conference. Visiting Toonz's new headquarters in Technopark in 2000, the first and largest technology park in India, Coleman assessed the facilities: "There were 450-Megahertz machines, faster than what we have at ILM. They had the latest Animo and Toon Boom software and 3D Studio MAX. They also asked very informed questions. But behind the questions, I could sense that they were worried they're behind us. They actually didn't believe me when I told them that their equipment is right up to par. Though they've recently gotten Internet access and are now reading about visual effects on various Web sites, I guess because of everything else in their world, they think they must be behind."[66]

Here, Coleman reproduces one of the mantras about the enabling effects of information and communication technology in the Global South: the idea that information and communication technology offers India a way to "leapfrog" the West in technological superiority is a potent ideology of economic globalization. However, such sentiment, offered fifteen years ago at the dawn of an Indian media outsourcing era, has not diminished long-standing structural inequalities in the division of cultural labor.

The most significant criticism leveled at Indian media process outsourcing firms is over a perceived "lack of quality." Most American producers outsource repetitive, labor-intensive postproduction tasks to Indian outfits, like wire removal, digital mattes, basic compositing, and rotoscoping. This has opened a "creativity versus execution" divide in the effects and animation industry, with Indian labor reduced to performing relatively mundane digital tasks while U.S.-based designers make the aesthetic decisions.

While a few American productions are produced from conceptualization to postproduction in India, most projects reproduce the classic labor–management divide, with Indians occupying the role of technician and Americans the role of artistic director. Studios seem to be unabashed about this ethnicized cultural calculus. For example, the head executive at Geon, which opened a studio facility in Bombay in late 2008 with funding from the Indian conglomerate Sahara, notes that the studio is looking to hire fifty more artists, but with only one "Westerner" for every five to ten Indians.[67] Similarly, a U.S. team manages the new Reliance/In-Three partnership, designed to coordinate one thousand Bombay-based technicians in the labor-intensive task of converting Hollywood's back catalog to 3D. One of the technical heads of the new outfit notes that "you can't just press a button and have a computer do it. You have to take artistic decisions, such as what is going to appear in the foreground . . . it's labor-intensive, but you don't need 300 Leonardo da Vincis. Key decisions can be made by a handful of people."[68]

Some in the Indian industry are resisting the execution/creativity divide as part of their mandate. Arguing that Indian digital artists and animators are tired of doing routine cleanup tasks for Hollywood, an executive at Eyeqube notes that "we don't want to be jobbers. We want effects designers as part of the daily set, thinking of scenes along directors."[69]

Clearly, the symbolic proximity brokered by new technologies of management has reinstituted old labor hierarchies and tensions. As a result, we seem to be at a tipping point in the Indian recruitment of Hollywood production, with the United States pushing back against outsourcing as well. During his November 2010 trip to India, Barack Obama promoted increasing Indian exports to the United States and creating American jobs as a way to balance American jobs lost to Indian outsourcing. Accompanying—if not complicating—these criticisms of outsourcing in terms of labor and national identity, there are a number of new industrial alignments attempting to "respatialize" media production.

One such respatialization is the Indian "one-stop shop." The common global perception that *Slumdog Millionaire* was a Hollywood film— "It was the first time that a film made by a Hollywood director on an Indian theme had gripped audiences in the West," noted the *Business*

Times Singapore[70]—has created the impression that Hollywood location shooting in India can be combined with Bombay cinema's new focus on rationalized and efficient production. While there are some Indian companies, like the Bombay-based On the Road Productions, that can help international producers with line production, location shooting, local technicians, and streamlining government clearances, the real turning point has been the building of one-stop facilities marked as "cost plus quality" outfits, where projects can be taken from pre-visualization to postproduction. Yash Raj Film's Bombay studios, Subhash Ghai's Mukta Arts, and Sandeep Marwa's Noida-based studios all advertise themselves as cost-saving one-stop shops for Hollywood, Indian, and international production. Foremost among these shops is the massive, thousand-acre Ramoji Film City (RFC) in Hyderabad, which has the capacity to support close to one hundred productions simultaneously. As Shanti Kumar notes, in its recruiting of Indian and international productions, RFC "represents a new kind of entertainment-based culture in India that is partly invested in claiming a share in the transnational enterprise of film and television, and partly interested in creating an alternative to the Hollywood-centered world of capitalist profit and pleasure."[71]

"Respatialized" media production has the potential to radically alter the geography and identity of Hollywood. This reorganization begins with the widespread acknowledgment that Hollywood's recent forays into Hindi filmmaking have been high-profile flops. As we saw in the previous section, Sony's *Saawariya* (2007), Hollywood's first film made for Indian audiences, and Warner's *Chandni Chowk to China* (2009), both exhibited the pitfalls of Hollywood-supported big-budget filmmaking in India. Indian producers took note of these failures, too, and there seems to be a shift in international co-venture strategy.

Outsourcing's geographies of production map onto national territories—and often "special zones" within countries—in order to maximize productivity gains through the global distribution of cultural labor. Despite the material transformation of work enabled by global deregulation, the national clearly remains an important marker of cultural and geographic difference. Hollywood has attempted to manage stereotypical national characterizations of labor by deploying the fiction of co-presence implied in the name of "Hollywood" itself, which, as a set of varied textual, spatial, industrial, and institutional practices, operates under the sign of a comfortable singularity. Yet what some are calling the contemporary "Indianization" of Hollywood shows how the casual exoticism deployed in the identification of labor competency might strike back at the center.

As the previous section demonstrated, anxieties over the national and ethnic attribution of labor are prominent features of contemporary outsourcing discourse and practice. The structural transformation of cultural labor, predicated on new technologies of remote management made possible by a neoliberal alignment of government and industry, institutionalize older labor prejudices even as they disaggregate discrete spheres of cultural production. Hollywood's interest in reinforcing institutional consolidation motivates contact between nations, industries, and laboring subjects. The justification for transnational labor contact, according to the technocratic discourse of outsourcing, lies in the productivity gains enabled by technologies of remote management.

However, this chapter suggests that the transactions and shifting contours of finance geographies complicate straightforward stories of the economic bottom line. Across the history of an emerging Indian conglomerate interest in Hollywood, through currency flows and fiscal crisis, and in coproduction, crossover cinema, and contemporary outsourcing, this chapter has focused on the material circuits of exchange beyond the conventional rhetoric of media industry convergence. Tracing these material circuits demonstrates the uncertain cultural politics of influence and interoperability in the global media industries.

3

The Theater of Influence

Reimagining Indian Film Exhibition

Now, PVR Saket is the scene of a big cinema, which shows
ten or twelve cinemas at the same time, and charges over a
hundred and fifty rupees per cinema—yes that's right, a hundred and fifty rupees! That's not all: you've also got plenty of
places to drink beer, dance, pick up girls, that sort of thing.
A small bit of America in India.
Arvind Adiga, *The White Tiger*

For all its contemporary connotations, addressing the multiplex as a
"small bit of America" recalls historical associations between Indian
public culture and the United States. As early as the 1910s, with foreign pictures dominating Indian screens, the movies were seen as "the
American shrine" that threatened to pull audiences away from more
traditionally religious forms of congregation.[1] The recent rise of the
multiscreen theater in India engages this long-standing connection
between public exhibition, social life, and economic aspiration.

The object of fascination in the epigraph above, Priya Village Roadshow's (PVR) Anupam 4, opened in the South Delhi neighborhood of
Saket in June 1997. Beyond its multiple screens, the glitz and glamour
of India's first multiplex also symbolizes the nation's much-vaunted
economic miracle. However, "behind the last shining shop begins the
second PVR," notes *The White Tiger*: "Every big market in Delhi is two
markets in one—there is always a smaller, grimier mirror image of the
real market, tucked somewhere into a by-lane. This is the market for the
servants. I crossed to this second PVR—a line of stinking restaurants,
tea stalls, and giant frying pans where bread was toasted in oil. The men
who work in the cinemas, and who sweep them clean, come here to eat.
The beggars have their home here."[2]

Here, the multiplex is a façade rather than the frontier of global India, representing the precariousness of contemporary urban life. Over the past fifteen years, the multiplex has assumed a prominent place in the Indian theatrical landscape, transforming film production and distribution. The multiplex is the primary entry point not only for new film genres and foreign cinema, but also for the new economic cultures of corporatization and multinational investment in the Indian film industries. Where traditional single-screen exhibition was chaotic and fragmented, the multiplex business is highly rationalized and dominated by a handful of companies positioned to benefit from international investment. These companies have prioritized theatrical innovation in India, focusing on architectural design, dynamic ticket pricing, concessions, and promotion, while maximizing occupancy-per-screen rates, upgrading projection and sound systems, and capitalizing on new technologies from IMAX to 3D.

The multiplex theater has become both a monument and a portal to the world of conspicuous consumption in late modern India. Multiplexes are "abstract" spaces that facilitate and imagine consumer mobility with global commodity culture.[3] With its polished stone, mirrored surfaces, and ergonomic plasticity, the multiplex integrates design elements of contemporary consumer-oriented architecture in the airport, mall, and hotel. In its facilitation of easy consumption, the multiplex resembles the fast-food restaurant; in its seating it recalls both the high-end suite and the aircraft cabin. Part sanctuary and part spaceship, the multiplex prioritizes design, utility, cleanliness, order, and rationality—in short, all those things that are supposed to be absent in the chaotic world of everyday life in the Global South (see fig. 3.1).

This chapter analyzes the cultural politics of the new Indian movie theater and its iconic display of modular forms of consumer mobility. Designed to offer a premium service built around the coordinated release of big-budget domestic and foreign features in major urban centers, multiplex theater construction in India arose alongside the reconsideration of urban space in the national imaginary. This imaginary is informed by violent changes in the urban landscape as mall-like shopping centers were erected on the remnants of slum communities that surrounded and permeated the traditional market sites of the bazaar. The multiplex also joins two major events that accompany glo-

Figure 3.1. PVR's Priya theater in South Delhi, in the early 2000s.

balization in the Indian context. First is the growth of the middle class, whose greater disposable income and leisure preferences are linked to consumer mobility and affluent display. Second, Indian urban life has been gradually transformed into an internationally recognizable locus of consumer culture. Hollywood functions as a signifier of transformation within the spaces of consumption, part of a much larger constellation of post-globalization shifts in the iconography of Indian middle-class life and its related commodity forms. In this chapter, I explain how the multiplex came to represent a new architecture of urban visibility, a monument to conspicuous consumption, and a transit point for Hollywood in India.

The 2010 FICCI/KPMG *Entertainment Industry Report* lists multiplex development among the main reasons for Hollywood's contemporary interest in India, alongside dubbing in regional languages and new technological innovation.[4] However, the multiplex is a relatively recent manifestation of theatrical innovation in India, a history in which Hollywood has played a critical role. In the first section of this chapter, I trace the history of American influence on transformations in the environment and imaginary of Indian exhibition. Hollywood has long been interested in establishing Indian theater chains as a way to enhance the distribution of American cinema. This history of American interest in the Indian exhibition infrastructure is bookended by two key failures: first, Universal's failed bid for Madan Theatres in the 1920s; and then, seventy years later, Warner's failed attempt to build a multiplex chain in Maharashtra in the mid-1990s.

The second section of this chapter places the Indian multiplex in the context of a broader retail transformation in India. The Indian government once gave relatively low priority to cinema construction, focusing sparse steel and concrete resources to projects more amenable to developmental modernism like dams, roads, bridges, and other civil infrastructures. Now, however, nationwide investment in the retail sector places the multiplex alongside commercial spaces like the shopping mall. In this section, I locate the Indian multiplex within a grid of public amusements that produce forms of elite urban sociability. Collapsing the space of the mall and the multiplex marks both a portal "into" the West and a gateway into the globalization of Indian life.

In the third section of this chapter, I focus on Delhi's Chanakya movie hall, a modernist architectural landmark and iconic theater for Hollywood exhibition in India recently razed to make way for a new multiplex theater. That a beacon of architectural modernism was itself subject to the logic of modernization attests to the rapaciousness of urban development in the postcolonial city. Chanakya's demolition and the protests around it engage the ironies of progress that suffuse the multiplex era.

Radiating in All Directions: Hollywood and Innovation in Indian Exhibition

The uptick in overall worldwide theater construction in the early twenties failed to fully reverse economic decimation in the film industry and the lack of building after World War I. This gap in international construction led some Hollywood studios to develop plans for international exhibition networks. India emerged as a candidate for American investment in the early 1920s, partly because British colonial authorities supported small-scale theatrical subventions. Addressing chronic theatrical underdevelopment in South Asia, measures like low-cost building loans to builders and improving domestic exhibition were designed not only to improve the industry but to enhance education and the inculcation of proper citizenship.

In the early 1920s, Hollywood was optimistic about its future in India. With global Hollywood still in its infancy, *Photoplay* magazine observed that an "important step in the world-wide conquest of the American movies will be taken this year when Western Asia and India will be exploited on a large scale . . . India, while it has been developed on a small scale will be the center of important film activities, which will radiate in all directions."[5] The Hollywood trade press made it clear that Hollywood studios with international aspirations would do well to take note of prospects in India.

Famous Players–Lasky (FPL) was one of the many Hollywood companies interested in India. In 1920, FPL planned to enhance its international trade network by acquiring film theaters overseas. Formulating an "Indian project" to launch its international initiatives, FPL proposed a US$3 million venture funded by a syndicate of British and Indian banks to produce films in India. Tarkington Baker and Frank Meyer launched the project by sailing for Bombay in May 1920 on a planned six-month tour. FPL acquired Lowji Castle in Bombay as a studio site to be completed by early 1921. The proposed Indian Empire Famous Players–Lasky Film Co. Ltd would be part of a Lasky production network spread between Long Island, Hollywood, London, and India. Consisting of laboratory and studio production facilities, the network also planned to distribute its films through a new Indian exchange network. Jesse Lasky appointed Walter Wanger as head of FPL's myriad production units, including the proposed one in India. The *Film Daily* covered the expansion plans on its front page, although, in the end, the deal never materialized.[6]

Indian demand for American pictures steadily increased through the mid-1920s. Even before the release of *The Thief of Bagdad* (1924)— for decades considered the most successful American film screened in India—Indian audiences were drawn to daredevil and slapstick features and serials. American commerce reports claimed that 90–95 percent of Indian theatrical exhibition was dominated by Hollywood. However, with Indian production on the rise and more theaters being built in urban centers like Bombay, there were indications of trouble ahead. By the mid-1920s, perhaps the most ominous sign of future difficulties was the strenuous application of Indian censorship, as colonial authorities were becoming nervous about the erosion of white authority in Hollywood comedies and more risqué films.

In many ways, the mid-1920s was a period of contradiction. American feature film imports were at a high point but India revenues accounted for less than 1 percent of global Hollywood sales.[7] Yet, domestic production was also on the rise. As one American report noted, the "signs are not lacking that the people of India prefer to patronize their own pictures if these are at all capably produced."[8] For Bombay exhibitors, Indian films were becoming more profitable than foreign pictures. New production companies were being founded and there was a flurry of new theater openings in and around Bombay, demonstrating, as Kaushik Bhaumik succinctly puts it, that the "industry was ready for take-off."[9]

Hollywood was also concerned about ongoing competition from British cinema, particularly as the 1926 Imperial Film Conference considered quotas and other measures to protect British cinema in the subcontinent.[10] Furthermore, Indian press accounts railing against the tide of American films "plaguing" India helped to strengthen emerging alignments between Indian cinema and British distribution interests. In a fairly colorful response to this "plague," the scenarist and director Niranjan Pal claimed that six Indian princes had offered the equivalent of US$5 million to fight the monopoly of American cinema in India. The princes wanted to build three hundred theaters in India dedicated to Indian and British features and had plans to establish reciprocal relations between British and Indian exhibition.[11]

It was at this moment of conflict that Hollywood made another play for theatrical exhibition in India, with Universal looking to acquire Madan Theatres, one of the most powerful chains in the country. Madan Theatres were the Indian distributing agents for United Artists, the studio behind *The Thief of Baghdad*. Madan's founder, J. F. Madan, helped pioneer theatrical exhibition in India starting with temporary sites and moving into permanent theaters in the 1910s. The Madan family business was also the primary importer of foreign film and camera equipment into India. By the early 1920s, J. F.'s son, J. J. Madan, was managing director of the media enterprise. Throughout the 1920s, there were rumors that Madan Theatres would be bought by an American film company, rumors that were substantiated by news reports of J. J. Madan's many trips to the United States and Europe. As Barnouw and

Krishnaswamy note, "On one of these, he negotiated with Carl Laemmle, president of Universal Pictures Corporation. They agreed on sale terms, subject to approval by their respective companies. But when he returned to India, J. J. Madan found his brothers unwilling to approve the negotiated price."[12]

Widely reported in the American trade press, J. J. Madan's trips to the United States in the mid-1920s included a two-week study of production methods on the West Coast, a stint to buy lighting facilities for production, and the purchase of a house organ for one of Madan's theaters. He stayed for two months in Hollywood, where he bought two years of product for Indian theatrical exhibition. Casting his lot in with Hollywood on these trips, Madan was vocal about the "superiority" of American over British film technique.

Film Daily announced on March 30, 1927, that "both an American and British concern are dickering for the purchase of the Madan circuit."[13] In a follow-up story in May, *Film Daily* notes that the "largest theater owners in the Far East are reported to be entertaining competitive offers from British and American syndicates," that "the American offer exceeds the British offer by over $200,000," and that J. J. Madan was now "likely to close the deal."[14] A June 23 article notes that the deal was on for an American offer of US$3 million for all of Madan's theaters in India, Ceylon, and Burma.[15] The deal fell through, but the Indian Cinematograph Committee (ICC) report voiced a strong concern for foreign theater ownership, casting the failed Universal–Madan deal as evidence that "powerful interests concerned in production in other countries might try to capture the market by acquiring control over the cinema trade here."[16]

A November 1928 exchange in the *Times of India* (*TOI*) indicates the depth of mistrust that came out of the failed acquisition talks. J. J. Madan voiced concern over testimony given to the ICC by Universal's Bombay representative. The representative, Madan claimed, had characterized Madan's theatrical enterprise as a monopoly in India. Additionally, the Universal representative pressured Madan Theatres to release its foreign film print holdings in India. According to the *TOI*, J. J. Madan claimed that the Universal's ICC statement was "calculated to disguise the serious consequences of the American invasion" of film in India. Marking a savvy shift from internationalism to indigeneity, J. J. Madan also insisted on the increasing popularity of Indian films over Hollywood product, adding that, because Western methods were well-known, little further Hollywood aid was required.[17]

A few days later, L. Prouse-Knox, the aforementioned Universal representative in Bombay, responded in print to J. J. Madan's charges. In a letter to the *TOI*, Prouse-Knox expanded on the term " virtual monopoly," explaining that 75 percent of Hollywood's revenues came from "high-class theaters" in twelve Indian cities that fell under limited ownership. The dearth of independent exhibition in India, Prouse-Knox maintained, curtailed foreign film's profitability. Further, Universal's representative downplayed the ICC's harsh assessment of the possible Madan sale, insisting that "the proposition had no hope of achieving finality on the terms and conditions proposed." Prouse-Knox closed by addressing Madan's rejection of "Western aid" to the Indian film industry in a statement that summarizes Hollywood's interest in Indian theatrical development at the time: "The reading public who are [Madan's] patrons also travel abroad, and know the class of entertainment offered in other countries, and the local article compares very unfavorably as an evening's entertainment from many standpoints. [Is] the picture going public to assume from this that the present entertainment they are offered is the highest standard they may expect now and in the future?"[18]

Defending itself from Madan's charges of invasion—which echoed the sentiments in the popular press—Hollywood was throwing down the gauntlet: it was in the business of enhancing Indian cinema, not competing with it. This was a convenient defense, given that Hollywood was already on the wane in India. Hollywood was understandably frustrated by its low revenues in a country where American cinema remained popular. The problems of poverty and print duplication piracy were referenced as partial causes, but the major culprit was seen as the growth in Indian cinema production and exhibition. By 1928, the *New York Times* was reporting that the "majority of Indian theater managers" said that they "drew from 40% to 50% bigger houses with local productions and comparatively the same increase in box office receipts."[19]

In the late 1920s, then, there is a dawning recognition that Hollywood's heyday in India is drawing to a close. That it would never recover again could not have been clear to anyone at the time, but this is precisely what happened. Yet, Hollywood's slow downturn did not curtail American interests in Indian exhibition over the ensuing decades. Hollywood remained a signifier of innovation within the Indian theatrical sector, particularly as exhibitors continued to call for new construction, up-to-date equipment, and improved facilities.

In the 1930s, one trade advocate noted that the U.S. could address Indian film industry needs by encouraging theater construction: "The USA film industry spends nearly thirty million dollars per year on foreign advertisement. Only a small part of it is spent in India, showing the Hindoo [sic] exhibitor and the theatre owner the American ways and methods of running theatres [like] sale of theatre equipment on [an] installment plan. [The] giving of advice on theatre building will bring back many dividends in the increased sale of American films and theatre equipment to India."[20]

During the 1930s, a few theaters in major urban centers like Bombay's Regal were furnished with cooling systems, high-quality sound, and projection equipment. These iconic theaters were easily accessible via public transportation.[21] However, most theaters existed on a bare subsistence level, with concessions and theater bars providing much-needed revenue.[22] A decade later, India was home to over two thousand theaters, with continued calls for more construction. In 1947, for example, an Indian regional representative on a visit to the United States claimed a need for more prefabricated theaters as well as American projection and sound machinery. According to the representative, not only did India offer a low-cost alternative for American feature production, but impending independence offered new prospects for American film distribution in the 750 Indian movie theaters that were showing American films at the time.[23]

As discussed in the previous chapter, Hollywood used its extensive blocked funds in the 1950s to fund theater rentals and to upgrade the old movie palaces. However, Hollywood also aligned itself with Indian exhibitors looking for greater variation in seating and screen size—initiatives that would reappear in the drive for multiplex construction in the 1990s.

In 1963, the *Motion Picture Herald*'s V. Doraiswamy claimed that the mass production of prefabricated structures would help add to India's five thousand theaters, particularly because five-hundred- to seven-hundred-seat cinemas "would use the minimum of iron, steel and cement, prov[ing] a blessing to developing countries."[24] The availability of building materials—funneled toward government development projects like housing, office buildings, and dam construction—was sparse for relatively low-priority theater construction. However, partial lifting of restrictions on theater construction in the 1960s helped to put greater emphasis on innovation in theater design.[25] In the early 1960s, the president of the Motion Picture Export Association of America (MPEA) Eric Johnston made the argument that India needed more theaters to show American films. Ongoing trade agreements between the MPEA and the Indian government reflected this commitment to theatrical construction. The shortage of building materials was partially addressed by the liberalization of construction rules in South India, with the result that new theaters were under construction in the late 1960s. However, fluctuating domestic film production contributed to the uneven pace of permanent theater construction, although mobile theater numbers increased more dramatically.

By the mid-1970s, with over 3,200 mobile cinemas and almost 5,500 permanent theatrical sites in India, the government began to focus more attention on theater development in rural areas, encouraging entrepreneurship and the creation of building cooperatives to facilitate new construction.[26] In the mid-1970s, the Indian Film Finance Corporation optimistically set its sights on thousands of new theaters over the next ten years but these plans remained on paper.[27] Taking advantage of the call for greater theatrical construction in India during the 1970s, Hollywood's foreign distribution cartel, the MPEA, began to explore using blocked funds for investment in the Indian hardtop sector. Beholden to the logic of import-substitution industrialization, which emphasized replacing imports with indigenous industrial development, the Indian government refused to allow Hollywood investment in theatrical construction. Hollywood would have to wait two more decades for Indian governmental largesse.[28]

Meanwhile, multiplex innovation was taking off in North America. In the 1970s, Cineplex Odeon branded a cinematic experience distinctive from home cable and the usual multiplex viewing by updating theater design, offering a wide array of concessions, and screening a variety of films in theaters with up to eighteen screens.[29] With the American financial and lending community responding positively to the economics of multiplexing, a number of Hollywood studios acquired theater chains in the 1980s, transforming the American multiplex into a themed entertainment destination that built on the amusement parks of the past. Charles Acland notes that the key features of this new "megaplex" revolved around programming and consumption options, the prioritization of customer service, and sheer enormity of scale, with grand physical structures containing upward of fourteen screens, some of them equipped for 70mm projection and digital sound. The megaplex also used ergonomic stadium seating with clear, unobstructed sight lines and sometimes housed video game arcades, party rooms, small retail outlets, cafes, and bars on site.[30]

Given the consolidation of the U.S. market and the reentry of Hollywood studios into film exhibition, it is not surprising that the multiplex chains would look overseas. Throughout the 1990s, the U.S. majors financed much of the global expansion of the multiplex, particularly in Europe and the Asia-Pacific region. In *Screen Traffic*, Acland also charts the successes of international multiplex construction in the late 1990s in Latin America. Box-office sales rose 50 percent in Mexico in 1997 at the same time that Hollywood's exhibition domination drove Mexican film production to its lowest levels since 1930.[31] This begged a question: would multiplexing be a solution for Hollywood's perennial problems in India?

In India in the mid-1990s, Hollywood faced a backlog of releases in limited theatrical venues in major Indian urban centers. While Bombay cinema surged, driven by the success of films like *Dilwale Dulhania Le Jayenge* (1995) and *Rangeela* (1995), Hollywood found the exhibition landscape too clogged to take advantage of a post–*Jurassic Park* (1993) wave of Indian interest in American cinema. In a number of popular theaters in Bombay, for example, owners raised ticket prices to take advantage of the huge demand for the new Bollywood releases but patrons were unwilling to pay the same high prices for Hollywood films. Hollywood releases like *Die Hard: With a Vengeance* (1995) were allowed only limited runs before having to make way for the next delayed Hollywood film in the pipeline. Given the narrowing bottleneck of exhibition opportunities for American film, it wasn't surprising that some Hollywood executives in India felt that "multiplexes may be the only solution."[32] Bolstered by the new possibilities of Hindi-dubbed Hollywood releases, Warner Brothers International (WBI) began to put out tentative offers to build movie theaters in India in the mid-1990s, as part of a larger plan to build a five-hundred-screen international circuit.

WBI was well aware that Indian theatres were closing and the old movie palaces were in a sorry state of disrepair. Indian exhibition suffered the growing popularity of electronic media and the ongoing rise of home entertainment options that had taken off with the introduction of VCR in the 1980s and cable television in the 1990s. New theater construction was also stymied by an intricate regulatory structure that slowed investment and delayed profitability. As Manjunath Pendakur has argued, building contracts often fell through in the absence of construction loans to theater manufacturers.[33] Furthermore, skyrocketing real estate prices made new land acquisition difficult and developers were becoming more interested in repurposing existing commercial properties. The old family exhibition dynasties were passing onto a new generation less invested in the glories of the past and driven more by a vision of modern retailing, with clean toilets and functioning air conditioning deemed as critical to the theatrical experience as what was being shown on-screen.

Of course, Hollywood's successes in the mid-1990s were also generating interest. Following the relaxation of dubbing restrictions and other import liberalizations, Universal's *Jurassic Park* was released in 110 prints in India in 1994, with 82 prints dubbed in Hindi. The film's US$6 million Indian gross piqued the interest of the other Hollywood studios. In 1994, both WBI and 20th Century Fox were focusing on the Indian market, planning to release twenty to thirty films per year, many in simultaneous release across the country. The same year, Sony announced the launch of a US$140 million Indian company focused on manufacturing broadcasting and software components. Building on the success of *Jurassic Park*, the Warner Brothers action film *The Specialist* (1994) was also dubbed in Hindi.

WBI's plans for expansion in India took the shape of a US$60 million interest in building theaters in Maharashtra. In 1994, WBI announced a local partnership with the Maharashtra Film Stage and Cultural Development Cooperation. WBI had originally planned a joint venture to modernize Bombay's Film City infrastructure when the multiplex plan was conceived and the company was now ready to sign a memorandum of understanding with the government of Maharashtra to establish one hundred screens across ten "multiple entertainment complexes" in suburban Bombay and nearby cities. Subsidized by generous tax and building exemptions, the new multiplexes would have a massive advantage over local theaters. Branded together under the moniker of "Destination Entertainment," each new theater was to have one screen reserved for local Marathi-language films and two for smaller-budget films. In this way, Hollywood could encourage the distribution of Indian cinema more broadly. The plan was for WBI to put up construction funds and manage the finished theaters, while the state government procured and leased the land. A front-page story in a September 1994 issue of *Screen*, the leading Indian film industry trade publication, captured the sense of excitement engendered by the deal: "If everything goes as planned, the multi-screen, multiplex theatre complexes will be a reality in India. Today, the maximum screens a theatre has in India are five, like Devi cinema in Madras. Thanks to Warner Bros. International Theatres, a subsidiary of Time-Warner group of Hollywood, which has offered to construct a chain of entertainment centres in different parts of India, the cinegoers of the country will soon be introduced to a new concept in entertainment, including that of watching films."[34] The plan was for the theaters to range in capacity from 150 to 700 seats, featuring computerized ticketing and Dolby Digital sound, and to be situated close to shops, eateries, discoes, pubs, video game parlors, and live-performance venues.

Hollywood's role in revitalizing exhibition infrastructure met with great excitement, especially after five hundred Indian cinemas closed in 1994. There was also a sense that Hollywood investment could give a boost to regional cinema by stepping into a venture that the Indian private-sector industries had largely avoided. "Naturally, while they slept, Warner Bros. seized the opportunity," noted a *Screen* editorial, "realizing fully well that in the coming years India's entertainment market will rise manifold for it to reap the harvest."[35]

After much fanfare, WBI's initial foray into Indian multiplex construction hit inevitable bureaucratic snags. However, the bell had sounded among other Hollywood outfits. A United Pictures International executive insisted in early 1995 that Indian multiplexes would "revolutionize the business for everybody, be it the Hindi film producers or the foreign film producers—American, British, or French. There will be screens that people would want to go to. Comfortable seating, great projection, and excellent sound has helped bring back audiences to theatres the world over."[36] The same year, United Artists Theatre Circuit announced a US$280 million co-venture with the Indian conglomerate Modi to build twenty-three theaters across Indian cities in the following five years.

In 1996, with films like Fox's *Independence Day* reaping profits for Hollywood throughout Asia, WBI reaffirmed its Indian ambitions, announcing an Rs.2 billion foreign direct investment in the Indian theatrical sector. By then, the Indian film industry had jumped aboard the multiplex bandwagon, with *Screen* announcing that "the romance is over" for films screened on television, as audiences were coming back to the movie theater.[37] This return to the big screen had spillover effects among single-screen theaters, which were renovated with new seats and flooring in anticipation of increased business.

As Warner Brothers continued to negotiate with Bombay cinema's home state of Maharashtra to build ten multiplexes with ten screens each, new problems began to emerge. Conservative national cultural organizations with ties to the Hindu right wing, like the Swadeshi Jagran Manch and Sanskar Bharati, began to agitate against Hollywood investment, demanding Marathi-language films on at least one screen in each multiplex.[38] Furthermore, local theater owners protested the subsidized tax and land rates being offered to a foreign multinational. When WBI dropped out of the Maharashtra multiplex ventures in 1996, after nearly two years of negotiations, it blamed the lack of government-owned land available for lease in the state. With WBI backing out, the Indian television network Zee TV quickly put in two bids and United Artists indicated renewed interest.[39]

WBI's withdrawal signaled a shift in focus, as the direct support of Hollywood studios in Indian multiplex construction faded and Hollywood turned its attention to funding theater construction in China. However, multiplexing found ready allies in Indian retail developers who saw the potential in the shopping mall's aspirational allure and the rise of discretionary income spending in India, particularly among middle-class youth.

In the vacuum created by Hollywood's exit, other foreign outfits entered the Indian theater space. In the late 1990s, Australian exhibitor Village Roadshow (VR) formed a joint venture with New Delhi–based Priya exhibitors to build fourteen multiplexes. VR's Indian expansion was part of larger Asian push in Thailand, South Korea, and Singapore, among other countries. VR eventually entered into a partnership with Warner's new initiatives in Taiwan, although VR was challenging the U.S. majors' theatrical plans elsewhere, especially in Europe.

By the time India's second multiplex opened in Ahmedabad, national creditors like HDFC Bank and ICICI Bank began to form equity investments with multiplex developers. Over forty multiplexes were built in 2001, and six hundred more were planned over the next five years.[40] Some in the Indian industry feared that the economies of scale in the multiplex industry favored the marketing of films with smaller audiences (i.e., Hollywood and other "foreign" cinemas). Nevertheless, multiplex contracts continued to be drawn up in major Indian urban centers and, increasingly, in smaller cities and towns.

While Warner Brothers dropped Indian theatrical development plans in 1996, U.S.-based IMAX Entertainment began a major push into India as part of a larger global initiative. The first IMAX theater opened in India in 2001, launched by Manmohan Shetty, a founder of Adlabs, one of India's most prominent film companies.[41] India's first IMAX 3D theater opened in Gujarat in October 2002. Ten IMAX theaters were planned for the next few years, often in conjunction with new multiplex construction and with ticket prices at the upper end of the multiplex range (Rs.150). This was part of a major Asian push for IMAX as it planned to build over fifty IMAX theaters in South, Southeast, and East Asia over the next few years. To support this expansion, IMAX planned to move away from its traditional documentary fare and expected Hollywood to develop six to ten films a year for the specialized theatrical format.[42]

In 2002, IMAX announced that it had developed digital remastering (DMR) technology to transfer 35mm film to the IMAX format, allowing them to repurpose Hollywood films like *Apollo 13* (1995) for new theatrical exhibition. In 2003, both Warner Brothers *Matrix* sequels were released on IMAX within two weeks of Indian theatrical release (taking advantage of quick transfers via DMR). IMAX has also exploited areas where Hollywood films have driven multiplex construction, especially in the South, where English is central to regional public culture. For example, some Bangalore exhibitors decided in 2002 to show only English-language films after the successes of *Spider-Man, Bend It Like Beckham* (the most successful film in India that year after *Devdas*), and *Harry Potter*.[43] Capitalizing on interest in Hollywood in the South, IMAX entered into a joint venture with Prasad Media and opened South India's first IMAX theater in Hyderabad (635-seat capacity with a twenty-one-meter 3D screen), part of a complex that also includes a four-screen multiplex, restaurants, shops, and gaming establishments. IMAX planned to provide technological and marketing support as well maintaining the theater, which was designed to show both educational films and fiction films including Hollywood releases.[44]

IMAX represents one of the key trajectories of innovation that are dictating new theatrical construction in India. These new multiplexes are branded, themed spaces that have exaggerated differences with contemporary Indian theatrical exhibition. These new screen experiences are not simply the physical creation of new technologies and materials. They represent a fundamental shift in retail philosophy, focusing on lifestyle changes and consumer affirmation. The next section details these shifts and the central role of the multiplex in the Indian retail revolution.

Multiplexes and the New Retail Economies

Built by the J. Arthur Rank Organization, downtown Kolkata's Lighthouse cinema has been showing English-language films since the waning days of British rule. Granted "heritage" status in 2004, the formerly named "Empire" cinema has the historical distinction of being the first theater in the region to show a full-length sound film. The Lighthouse is near the New Empire, another landmark cinema house in Kolkata (formerly Calcutta) run by Warner Brothers after World War II principally to exhibit Hollywood films. Designed by the Dutch architect Willem M. Dudok in the mid-1930s, the Lighthouse's façade retains an Art Deco feel but also recalls the blocky abstraction of the International Style, whose rectilinear combination of form and function once served as a sign of urban architectural modernism in Indian theater design. The Lighthouse opened in 1939, with a screening of *Algiers*, the United Artists remake of Julien Duvivier's narrative of French colonialism, *Pépé le Moko* (1937). Hollywood films were always prominently on offer. For many years, the Lighthouse's longest-running film was American director John Hughes's 1994 film *Baby's Day Out*, which ran for seventeen weeks. Upon visiting the Lighthouse for the 1999 Calcutta Film Festival, American film critic and thumb-impresario Roger Ebert gleefully recounted his experience and meeting with the theater's Indian–Swiss owner: "The street outside is a riot of joyous capitalism. There are luggage stores, motor-scooter repairmen, clothing merchants, a used bookstand, a sari shop and countless fast-food vendors cooking bread and savories over small stoves in the open air. That's just in the street. The sidewalks are also jammed. There are no American chains here, perhaps because opportunists would open fast-food stands right there inside McDonald's to supply snacks to the people waiting in line."[45]

Just a few years after the Calcutta Film Festival, the Lighthouse's owners decided that new "modernization" initiatives were needed to augment previous efforts, which had included outfitting the theater with over a dozen Coca-Cola dispensing kiosks. The 1,400-capacity hall, one of the largest in India, was converted to a multiplex after continual losses: for many years, the conference room upstairs from the main theater had made more money than the cinema hall.[46] Hollywood's role in the remodeling of the Lighthouse Theatre began in early January 2002, when a number of the Hollywood majors, including Warner Brothers, 20th Century Fox and Paramount, stopped releasing their films in the Lighthouse Theatre because of its perennial under-capacity and the negative publicity that came with it.[47] The same year, the theater was converted into multiplex—influenced by American retail design—with a restaurant, skating rink, and bowling alley on the ground floor and on the upper levels, five hundred- and three-hundred-seat cinemas featuring automatic reel-change platter systems and projection lamps imported under new government tax-exemption initiatives.

The Lighthouse's conversion illustrates the broader dynamics of the multiplex revolution and Hollywood's role in the transformation of exhibition culture in India. As we saw in the previous section, Hollywood's interest in Indian theatrical innovation has a long history. As a relatively recent manifestation of this long-term trend, new theater initiatives are inscribed within cultural assumptions associated with the multiplex. American entertainment magnate Sumner Redstone, often credited for coining the term "multiplex," succinctly articulates these assumptions: when Redstone charged his majority-owned National Amusements to partner with a Russian company to open an eleven-screen cinema in

Moscow in 2003, he insisted on bringing "a Western style approach to the theater."[48] As we shall see, this "Western style" combines an international architectural aesthetic with a retail imaginary designed to create new spaces of consumption. These retail transformations were central to the multiplex's emergence in India.

In March 2000, the Federation of Indian Chambers of Commerce and Industry (FICCI) issued a report describing the relative underdevelopment of Indian theatrical exhibition.[49] With five billion admissions per year, India still had fewer than thirteen thousand theaters, an average of 12.9 theaters per one million population (as opposed to the 116 theaters per one million people in the United States). By the late 1990s, a revenue crisis in mainstream Hindi cinema was foreshadowed by a two-decade-long downturn in traditional theatrical ticket sales. Thirty-year-old movie palaces were teetering on the brink of collapse, suffering declining admissions due to the rise of cable television, alternative entertainment choices made possible by new information technologies, and quick turnarounds in the sale of video rights designed to curtail piracy.

Responding to the declining fortunes of existing theaters, state governments created a series of incentives to spur new theater construction. In many cases, 100 percent entertainment tax waivers were granted to multiplex owners for the first three years of operation, with a 75 percent waiver approved for the subsequent two years if they filed by mid-2002. Some states like Gujarat announced a seven-year tax holiday for multiplex owners in the late 1990s. Other incentives included charging industrial rates for electricity for five years rather than the higher commercial rates, and waiving sales taxes on the purchase of cinematographic equipment (alongside lifting import duties on projection equipment). However, relaxed entertainment taxes remained the biggest incentive.

The Indian theatrical sector has complained about entertainment taxes ever since they were instituted in the early 1920s. While countries like France and Malaysia set subsidies and taxes at the national level, Indian entertainment taxes are generally set at the local and regional level. In the late 1990s, a number of states announced multiyear tax exemptions for new multiplex construction. While limited entertainment tax waivers incentivize multiplex construction, they also invite the kind of transparent reporting of ticket sales that municipal and state governments have wanted for years and that investors have pushed for more recently.

Theater owners were also encouraged by big tax breaks to retrofit single-screen theaters to accommodate multiple screens in smaller venues. By 2004, Indian multiplex construction had driven up earnings for Hollywood in the previous eighteen months by as much as 75 percent (to US$20 million) and Bombay cinema's box-office revenue by as much as 60 percent (to US$250 million). Fifty more multiplexes with two hundred screens were planned for the next two years.[50] Indian multiplex innovation was so successful that a 2004 Chinese delegation supported a confidence-building measure to work with Indian entrepreneurs to develop multiplexes in mainland China. By 2007, there were 325 multiplex screens in India: by 2010, 900 screens. Film distributors now consider the multiplex so crucial to domestic box office revenues that a 2009 multiplex strike resulted in virtually no new Hindi and Hollywood films released in India for almost ten weeks.

However, economic incentives alone cannot account for the transformation of the Indian theatrical imaginary. For that, we must turn to the consumption imperatives inscribed within the logic of the multiplex itself. John Robertson, an architect with international multiplex design experience, suggests that the multiplex experience begins with the theater exterior. The façade serves as the first opportunity to "create an impression of excitement and anticipation" while affirming the "signature identity of the theatre."[51] Echoing these ideas, Prakash Chaphalkar of Pune's City Pride multiplex notes the importance of lifestyle affirmation in the multiplex: "Now what happens [in the multiplex] is that the moment you come here, the ambience is good, everybody is dressed well . . . naturally the people are induced to buy more."[52] "Ambience" is a catchall term that refers to new design aesthetics in cinema construction prioritizing an aspirational consumer mobility.

The multiplex coordinates three consumption heterotopias: the urban exterior, the theatrical interior, and on-screen space. Multiplex developers in India have taken advantage of skyrocketing private vehicle ownership and traffic congestion to create cordoned-off zones where the Indian middle-class consumer can stop at a single location for all their entertainment and shopping needs. The coordination of consumer options in the mall and the multiplex create a total environment akin to the theme park, what Susan Davis calls "a virtual maze of advertising, public relations and entertainment that is exhaustively commercial to the core."[53] While the Indian multiplex lacks the theme park's continual affirmation of a global corporate parent's cultural identity, the spatial philosophy of the Indian multiplex involves the assistance of corporate sponsorship designed to move the moviegoer though a unified consumption environment—a "rich variety of artifacts, cultures, histories, styles, texts, architectures and performances, within a framework of overall uniformity of message."[54]

My conversations with multiplex developer Shravan Shroff during the early days of the Indian multiplex boom illustrate both the patterns of innovation in the Indian multiplex and its place within the cultural logic of middle-class aspiration in India. Shroff is part of a new breed of multiplexer, involved in film production, distribution, and exhibition. The third generation of a family-owned distribution business, Shroff originally planned to go to film school but received his MBA in marketing from the University of Melbourne in the mid-1990s, just as the Indian multiplex boom was taking off. After working for three months at the Australian theater chain Greater Union, staffing concessions and the usher stand, Shroff looked into the Indian exhibition trade and noticed the dearth of well-maintained Indian cinemas and the limited number of multiplexes.

Shroff notes that when Shringar Cinemas began in 1997, "the middle class was growing and spending more, but, while foreign brands were being launched, the quality of service and profitability in the exhibition business remained poor."[55] In late 2000, Shroff entered into his first multiplex deal, a fifty-fifty venture with the Bombay-based film processing company Adlabs, which resulted in the five-screen Versova multiplex in Bombay. Differing from the PVR philosophy of acquiring foreign joint-venture capitalization, Shroff and his Shringar Cinemas have focused on all-India deals. Shroff claims:

> We don't really see the benefits that a foreign venture partner could bring in. In fact, I see a detriment in tying up with a foreign partner. They usually have very deep pockets and are coming off a bad run in America that's continued to the U.K. and now there is saturation in Southeast Asia. That puts incredible pressure on a company like Village Roadshow [VR] to perform . . . It's very easy for VR to make a US$10 million commitment in India [but while there is] a certain type of sex appeal in associating with a foreign partner, you have to walk their walk, talk their talk—it's a

dangerous trend . . . Hollywood movies only constitute 5 percent of the box office, so why do we need an international chain?[56]

Multiplexes, according to Shroff, are a fairly straightforward business: one simply takes "the McDonald's model and brings that forward." Here, the constituent feature of the McDonald's model is its standardization of experience, taste, and quality, not its standardization in construction costs or commodity purchase prices. The standardization of experience, particularly "ambience," is a determining factor in the Indian multiplex, with branding and revenue possibilities in seating, uniforms, lighting, and projection equipment, as well as the general standard of service. Shroff notes that a key element in the McDonald's philosophy is "clean toilets wherever you go—that's extremely important as far as the Indian context goes. [It's] not difficult to keep your toilets clean, it just requires commitment, dedication, and supervision." Claiming that toilets are poorly maintained in Indian public space, Shroff notes, "That's one area that I look into personally, whenever I'm doing a round of my theaters."

Many commentators have noted that McDonald's entry into Asia was marked by the "invention of cleanliness" that connected the fast-food experience to the space of the luxury hotel.[57] For example, James Watson claims that the clean McDonald's restroom directs Hong Kong consumers to make the "mental equation between the restaurant's toilets and its kitchen."[58] As in the Hong Kong McDonald's, the Indian multiplexes' pristine public restrooms invite the consumer to identify the cinema as another space of social exclusion, based on a propriety founded on the divisions of class and caste. Here, the "public" restroom is a kind of utopian space, off-limits to the lower classes, except perhaps for the janitor who is responsible for its sparkle. The multiplex toilet elides the forms of "degraded" urban experience deemed antithetical to the project of the newly globalized Third World city. Simultaneously *of* the city and *outside* the city, the multiplex's public restroom is a strange kind of oasis, a denial of an alterity that threatens to contaminate the global city from within. Enveloped in the multiplex's antiseptic confines—its smooth, white functionalism—the spectator can fantasize, however briefly, on the joys of middle-class consumption even as he or she produces its waste.[59]

For Shroff, the Shringar programming philosophy is structured around screening films in Hindi and English, but one screen is reserved for "world cinema." This reservation is more common in Southeast Asian multiplexes, where a single screen might be reserved for "art" films or uncensored pictures. Shroff claims that "as Indians become more educated, with more global reference points," it would make sense to have one screen devoted to world cinema in the Indian multiplex. However, "world cinema" is a complex category that can sometimes exclude Hollywood while including regional Indian cinema. For example, Shringar took a South Indian film (starring future Bollywood actors Aishwarya Rai and Tabu) and instead of dubbing it when it was shown in Bombay, Shroff subtitled it, trying to tap into the world cinema audience. The film's success prompted Shringar to "go after more world cinema." And while "world cinema" might include a French, Indonesian, or Hong Kong film, it rarely includes Hollywood. The insertion of non-Hindi Indian commercial cinema into the rarefying logics of world cinema signals the multiplex's complex cultural position within media globalization.[60]

As Adrian Athique notes, Shringar is like most of the big contemporary multiplex companies, which operate most of their theaters through lease agreements rather than owning them outright. These multiplex operators have used the exhibition sector to launch a broad program of media conglomeration. PVR has moved into distribution and mall development, as has Shringar, which also plans to move into the broader hospitality industry, including the food court business.[61]

Nowhere else in the world is the multiplex so associated with commercial retail spaces than in Indian cities and suburbs. Leisure consultants note that cinema-going, eating out, and shopping rank highly for Indian consumers. One Indian business publication, remarking on the "joys of that only the market can bring," notes that "marketers rushing into these towns [are] helping unleash the entrepreneur shackled in Small Town India. Rather than migrate to cities or overseas for better opportunities, many of these well-educated youth are exploring the huge franchising opportunity that's emerging—be it for a Baskin Robbins ice-cream outlet, or a Compaq reseller or a McDonald's or a Pizza Hut."[62] McDonald's opened its first Indian outlet in 1996 and operated fifty outlets by the end of 2003. Other U.S.-based multinationals have also found promise in the Indian mall retailing. While PepsiCo India targets on-site soft-drink sales for 15–20 percent total sales in India, Coca-Cola has exclusive sales arrangements at DLF Galleria mall complex just outside the Delhi suburb of Gurgaon and also at Delhi's Ansal Plaza (Ansal also houses a McDonald's and other fast-food eateries that sell Coca-Cola soft drinks exclusively).

The new Indian urban retail space shares some similarities with its American counterparts, but there are also important distinctions. The American multiplex was designed as a functional exhibition space that approximated the anonymity of the shopping mall. The Indian relationship between the multiplex and the mall, however, is motivated by the public display of consumption. So, while Gary Edgerton can claim that the "contemporary movie theatre is no longer an exclusive showcase for dreams," and that the "evolution of theatre design from movie palace to multiplex is a switch in emphasis from consumer dreaming to buying," in the Indian multiplex the emphasis is on *dreaming to buy*, and the aspirational imperative is still highly prioritized.[63]

Indian multiplexes are closely aligned with the shopping mall's spectacularization of consumption, which may have something to do with the political economy of Indian multiplex ownership. In the United States, the standardization of the multiscreen exhibition is tied to their location within massive multiplex theater chains. Like a fast-food franchise, American theater chains attempt to duplicate a consistent consumption environment from place to place. In India, however, unlike the large consolidated cinema circuits in the United States and in many Asia-Pacific countries, chains are small, with the largest group owning just nineteen theaters. Without a corporate theatrical parent serving to anchor the multiplex brand, the spectacularity of new forms of consumption deployed by the Indian multiplex is conveniently attached to the global mobility of the shopping mall. In fact, in many multiplex-centered shopping malls and arcades in Delhi and Bombay, retail sales actually surpass film ticket proceeds. As one marketing executive puts it, "The Indian customer is still time-rich and likes shopping leisurely. The coexistence of shopping and entertainment will soon emerge as a new way of life."[64]

These consumption spaces engage the markers of affluence and mobility as modes of social differentiation. In this way, multiplexes are linked to the management of caste and class difference throughout the history of Indian exhibition (see fig. 3.2).[65] Furthermore, multiplex au-

Figure 3.2. "Class" difference in ticket prices at the Priya PVR theater in South Delhi.

diences are assimilated into contemporary zones of consumption. As Charles Acland has put it, "Such zones mark a tacit agreement that public membership in a transnational context has its own admission price."[66] Despite the consumer revolution's insistence that all are invited to participate in the retail party, the multiplex demonstrates clearly how certain theatrical practices are inscribed in elite forms of sociality.

In *Shoveling Smoke*, anthropologist William Mazzarella argues that the recent consumer shift in India marks a fundamental transformation of the older logic of developmentalist self-sufficiency, represented most strongly in India's import-substitution initiatives during the 1970s. Mazzarella notes that the opening of Indian consumer markets and the influx of foreign brands after the late 1980s have completely reorganized the infrastructure of Indian marketing. One of the most unexpected outcomes of the post-developmental aspirational allure of a "consumption-led path to national prosperity," Mazzarella suggests, is the alignment between Indian self-sufficiency and the recruitment of foreign investment.[67] In other words, according to the logic of globalization, the *foreign* can function as a signifier of the national when once it functioned as its antithesis. Mazzarella insists that in India, the awareness of global brands has outstripped their widespread availability: "Western brands became important markers of social distinction for a small elite. But I want to note just how much the mystique associated with these goods depended on their capacity to serve as physical embodiments of a source of value that was understood to reside elsewhere. This somewhere might in shorthand be called 'the West,' but in fact it was conceived as at once concrete and abstract, as a real place and as a mythical location."[68]

As India's exhibition revolution suggests, the multiplex frames "the West" as a heterotopic space, assimilable within the confines of Indian retail environments. But surely there are slippages and resistances to the meanings associated with the multiplex, places where the occasions of viewing collide with the social and textual forces that organize urban leisure (see fig. 3.3). The next section focuses on the consequences of this friction between the phenomenologies of engagement and geographies

Figure 3.3. Old retail meets new retail in a South Delhi multiplex complex.

of exhibition. It tells the life history of Chanakya, a landmark theater known as one of the gateways for Hollywood in India. Once a symbol of India's medieval past and modern aspiration, Delhi's Chanakya theater was recently demolished to make way for a new multiplex. As Igor Kopytoff suggests, "Biographies of things can make salient what might otherwise remain obscure."[69] What can we learn from the *death* of things, and how might we read the event signified by Chanakya's destruction?

Chanakya's Death: Modernism as Relic

The movie theater is a space where the global can be located, materializing in the built environment that configures the experience of a place. When thought of as a quintessentially urban form, the theater draws cinema into the city, embedding media networks within preexisting forms of transnational public culture. India's capital city of New Delhi has its share of landmark movie theaters. Now living (and dying) together in the city, landmark Delhi theaters are a hodgepodge of shifts in building fashion. The capital's theatrical cityscape is a design collage of architectural styles with distinctive histories.

Take, for example, the Regal theater, one of Delhi's first permanent cinemas. Opened in 1932, Regal was designed by Walter Sykes George, who also worked on the surrounding commercial center of Connaught Place. Regal's classical style stands in stark contrast to the modernism of the Shiela theater, located in Paharganj. Constructed in 1961, Shiela was designed by Ben Schlanger, who also played a role in designing the General Assembly of the United Nations. Shiela's iconic exterior—a curving expanse of concrete suspended above the marquee—mirrors the theater interior, which housed India's first 70mm projection system. Named for owner D. C. Kaushish's wife, Shiela was built in a working-class district, but theater management wanted to draw elite audiences from nearby Connaught Place.[70] Hollywood recognized Shiela's promise early on, and Warner Brothers invited Kaushish to see the filming of *My Fair Lady*.[71] The film was a huge success when it screened at Shiela and the theater ran English-language films almost exclusively during its first fifteen years of operation.

Like Shiela, the Chanakya theater has had an important role in the foreign film culture of Delhi and served as a key exhibition site for Hol-

Figure 3.4. Delhi's Chanakya movie theater, shortly
before its demise. All Chanakya photographs by
Debashree Mukherjee.

lywood in India. Chanakya was built in 1970 in Delhi's diplomatic enclave of Chakayapuri. In an interview conducted with a Sarai research
team in 2003, Rajesh Khanna, the proprietor of Chanakya, spoke fondly
of Sheila and Kaushish's ambition in opening a theater in what seemed
to be a less than lucrative location. He waxed poetically: "Kaushish
saab was no doubt, one of my ideals. The way he ran the Shiela cinema.
My ideal was D. C. Kaushish. That inspired my success at Chanakya. I
thought to myself that if ever, someday, I ran a cinema, I would run it the
way D. C. Kaushish has run it. Because that guy has run that cinema, in
Paharganj, in a locality where the entire trade was laughing at him when
he said he is going to run English pictures."[72]

Chanakya's combination of Hollywood screenings and its location in
a diplomatic enclave offered Delhi audiences a particularly appealing
configuration of cosmopolitanism (fig. 3.4). As Ipsita Sahu has argued,
Chanakya was a nodal point for Delhi's urbanization and aspiration as
a global city.[73] Hollywood played an important role in this aspiration.
Screening reruns of American films even during Hollywood embargoes, Chanakya offered movie audiences engagement with a cosmopolitan lifestyle even as Western commodities were restricted under Indian
import-substitution industrialization during the 1970s.

Built by the New Delhi Municipal Council (NDMC), Chanakya was
planned as part of a complex of shops, a cultural center and a hotel. The
theater opened in December 1970 with a screening of Raj Kapoor's *Mera*

Naam Joker. Early on, the theater showed mainstream Hindi films, "parallel" cinema, and the occasional English-language feature. However, Chanakya eventually became known for its foreign cinema screenings, though it shifted to big-budget Bollywood during its last decade of operation. As David Vinnels and Brent Skelly note, Chanakya was "designed from the outset as a prestigious venue, hosting diplomatic functions and the world premieres of Merchant-Ivory's *Heat and Dust* in 1982 and *A Passage to India* in 1984."[74]

Considered to be on the outskirts of the city when Khanna entered into a long-term lease, Chanakya was primarily accessible by car, with a rare on-site parking lot further encouraging private transportation. In later years, the expanding public transportation system created better integration with the city, allowing college and secondary school students to attend screenings. Before it deliberately shifted to elite family audiences, Chanakya was an important recreational spot for students at the Indian Institute of Technology and other Delhi universities and colleges. Chanakya's house restaurant Nirula's became popular as a hangout for Delhi undergraduates: a place to snack and play video games after—or during—school.

Over the years, Chanakya also functioned as an important venue for film festivals, essentially serving as the gateway to world cinema in the capital. Chanakya housed an early 70mm cinema screen and it pioneered other theatrical innovations in India, including a very early Dolby sound system. Despite this integration into global film circuits, Chanakya's proprietors assembled its famous stand-alone projector by hand with parts secured from locations throughout Delhi. In the late 1990s, as multiplexes increased in popularity, Chanakya invested in upgrading its décor, renovating its exteriors and installing new sound and air-conditioning systems.

In late December 2007, after almost forty years in operation, Chanakya held its final screening, Bollywood star Aamir Khan's directorial debut, *Taare Zameen Par*. Chanakya had been deemed obsolete and was to be replaced with a mall and a multiplex. Under competitive pressure from the Anupam PVR multiplex, plans to convert Chanakya to a multiplex began in October 2000 when it came time to renew its ten-year license agreement.[75] In Delhi, most of the city's single theaters had fallen to an average daily occupancy rate of between 30 and 40 percent. These low occupancy rates justified the logic for the multiplex because the exhibitor could rotate underperforming films while engaging different economies of scale (unlike the traditional halls, multiplexes have a break-even occupancy rate of 45 percent).[76] Multiplex conversion increasingly was seen as a fix for a stagnating exhibition sector. Supported by this rationalization, hundreds of single-screen halls have closed or converted to multiscreen theaters across India over the past fifteen years.

When Chanakya's lease expired shortly after the new millennium, the NDMC refused to renew it, claiming that the renters were profiting over Rs.15 million on a property valued at over Rs.1 billion, while the annual license fee paid to NDMC was only Rs.1.55 million.[77] The protracted legal dispute between the NDMC and Aggarwal and Modi Enterprises (which had run Chanakya for decades) spilled out into the public domain, as the proprietors insisted that *they* had originally come up with the multiplex conversion idea. After a legal dispute, where Aggarwal and Modi Enterprises claimed that their plans to redevelop the theater were denied through "an illegal closed bid tender system,"[78] the Delhi High Court ruled against their plea for a public auction, ruling instead in favor of the NDMC to build a multiplex and a shopping complex in time for the 2010 Commonwealth Games.

Considering the case on appeal, the Supreme Court refused to stay the High Court order but asked that the NDMC give the former tenants the first option to bid for the new multiplex construction and operation. By early 2008, reportedly twenty-five firms had bid for the redevelopment, including a rumored sale to DT Cinemas for an estimated Rs.2.5 billion. NDMC awarded the Yashwant Place redevelopment project to Delhi Land Finance (DLF), the massive commercial real estate developer that had been constructing residential colonies in Delhi since before independence. DLF planned to build three multiplexes on the Chanakya site and demolition work began in September 2008. Chanakya was finally razed at the end of 2009 (see fig. 3.5). Chanakya's survival as one of the few remaining single-seat theaters in the multiplex era was over. By this time, some twenty-five single-screeners had closed in Delhi, leaving about the same number in operation, many in disrepair.

Chanakya's demolition signaled a shift in the Indian theatrical imaginary, where one vision of globalization was exchanged for another. Named for the fourth-century B.C.E. diplomat and political strategist

Figure 3.5. The Chanakya demolition in progress.

who helped defeat Alexander the Great, Chanakya was not able to turn back the invasion of the multiplex. In essence, multiplexes are schemes designed to modernize exhibition, promoting and maximizing customer loyalty.[79] Ironically, once an icon of modern exhibition technology and practice, Chanakya had been betrayed by modernization itself, falling victim to its rapaciousness.

If Chanakya was a theater that staged and visualized the modern, what did its death signify? The theater's origins offer some clues to reading its demise.

In terms of Chanakya's placement in the city, the surrounding green spaces gave the area an artificially bucolic sense of clubs, parks, and polo grounds, trading on the elite exclusivity of the diplomatic enclave. This placement mapped a projection of Indian diplomatic ambition that was itself rooted in a sense of India's history. In its very name, then, Chanakya signaled the diplomatic glories of India's premodern past as well as the possibility of Indian political modernity in the global present.

Chanakya's engagement with the spatiality and temporality of modernity is apposite given how the modern is characteristically understood. As Timothy Mitchell astutely notes, two concerns dominate our engagement with the modern: first, the question of modernity's belatedness as a "stage of history through which we have already passed"; and the second question is "concerned not with the passing of modernity but with its placing, not with a new stage of history but with how history itself is staged."[80] In mapping across the historicity and significance of the modern, Chanakya's story demonstrates how ideas of progress materialize in particular built environments.

Chanakya is often described as a symbol of Nehru's vision for modern India, its monumentalism designed to promote and memorialize the first prime minister's aspirations of Indian industrial development. The theater's reinforced concrete construction reflects the influence of post–Le Corbusier modernism, specifically the Brutalist style, which spread extensively through India (see fig. 3.6).

Figure 3.6. The theater's reinforced concrete construction reflects the influence of post–Le Corbusier modernism.

Le Corbusier's shift to the Brutalist style in the 1930s was prompted, according to Charles Jencks, "by a rediscovery of natural orders, primitive societies and a sexual relation with women unconstrained by conventional etiquette, sophistication or snobbism."[81] The city was to be the laboratory for Brutalism, motivated by the restoration of nature lost in the constraints of civilization. When it came to its stylistic travel to the tropics, Brutalism invoked a "vernacular modernism": inaugurated by the modern's fascination for barbarism, brutalism's Indian transposition confirmed a vision of the future.[82] Commenting on Le Corbusier's most prominent Indian constructions in Chandigarh, Ravi Kalia notes that his "experimental architecture" aligned with Nehru's vision of modern, industrial India.[83]

As Gautam Bhatia notes, modernism has been the default style for Indian institutional architecture: "Built by government construction agencies, municipal authorities and city Works Departments, public architecture became synonymous with bureaucratic citadels—inefficient, cumbersome and faceless."[84] As in many cities, architectural modernism attests to the uniformity of state power—erasing subtlety in the blunt application of concrete surfaces. Assuming prevalence in the 1960s, architectural modernism in Delhi was a rationalization of state power. Chanakya was a symbol of this political modernity.

Yet, as a symbol materialized in the built environment, Chanakya had been decaying long before its demolition, signifying a modernity always already in ruin.[85] Given the corrosion and abrasion related to the permeability of concrete, decay was actually inscribed in the material fabrication of Chanakya. As Curt Gambetta notes, the Indian building and architecture establishment was not sure about reinforced concrete early on, and it took a concerted effort by the Concrete Association of India and the Cement Marketing Company to institutionalize concrete as the preferred material of the "national modern."[86] However, as Gambetta argues, in "architecture produced in the so-called developing world, decline is the concept that marks these displacements and erasures associated with the experience of the modern."[87]

While concrete was valued as a durable building material, capable of sustaining a vision of the modern, as Indian building standards shifted priorities from durability to strength in the constitution of concrete mix in the 1950s, adverse exposure to degradation problems increased.[88] One of the significant features of reinforced concrete construction is that it almost immediately begins to deteriorate in less-than-temperate climates. This environmental degradation is exacerbated by the intensity of the South Asian monsoon, resulting in a rotting from inside due to metal corrosion, and on the outside from environmental abrasion. In other words, at precisely the time that concrete is key to the vision of modern India, obsolescence was already part of the mix. As a vision of architectural modernism, Chanakya was already rotting from the inside out—as if marked for death from its origins. As I noted above, Chanakya's slow, steady decay from Delhi's climate and pollution, well before its final demolition, attests to the ways in which *ruin* is a permanent feature of the architecture of the modern. Chanakya's demolition signals that certain features of modernism might already be receding from view.

Chanakya's death engages a global present that is haunted by the fear of obsolescence—a modernity that is subject to being replaced, even *modernized*. There are two critical spatial antecedents for this dramatic historicity. The first spatiality marks Chanakya as a "non-space," described by Marc Augé as an intertwining of premodern places— characterized by "the presence of the past in a present that supersedes it but still lays claim to it"—with the non-places of supermodernity, forms of spatial excess, "landscape-texts" inscribed in transit, such as the motorway, the airport transit lounge, the supermarket checkout line, tollbooths, and rest areas.[89] The second spatiality is that of Ackbar Abbas's concept of "disappearance," which marks the "reinvention" of urban space in postcolonial contexts.

Following Walter Benjamin, Abbas testifies to the intimate relationship between architecture and the identity of the city, detailing three features of postcolonial urban practice that relate to the culture of disappearance: the first is the city's receptivity to a diversity of architectural styles; the second is the constant reinvention of the urban space through interminable construction; and the third is the city's intense density.[90] As non-space and space of disappearance, Chanakya's death can be read as an allegory for the past's complex imbrication in the postcolonial present.

Yet Chanakya's decay and demise, while inevitable, was not immune to memorialization. On January 30, 2008, on the sixtieth anniversary of Mahatma Gandhi's assassination, a candlelight vigil was planned by

Figure 3.7. Protests were held by conservationists, architects, and students engaging in "Gandhigiri" to save the Chanakya cinema hall.

the "People for Chanakya," composed primarily of conservationists and architects who, when interviewed, said that they planned to indulge in some "Gandhigiri" (see fig. 3.7). "Gandhigiri" is actually an older term referencing the tenets of Gandhianism recently resurrected and translated into the cinematic vernacular by Sanjay Dutt's performance in the 2006 Hindi film *Lage Raho Munna Bhai*—coincidentally, the first full-length Hindi film to be screened at the United Nations. *Lage Raho* was widely celebrated as "bringing Mahatma Gandhi back into public consciousness."[91]

Ashis Nandy finds that the recent invocations of Gandhi in mass culture allow for a break with elite politics, reinvigorating everyday contestation within the domain of the popular.[92] Perhaps less charitably, Joseph Lelyveld notes that, "in India today, the term 'Gandhian' is ultimately synonymous with social conscience."[93] By shuttling between sacred and profane worlds, however, "Gandhi" resonates with the public in more mercenary terms as well. The marketing of Gandhi's image has long been a part of popular advertising around the world. William Mazzarella finds that the transnational circulation of the Mahatma's image, a certain form of "Gandhian publicity," invokes "Gandhi as a public cultural signifier in a consumerist age."[94] For example, following the appropriation of his image in advertising after 2002, Gandhi's great grandson sold image rights to the U.S.-based CMG Worldwide for US$60,000. This sale caused widespread public consternation and bemusement in the Indian public domain. The more righteous considered the sale an adulteration of a national icon and a violation of his principles of asceticism and renunciation, while the more cynically minded felt that the sale was a sign of the utter banality and exhaustion of Gandhi in the neoliberal era. Mazzarella finds that the corporate resignification of "Brand Gandhi" had strangely confirmed Gandhi's charismatic authority over mass mobilization, redeploying the reconciliation of materialist and ineffable worlds toward corporate goals.

Clearly, the Chanakya memorial was partaking in a broader "repackaging" of Gandhi for twenty-first-century consumption.[95] The Chanakya vigil was also held on the first anniversary of a major conference in New Delhi in 2007, celebrating one hundred years of *satyagraha* (the philosophy of nonviolence) in South Africa. It might seem a bit incongruous to celebrate Gandhi at the foot of an iconic expression of industrialized modernity, given his famous pronouncements on industrialization. Yet Gandhi never expressed a simple preference of tradition over modernity. After all, while he critiqued modernity as part of an incipient anticolonial nationalism following 1909's *Hind Swaraj*, he also admitted that his early career as a barrister framed an apprenticeship in colonial modernity. Furthermore, his political interventions artfully performed the modern and the traditional as theatrical—*staging* the modern within the theatricality of protest. Perhaps it's not surprising that the Chanakya devotees chose Gandhi as a way to keep vigil over a particular passage of the modern within their city.

Exhibiting Modernity

Architecture involves the interaction of style, environment, and use. Because architectural forms conjoin the local and the global in their form and function, they are productive sites to explore the idiom of influence. The three case studies in this chapter have mapped influence as a way to conceive Hollywood and other Western forms less as incursions and more as signifiers of innovation within the Indian mediascape.

Yet, it is important to recognize that the anesthetized and functionalist experience of the multiplex is in stark contrast to the experience of urban India that engages a chaotic, sprawling counterpublic generated by multiplicity of the crowd and vibrant with danger and opportunity. Everyday Indian life has been transformed by a rapacious capitalism that has devastated the urban poor and shattered the lives of rural migrants drawn to the city by promises long since broken. With average multiplex ticket prices at over Rs.120—as opposed to Rs.20–Rs.40 for single screens—these new theaters are indices of inequality. Buying their tickets in the lobby, enjoying concessions, and looking around the theater, multiplex patrons can confirm their social privilege.[96]

As Lakshmi Srinivas notes, "Theater spaces are saturated with value."[97] The multiplex signifies values defined by the implementation of disciplinary technologies and techniques. Like the shopping mall, the multiplex in India functions both inside and outside urban space. The multiplex transforms the lived, material chaos of the Third World city into a slick artificial global mobility, effectively collapsing uneven urban development onto a kind of mirrored, heterotopic projection both inside and outside the movie house. The Indian multiplex testifies to the power of cosmopolitan fantasies that support the metapsychology of global consumption, a form of engagement with commodity culture that promises a utopian equality of access yet is dependent on the rationalization and reproduction of forms of social difference.

Even as the traditional theater continues to assimilate a diversity of patrons under a single roof, in its exclusionary address the multiplex refracts the social hierarchy of Indian urban space. Lacking correspondence with the demographics of its neighborhood, the multiplex provides a space "free" from the urban crowd, creating a sociability predicated on the exclusion of diversity. Multiplexes are located at the intersection of consumption spaces that include hotels, shopping malls, pubs, restaurants, and bowling alleys, coordinating visible affirmations of class difference.

The MBA-dominated culture of multiplex operation, staffed by leisure and hospitality executives, sets itself against the chaos and intricate histories of the family-owned single-seaters, pitting the advantages of transparency and corporatism against familial dynastic intrigue. The multiplex, representing the vanguard in the formalization of the theatrical sector, produces a number of ancillary industries, from concessions, ergonomic seating, air conditioning (including humidity and "odor perceptibility" controls), and toilet facilities. While many Indian companies have found a niche in the multiplex market—such as Cinecitta and Monee projectors, which are used in the United States—the recent relaxation of import duties for projection and other exhibition equipment has created a lucrative market for foreign equipment manufacturers: German Kinoton projectors and Schneider lenses; American Strong projectors; Christie projectors and platters; Belgian Multivision Screens; xenon lamphouses (E-City multiplexes in India are branded "Xenon"); and JBL and Australian Monitor speakers.

Yet, even as the multiplex—and its spatial corollary, the shopping mall—attempts to congregate the middle class around a shared utopian consumer space, it substantiates the differences between spaces within the city. Relying on the displacement of long-standing slum communities and traditional forms of marketplace interaction, the multiplex and the mall are zones of assimilation dependent on racial, ethnic, gendered, class, and caste forms of stratification. Even as it projects the leading edge of Indian exhibition, every multiplex constructed in India is haunted by the nightmare of its future, its horizon limited by the three-, five-, seven-, or ten-year tax exemptions doled out by the central government. What will happen when these exemptions expire? If multiplexes serialize the consumption of time in the new Indian economy, perhaps they themselves mark only a temporary passage to new modes of exhibition. Perhaps, following in the wake of Chanakya's death, all multiplexes are destined for ruin.

4

Economies of Devotion

Affective Engagement and the Subject(s) of Labor

Between the largest free nations, one the youngest, the other
the oldest, there is a kinship of the spirit. A kinship that can
mean only good for all mankind.
Frank Capra on the relationship between Hollywood and
Bombay cinema, October 1952

This chapter focuses on the routes and routines of working bodies in
transnational screen culture. Drawing the historical into contemporary
practice, I attend to the question of how subjectivity and labor—marked
by racial, religious, class, and national difference—become defined by
various itineraries of contact between Bombay and Hollywood. My
interest here is in both the formalized trajectories through which labor
travels and the more extemporaneous processes that distribute the activity of real and represented bodies in the social worlds of work.

Cultural labor can be understood as process, artifact, interaction, and
imaginary. Labor expresses the body's relationship to power and experience, placing the working subject within larger social forces. At the same
time, labor is tied to the intersubjectivities of communicative exchange.
In this chapter, I show how the production of cross-cultural intimacy is
inscribed in industry exchange, creating forms of affinity tied to the circulation of laboring bodies between Hollywood and Bombay. Engaging
with these bodies can illuminate the ways in which work is materially,
socially, and culturally organized in the media industries.

This engagement with bodies and intersubjectivity maps onto recent
critiques of the global political economy, suggesting a shift from material to immaterial forms of work. For Michael Hardt and Antonio Negri,
the rise of "affective labor" in the new economy "produces or manipu-
lates affects such as a feeling of ease, well-being, satisfaction, excitement,

or passion."[1] Hardt and Negri suggest that this production of affect is integral to the proliferation of new service industries. In this chapter, I'd like to suggest that affect is part of a longer history of the "spirit of capitalism,"[2] where forms of identity and attachment coalesce around the anxieties of displacement that characterize the social world of work. Here I focus on the cultural politics of "traveling" bodies, detailing how categories of difference are inscribed within an "affect economy" of transnational media industries.[3]

The connections engaged by stars, fans, and industry representatives between Hollywood and Bombay cinema distributes emotional engagement across media worlds. In this way, laboring subjectivities become a key site of transcultural media encounter. In print stories, festivals, and correspondence, public and private expressions of devotion, proximity, and expressions of religious affiliation all become part of a social configuration in which attachment emerges as a symbolic resource.

Reading the journalistic, corporate, and fan archive, this chapter considers these "geographies of intimacy" across three case studies in the history of Bombay and Hollywood encounter.[4] The first two case studies show how interpersonal contact signifies industry relations in different travel narratives. The first case study addresses the promotional discourse of celebrity tourism that construes labor as leisure, garnering starstruck press and popular attention. I show how the common discourse of Hollywood star travelogues depends on tropes of comparison, particularly those predicated on a kind of racialized Otherness. My second case study looks at letters and other forms of correspondence that cast American and Indian media relations in informal, personal terms. As a frame for inter-industry relations, epistolary communication capitalizes on the "affective economies" of attachment.[5] Taken together, the first two sections show how institutional commitments between Bombay and Hollywood industries are sustained by the politics of interpersonal encounter. The third and most extensive case study engages devotion in a more historical register, focusing on the popular characterization of Indian film work as "Hindu" at the same time that religious caste is used to characterize tensions between labor and management in interwar Hollywood. This parallel trajectory of appropriation points to the historical conjuncture between the social worlds of Indian and

American labor, even as anti-Asian nativist anxieties proliferated in the United States before and after the formation of Hollywood.

This chapter's critical interrogation of the tropes of celebrity association, the exchange trajectories of epistolary correspondence, and the role of religion in the configuration of work show how subjectivity is enmeshed in the comparative politics of screen labor. At the same time, these case studies demonstrate the intimate entanglements between industries: the modes of comportment that orient one industry to another in moments of encounter.

Orienting Hollywood, Part 2

Over the years, Hollywood stars have traveled to India for reasons ranging from spiritual uplift and tourism to social advocacy and shopping. Goldie Hawn is perhaps the archetypal Hollywood star in this regard (see fig. 4.1). An Indian media darling for her frequent visits, her predilection for bright saris and other fabrics, and her avowed interest in Hinduism, Hawn's well-publicized friendships with socialites like Parmeshwar Godrej have dramatized Bombay–Hollywood contact for decades. For example, Hawn and Godrej were critical to creating Hollywood excitement for *Lagaan* in the run-up the American Academy Awards, helping to garner a foreign-language nomination at the Oscars in 2002. In this way, Hollywood attendance at Godrej's and other opulent Bombay parties instantiates a kind of crossover stardom. These forms of celebrity contact align with eagerly solicited Hollywood platitudes on "the Indian experience," which Sally Field called "wonderful" on her first trip to India in 1994. She was chaperoned by none other than Goldie Hawn, then on her third Indian trip.[6] While Hawn may have been the reigning queen of celebrity Hollywood in India, there are new contenders for Goldie's crown.

When Julia Roberts announced her conversion to Hinduism in *Elle* magazine a few years ago, she joined the ranks of American celebrities famous for their public professions of religious affiliation. From Mel Gibson's Catholicism, John Travolta and Tom Cruise's Scientology, and Richard Gere's Tibetan Buddhism, to George Lucas's "Buddhist Methodism," Madonna's Kabbalah, and Marie Osmond's Mormonism, devout

Figure 4.1. Goldie Hawn shops for silk in Varanasi, 2009. Source: Associated Press.

stardom aligns public expression with private belief. For many Hollywood celebrities, religion situates the star between missionary and mercenary worlds, connecting the profane with the sacred. For Hollywood's most publicly manufactured subjects, religious devotion references an essential, inalienable self that is both inside and outside commodification. The shuttling between the interiority and exteriority of celebrity characterizes the work of stardom, which is why something as intangible as belief can testify to the material reality of the star.

So perhaps it's not surprising that much of the conversation around Julia Roberts's conversion has been about intention: Was her Hinduism driven by faith or was it a brand accessory to gendered stardom, like henna, *bindis*, or tattoos in Anglicized Devanagari script? Was Julia's Hinduism driven by belief or was it a publicity stunt—in short, was it about conviction or career? Such queries are common to the culture industry of stardom, which frames (and monetizes) the gap between authenticity and performance. The theater of religious intimacy seems ideal for the staging of stardom because, as Chris Rojek claims, the cultish identification mobilized by celebrity worship is substantiated in a language of sacralization.[7]

Julia's religious sincerity aside, the fascination with Hindu conversion is part of a much broader cultural logic, located in the anxieties about identification and alterity in the international division of labor in the screen industries.[8] Julia's public conversion demonstrates how self-presentation and brand management have become the front-stage work of celebrity. Ernest Sternberg notes that in the labor of "personal composition," stars can position themselves in a market by "mobilizing demeanor and conduct so they reference a realm of meaning that consumers find evocative."[9] The self as brand increasingly defines the celebrity commodity, and religious identification offers a particularly potent form of self-branding, especially when it is associated with a public rite of conversion.[10]

Throughout the history of Hollywood, stars publicly committed themselves to family and charity work in order to mitigate the temperance and excess that characterized celebrity lifestyle. However, contemporary stardom, fueled by the fiction of instantaneous access and the hyperreality of global infotainment, demands new registers of intimacy. It is not enough that stars have a "private" life that is both distinct from and connected to our everyday; we must know their motivations and dreams as well. Our knowledge of the personal life of the star is rooted in this engagement with the interiority of desire. In Hollywood's globally mediated stardom, religion—along with transnational child adoption—helps to extend the brand afterlife of the celebrity commodity.[11] At the same time, the karma of celebrity folk negotiates the pressures of cultural labor as it is dispersed across various histories and places.

For decades, India has functioned as a location for spiritual transcendence and personal transformation for the Hollywood glitterati. Recently, however, with increasing institutional contact between Los Angeles and Mumbai, more American stars are traveling to India for work. At first, most of them seemed to be stars of a faded sort, working in India in order to resuscitate their flagging careers. With their stardom tarnished by flops, bad financial planning, and personal controversy, actors like Sylvester Stallone and Denise Richards have been redeployed in the service of high-profile Hindi productions like *Kambakkht Ishq* (2009). This kind of stunt casting suggests that Bollywood is becoming a dumping ground for Hollywood stardom.

However, working with Nicolas Cage and other "worn-out" Hollywood stars also provides Hindi film directors like Vidhu Vinod Chopra with the opportunity to break into English-language production. Alongside fallen A-listers, emerging American film stars from Brandon Routh to Ali Larter have taken their turns in Bollywood studios. More recently, however, established Hollywood actors like Drew Barrymore and John Travolta have expressed interest in collaborating with Hindi film producers, illustrating the productive potential of crossover celebrity. Far from serving as the graveyard of Hollywood stardom, Bollywood has emerged as a site for Hollywood reincarnation. In other words, Hollywood labor can be reborn in India.

By 2009, the stage seemed set for the highest-profile rebirth of all. The Indian and international press were delighted that Julia Roberts had worn a vermillion *bindi* during a January visit to the Taj Mahal, seeing it as a gesture of cultural respect.[12] Of course, it also helped that she was a yoga devotee and had named her production company "Red Om Films." Raised by Catholic and Baptist parents in Georgia but having occasionally practiced Hinduism for over a decade, Julia Roberts converted in India in autumn 2009 while filming *Eat Pray Love*, the adaptation of Elizabeth Gilbert's novelized advertisement for spiritual tourism. Reportedly, Roberts's full commitment to Hinduism was secured through a meeting with Swami Dharam Dev, who renamed her three children in honor of the gods for the duration of her India shoot. Some of the global faithful were incredulous at their celebrity convert, but Roberts was welcomed by the Universal Society of Hinduism (located in the United States).

Despite all the fanfare, the logistical challenges of a foreign shoot in India trumped any consideration Julia might have wanted to show to her newly found brethren. During the filming of *Eat Pray Love*, for example, hundreds of security guards attached to the production shut down Navaratri festivities at a temple near Delhi so that the film could be shot on temple grounds. Adherents wishing to perform their *darshan* were denied the opportunity even to see Roberts in the act of filming. Roberts might have publicly hoped to be reincarnated as "something quiet and supporting" after the hustle and bustle of celebrity life, but her film production obstructed a local religious observance.[13] What is curious here is less the disregard for local practice or the compromise of religious belief by professional obligation; after all, Hollywood celebrity demonstrates that the distinction between religion and work is hardly sacrosanct. What is more interesting is how the global economy of Hollywood manifests itself through the narrative of conversion. While stardom's negotiation between the elite and the everyday was illustrated by Julia's newfound religion, Hindu conversion also resonates as a metaphor for the mobility of Hollywood's cultural labor.

Of course, religion is only one form of devotion produced by inter-industry contact. The attachments to places and persons by stars and fans constitute everyday forms of contact between media industries. Celebrity travelogues and fan commemorations may seem ephemeral when compared to the more formalized political economies of inter-industry exchange but they establish schemes of regularity and purpose. In fact, these rituals of contact—modes of identification mobilized by "affective economies" of exchange—are productive sites for analyzing the ways in which media industries are both pulled together and pushed apart.

What is the cultural work accomplished by these forms of celebrity attachment and ambassadorship, and what is the repertoire of understanding engaged by and produced through the transnational circulation of screen labor? The production and representation of industrial co-presence is critical to the "transnational connectivities" that constitute the media world.[14] In this way, celebrity and fan discourse call attention to the "face-work" of encounter between global media industries.

The term "face-work" is most commonly associated with the work of the sociologist Erving Goffman, whose research into the rituals of face-to-face encounter called attention to the complex ways in which human behavior structures "the traffic rules of social interaction."[15] Goffman's work focused on the ways in which physical co-presence was embedded within social transactions, but the micro-politics of his fine-grained social descriptions have been directed toward wider implications, focusing on how trust and commitment are maintained in the abstractions of modernity. In his work on globalization and culture, for example, Michael Curtin extends Goffman's "face-work" to the media industries. Curtin claims that, despite the presence of new technologies of instantaneous access and electronic coordination, "creative labor also needs to congregate so as to build relationships of trust and familiarity" that can sustain the collaborative work of media industries.[16] Following Curtin, I argue that the trade of stars, photos, and letters between Bombay and Hollywood performs the face-work of global media exchange.[17] Staged by a theater of intimacy, this face-work enables the practices of contact through which Hollywood enters the Indian mediascape.

Touristic imperatives have predominated in the face-work of encounter, but Tom Cruise's publicly expressed desire to visit India in a *Times of India* interview on February 15, 2009, can be seen as part of an emerging trend of American stars traveling to India to work in the film industry as well. In 2011 alone, Naomi Watts and Liev Schreiber, Hugh Jackman, Josh Hartnett, and Rob Schneider all visited India for work and tourism. It has now become commonplace to ask any Hollywood star visiting Bombay whether they would like to work in the Indian industry. Their answers are often the same as the one given by John Travolta, who noted on a recent trip to India that he "would enjoy singing and dancing in Bollywood" and "India feels like being at home."[18]

Working in Hollywood has historically been seen as the ultimate validation for Indian-born talent, consolidating the stardom of M. Night Shyamalan, Shekhar Kapur, Ashok Amritraj, and others. Actors like Anil Kapoor, who played the quiz show host in *Slumdog Millionaire* (2009), insists that "everybody wants to make it globally, which means making it in the U.S."[19] However, many other Bombay stars—like Aamir Khan, Akshay Kumar, and, until recently, Bipasha Basu—have distanced themselves from Hollywood ambition, claiming that serving in minor, typecast roles in American film would tarnish their stardom.[20] Bombay stars' gestures of refusal, alongside American celebrities' resounding Indomania, constitutes a declaration of Bollywood independence at a time of growing alignments between Hollywood and Bombay industries.

The cultural observations of American stars on tour can be framed as individual perceptions masquerading as industrial validation. Here, sentiment can be read as an instrumental exercise, reasonably dismissed as part of the cynical machinery of branding. However, what makes celebrity discourse so effective is that stars signify densely interwoven networks of industry, genre, and narrative, validating the intensities of viewer attachment and identification.[21] Industrial reciprocity is established through these networks of exchange. At the same time, celebrity collapses these networks onto the body of the famous, implicating the star within larger historical frameworks. I turn to these frameworks below.

Travel stories of wealthy Indians visiting Hollywood before World War II framed a class discourse of racialized Otherness at a time of increasing anti-immigrant exclusion in American law and culture. The visits of doctors, bankers, industrialists, and other upper-class Indians were often covered in the Los Angeles press.[22] Most significantly, the idea of the royal or courtly personality framed the early discourse of

Indian celebrity, particularly for the *Los Angeles Times*, which diligently documented the various princes who visited Hollywood in the waning years of their Indian majesty. As early as 1915, an Indian visitor who had Anglicized his name to R. D. Surrey and who claimed to be a dispossessed Punjabi royal worked as a technical director for the Ince Picture Company. Entertainment reporter Grace Kingsley described him as a "a sensible and practical prince . . . not mooning over glories departed, but learning what he considers the greatest business in the world."[23] The son of the owner of Star National Theatrical Company in India, Surrey disdained the misrepresentations of "oriental motion-picture plays," but nevertheless publicized his royal ancestry as an entry point into early Hollywood.[24] Similarly, when Bombay producer Y. A. Fazalbhoy visited Hollywood in 1936, his trip was staged as a royal world tour.[25] These early industry encounters established equivalences between the "the ancient world" of Indian royalty and the mobility of Hollywood's modern aristocracy.

In the early years of Hollywood, Indian royalty helped to confer a mantle of respectability and an aura of refinement to the industry, further distancing cinema from its status as "lowbrow" entertainment. At the same time, royal identities eased over racial difference during a period of rising anti-immigrant American nativism. As labor, property, and citizenship laws continued to disenfranchise Asian Americans, Indian royalty provided a more manageable form of racial, ethnic, and national difference because these temporary visitors were clearly differentiated from the permanent Indian residents of the United States by virtue of their spectacular ancestry. I will have much more to say on the historical issue of labor and exclusion in the final section of this chapter.

After World War II, Hollywood's fascination with the Indian elite was displaced by an attention to "ordinary" Indians, particularly as American political science sought to promote and understand Indo-American Cold War relations through the prism of Hollywood representation. This alignment between popular culture and foreign policy exemplifies what Christina Klein calls "Cold War Orientalism."[26] In the early 1940s, while not calling publicly for the decolonization of British India, the Roosevelt administration quietly advocated for Indian independence in order to secure greater support for the Allied war effort. After independence in August 1947, the U.S. intelligence community assumed that the new Indian government, under Prime Minister Jawaharlal Nehru, would follow the British anticommunist position. This was not surprising, perhaps, since Britain initially guided much of America's strategic thinking on India. It came, however, as a "profound shock" that India, while sympathetic, would not steadfastly commit to the Western side of the Cold War.[27] As the United States accelerated diplomatic efforts to import more of India's mineral resources in the 1950s—especially manganese for steel production and monazite and beryl for the defense industries—Indo-American cultural perceptions were seen as significant objects of study. Notable among these studies is the work of Harold Isaacs, who conducted a series of interviews with American writers, politicians, and businessmen, soliciting their broad perceptions of China and India in the mid-1950s. Isaacs noted that the composite picture of Indians drawn up by the impressions of influential Americans tended to invoke a culture caught between competing traditions of modernity and tradition. These American impressions led to frustration and antipathy toward India, driven by its contemporary foreign policy but also affirming older American stereotypes.[28]

At the same time that American political science dismissed American cinema as the wellspring of Indian misperception, the U.S. State Department was actively recruiting Hollywood to its cause. Chester Bowles was serving as the U.S. ambassador to India and Nepal when he solicited film director Frank Capra's help to defeat Soviet and Chinese communism on Indian soil. Capra was a prominent member of the Hollywood establishment (ironically under suspicion for alleged communist sympathies) and a member of a State Department advisory group charged with promoting positive international perceptions of the United States. In early 1952, Bowles asked Capra to attend the International Film Festival in India to help gauge the level of Soviet and Chinese impact on India in the early years of political nonalignment. Capra was already known in India, his films having played an important role in the social consciousness of a new generation of Indian artists looking for political transformation through mass commercialized forms. Capra's attendance at the film festival, what he called his "introduction to the Orient," was just one of many coordinated displays of geopolitical friendship between the United States and India.[29] Garlands, trinkets, and various other honorifics were exchanged, to the great benefit of local merchants and florists.

In his autobiography, Capra claimed that the Russian and Chinese film delegations had bought up all the fresh flowers in Delhi in preparation for a ceremony at Gandhi's memorial. The next day, when it came time for the American delegation to pay its respects, Capra refused to be outdone and showed up with his grandchildren to maximize the emotional impact of the visit.[30]

Such gestures of reciprocity helped to manage industrial points of contact between Hollywood and Bombay media ecologies at a time of increasing geopolitical tension. So far, this chapter has focused on the high-profile moments when stars attempt the resuscitation of spirit, career, and diplomacy. But what of those less spectacular forms of transnational media that are equally crucial to the representation of exchange? In the next section, I focus on the traces of movement that linger in the exchange of photographs, autographs, and above all letters. These iconic, literary, and epistolary exchanges demonstrate how industrial motivations are caught up and made legible through interpersonal connection.

Epistolary Frictions

In a letter to the editors of the religious journal the *Christian Century* written in 1930, W. E. Sikes of Berkeley, California, argues that Hollywood in India is a "menace." Having spent five years in India during a time of increasing Hollywood export, Sikes found that American films "do more to lower the white race in the eyes of Indians than any other influence we can imagine." Sikes felt that Hollywood in India led to a wholesale misperception of the United States; worse, it undermined the work of missionaries while substantiating the prejudices of popular anti-Indian portrayals like Katherine Mayo's *Mother India*. "The point," Sikes concludes, is that "we are free to send either the best we have or the worst, and every decent consideration would justify sending to others only the best. American business has made tremendous strides in Indian markets, but they have been firms that gave India the finest products that have secured the widest field for them. Are the moving pictures the only representatives of the worst elements in life and in business?"[31]

The invocation of Hollywood in Indian film discourse proved to be more multifaceted than moralists like Sikes recognized. As Neepa Majumdar has shown, the publication of autographed photos of Hollywood stars in early film magazines helped propagate a parallel discourse of Indian stardom beyond the image itself.[32] The signed star image also generated the fiction of a personal relationship, an intimate intersubjectivity of contact that negotiated asymmetries between media industries. Paul Muni's autographed photo (fig. 4.2), published in a magazine that routinely criticized the American film industry, exemplifies these contradictions. *Filmindia*'s editor, Baburao Patel, became internationally known for his condemnations of the American film industry around the release of *Gunga Din* (1939). On a trip to New York in 1939, Patel called attention to "the smug serenity which has marked Hollywood's production of motion pictures slandering the Indian people."[33] Yet his magazine was full of photos of his trip to the United States, posing with Hollywood stars like Alice Faye, Lya Lees, George Raft, Gloria Dickson, and Don Ameche. For Patel, the iconic power of the Hollywood star, legitimated by personalized sentiment and an autograph, created a circuit of interpersonal exchange strong enough to remain uncompromised by what Hollywood did as an industry.

Baburao Patel's self-placement as a Hollywood intimate clearly aligns with his clever penchant for promotion. However, there is something more in the celebrity photo that is legitimated by Hollywood and also capable of circulating beyond it. The autograph authenticates the photo, testifying to the unique, material singularity of the star. Yet, the signed photo also enhances the circulation of the star-as-image. This conjoining of signature and image aligns the celebrity's body with the iterative processes of stardom, creating a figure of transit that negotiates between one industrial realm and another. Paul Muni's photograph is both of Hollywood and outside it, which is why Patel can repurpose it to promote an Indian publication without compromising its claim to cultural distinctiveness.[34] In short, Muni's star photograph is an artifact of Hollywood, yet it is partially insulated from its ideological effects.

While celebrity tourism, star photos, and geopolitical intrigue are privileged moments in the circulation of screen culture, everyday industry contact is also characterized by more mundane forms. What I am interested in here are the epistolary documents that frame industrial encounter in ways that gesture to both dialogue and difference.

Early on, American audiences were titillated by the occasional entry of strange Indian film customs through columnists like "Polly Perkins"

Figure 4.2. Through a photo and a personal note, Paul Muni reaches out to Baburao Patel. The caption reciprocates the sentiment. *Filmindia*, February 1940, 5.

at *Wid's Daily*, who told her readers that "Indian audiences always close their eyes during a kissing scene on the screen."[35] Conversely, many Indian magazines featured "Letters from Hollywood" or notes from "Our Hollywood Correspondent" alongside accounts of "Hollywood at Work" and "Cosmopolitan Hollywood." Prominent in this tradition is the writing of Sylvia Norris, who penned the "Film Letter from Hollywood" column for the English periodical *Filmfare* from the 1950s to the 1970s. She wrote of Indian star visits and delegations to Hollywood—fairly common during the Cold War—and provided her Indian readers with background on upcoming Hollywood productions. A combination of film reviewer, cultural attaché, and society columnist, Norris provided a translation point between Hollywood and Bombay cinema. For example, in a 1958 *Filmfare* column she described director–producer Mehboob Khan, whose *Mother India* was widely appreciated in the United States, as "the DeMille of India." Although she was only repeating a pithy and evocative description, Norris's reference would substantiate a moniker that was foundational to Khan's biography.[36]

Designating the work of foreign correspondents as "Letters" is a way of referencing epistolary forms validated by the intimacies of interpersonal exchange. However, the production of symbolic proximity can also serve as a mode of industrial contact. Such epistolary points of contact predate Hollywood.

For example, a December 1910 letter from Rajahmundry (then part of the Madras Presidency) to the editors of *Moving Picture News* explains the predominance of mythological epics on the Indian stage. The letter writer promised to provide linguistic and cultural assistance to American producers interested in cinematic adaptations for "one-third share of the net profits." The editors responded with the "hope that some enterprising manufacturer will be keen enough to avail himself of the opportunity now offered."[37] The teens saw the proliferation of such Indian entreaties, strategically phrased in the speech genre of genuflection, requesting new and secondhand prints, noting positive audience reactions to Hollywood film, and testifying to the importance of the Indian market. Such letters framed informal networks of international exchange that were critical to the institutionalization of technology and knowledge within both film industries.

The genre of the personal request as a means to promote and consolidate media institutions proved to be a durable strategy. For example, in a September 1932 letter to the president of the American Academy of Motion Picture Arts and Sciences, S. R. Kantebet, then chairman of the Technical Committee of the newly formed Motion Picture Society of India, proposed increasing India's international film profile by encouraging a "more scientific interest in the entire technique of motion pictures, both silent and talkie." After describing the archival, organizational, scientific, and experimental aims of the new Bombay-based Society, the writer asked for Hollywood's help in providing surplus "books, journals, apparatus, components, and in fact anything" that was "intrinsically of little value" to the presumably fully developed American film industry. In return for help in modeling the institutionalization of the

Indian film industry on its American counterpart, the writer offered Hollywood an opportunity for increased publicity in the subcontinent.[38]

While the work of journalists and media entrepreneurs legitimate institutional reciprocity through interpersonal relations, film audiences represent the most powerful symbols of attachment in the media world. Film fans in particular, whose intensity of attachment renders legible the forms of cultural labor that make audiences possible, represent the most heightened forms of spectatorial identification. This intensity of attachment can publicize the intimate, embodied relationship between industries. Published fan letters, common to media journalism, testify to an acknowledgement of the bonds of affinity established by the cultural labor of audiences.

For example, in a 1931 essay about the experiences of amateur scenarists around the world, the *North American Review* saved for last the "most extraordinary attempt to obtain an acting engagement at long distance." In a letter written from a young Nagpur man, who described himself as among the "Chatpavan Maharashtra Brahmins, one of the most envied castes in India," the writer "undertook to enslave himself to the film company for a period of two years in return for passage to the United States and an opportunity to enter motion pictures." He continued: "I am certain that in a short time and under expert direction I shall be another Rudolph Valentino, as the acting of his type suits me much. I will be useful to you for supplying your company with Hindu mythological, historical and social stories for film production and also for the customs and costumes required therein. I have for a long time thought over this point and am determined to devote my whole life to this precious art. I have great and lucrative schemes in my mind which I shall personally disclose to you in America."[39]

The American trade press delighted in such accounts of ardor, suggesting that they represented a more primitive and hence authentic mode of engagement. For example, the American trade journal *Film Daily* noted that "over in India, the natives buy ready-made 'fan' letters which gush adoration to the stars to whom they address them. This is not a time-saving device, simply an accommodation for the illiterate natives who have no conception of the English language."[40]

Another common form of contact between audiences and industries is the *unpublished* fan letter, sent directly to the studio's corporate office. These literary forms, cut off from public circulation but intimately tied to interpersonal reciprocity, help to demonstrate the limits of "face-work" in the institutionalization of media. In closing this section, I offer a brief set of examples.

In 1964, Gulab Singh Sengar, a mathematics lecturer at Lohia College in Churu, sent an aerogramme to Jack L. Warner, then president of Warner Brothers:

> You will be greatly surprised to get this letter from a stranger thousands of miles away. But I could not help it. I have tried my level best to get some information about a picture, DANGEROUS, produced by your studio in 1935. Bette Davis won her first "OSCAR" for this picture. I want to know the name of the person who directed this film. I have searched many magazines and Almanacs but could not find the name of Director of "Dangerous." I hope you can solve my difficulty. This is my humble request to you and I am sure you will help me out of this difficulty. I have become desperate after so many failures in my search.[41]

Within two weeks of her writing, Warner's director of international relations, Carl Schaefer, sent a short letter with the requested information.[42] What was the point of replying to a fan letter that was never circulated outside the studio? Before I attempt a tentative answer, consider the very different tone of another exchange with Jack Warner four months later.

Manharlal H. Chawda's August 1964 letter requests that Jack Warner meet with his brother Dhiraj, a color photographer who was on a two-month trip abroad. Dhiraj wanted to capture a portrait of Warner that would represent the "daily life of a big producer in Hollywood, and [show] it to India through the Indian film magazines." Promising to return the favor by introducing Warner to the Maharaja of Udaipur in order to develop the Lake Palace Hotel as a possible Hollywood shooting site, Chawda framed his letter to Warner as a request from one Rotarian to another.[43] The Rotarian connection is significant, because Indian Rotarians saw themselves as bridging East and West through the concept of fraternal service.[44] While enhancing international business relationships was a clear benefit of the elite Rotary mandate, Carl Schaefer received a terse memo from Jack Warner's office: "JLW [Warner] said for you to take care of these Indians (from India) when they arrive which should be soon now. If he calls I will transfer him to you. I gather that JLW does not want to be in town when they are at the studio."[45]

What do these examples indicate? A request from a fan is responded to positively, while an entreaty from a fellow member of an elite global fraternity is brushed aside. Here, the star system and audience attachment take precedence over a business alliance. Clearly, the epistolary figure speaks to the dilemma of physical exchange between Hollywood and India. Like the material singularity of the star that is displaced yet legitimated through its circulation, the epistolary form is predisposed toward the exchange of information rather than bodies. However, epistolary forms can also introduce the possibility of actually meeting the face behind the name, which is why the enduring feature of so many of these letters is that they remain unanswered.

In this section, I have focused on improvisational transactions often overlooked by the more calculating sociologies of industrial exchange. The face-work of textual travel creates transnational economies of intimacy in the exchange of cultural labor. Moreover, the gestures of reciprocity and refusal enacted through these transactions help to organize and rationalize the social life of media institutions. In the next section, I turn to one particular characterization of this social contact between industries, the coincidental categorization of Indian and Hollywood film labor as "Hindu."

The Making of Hindu Hollywood

In *Maximum City*, his book on the real and imagined landscapes of Bombay, Suketu Mehta describes the way in which Hindi cinema has taken up Hollywood and flourished beyond it. He dubs Hindi filmmakers "resourceful saboteurs," and observes that "when every other country's cinema had fallen before Hollywood, India met Hollywood the Hindu way. It welcomed it, swallowed it whole, and regurgitated it. What went in blended with everything that had existed before and came back with ten new heads."[46] Mehta's metaphor of consumption references common accounts of Hollywood piracy in India. What is different here is that while other commentators see piracy as anthropophagic— film journalist Subhash Jha, writing about Hollywood remakes, claims

that "Indian cinema continues to be unabashedly cannibalistic"[47]—
Mehta sees an even more radical transformation. Recast in the theater
of a demonic indigenous possession, Hollywood transmigrates into the
body of Hindi cinema and the rational imitation prescribed by the logic
of development proliferates out of control. Hollywood is devoured and
made anew.[48]

Part of a cultural repertoire of responses to Western media, the narrative of Hindu conversion actually informs the origin myth of India
cinema. During December 1910, D. G. Phalke had an epiphany while
watching Pathé's *The Life and Passion of Jesus Christ* (1906) at the
America–India Picture Palace. "While the life of Christ was rolling before my physical eyes," he narrated some years later, "I was mentally
visualizing the gods, Shri Krishna, Shri Ramachandra, their Gokul and
Ayodhya."[49] In the production of Phalke's *Raja Harishchandra* (1913), a
Western technology is internalized, with religion framing the discourse
of indigenization. As K. A. Abbas claims of its impact on the audience,
"The film may have been a foreign importation, but the figures they saw
on screen were ancient gods and goddesses."[50]

While some Indian filmmakers dramatized indigenization in terms of
Hindu conversion, religion also framed the Western travel writer's search
for Hollywood's Indian equivalent.[51] Notable among these accounts is
Beverly Nichols's conception of Bombay as the "Hindu Hollywood" in
Verdict on India, first published in 1944.[52] Like Western travel writers
before him, Nichols takes the reader on a tour of the Bombay film world:
stars sit cross-legged while naked "coolies" rest on the floor of the studio; film takes are interminable; equipment is hauled by bullock carts;
kisses are taboo; aside from the occasional social film, mythological and
historical subject matter predominate; film criticism is practically non-
existent. Embodying the "startling" difference between East and West,
Nichols claimed that Bombay "wasn't at all like Hollywood."[53]

At the same time, Nichols offered prescriptions for the success of Indian cinema as films got shorter in length, aided in part by wartime restrictions on film stock. For Nichols, at its most positive India abounded
with drama and diversity—it offered a multiplicity of stories, physiog-
nomies, and character types. However, Nichols's most significant repu-
diation is cast through his view that Bombay film production is "almost
entirely dominated by Hindu capital." Furthermore, he insists, Bombay

films are focused excessively on religious myth and untouchability at the expense of "Muslim traditions." So dominated is filmmaking by religion, Nichols insists, that Bombay is a veritable "Hindu Hollywood."

Nichols's evocation of Bombay filmmaking as "Hindu Hollywood" helps to substantiate the politics of *Verdict on India*. After all, the linking of religious identity to indigenous cultural production was designed to support Nichols's argument that India's domination by a Hindu majority required the creation of a South Asian Muslim homeland. However, Nichols's religious evocation resonates on a number of levels beyond communalist politics. His deployment of "Hindu" as a generic marker of Indianness exemplifies the common associations between Hinduism and Bombay filmmaking, especially with reference to Hollywood. In 1941, for example, the *Hollywood Reporter* claimed that "Hindus find filmmaking as screwy as Hollywood," and went on to claim problems specific to "the Hindu Hollywood": "a Mohammedan will not eat what a Hindu will; a Hindu of one caste will object if a Hindu of another caste prepares the food. It is hard to keep things straight, so [they] try to do very little location filming."[54] Similarly, the *Chicago Daily Tribune* carried photos of a Bombay film production under the caption "Hindu Hollywood."[55] International productions made in India, like *Shiraz* (1928), were sometimes referred to as "Hindu films," extending to a conception of the entire Indian audience as the "native Hindu market.[56] Furthermore, language collapsed onto religion through rather willful errors of transliteration, as in the *Los Angeles Times* assertion that "pictures made in Bombay have used only *Hindu* dialogue" (emphasis added).[57]

The language of the *Los Angeles Times* story, referenced above, is especially ironic because Bombay cinema's fluid movement between Hindi and Urdu offered an intervention in the language politics of decolonizing India. While Hindi purists demonized Urdu as an illegitimate Persian influence in the world of dramatic arts,[58] Bombay cinema opened up a fluid linguistic space that only partially reproduced the contentious Hindu–Muslim politics of the day.[59] While Bombay did not escape prevalent communalist tensions, Nichols's "Hindu Hollywood" was home to a number of progressive writers from varied religious backgrounds that were neither part of the nationalist mainstream nor beholden to its linguistic politics.[60]

Outside India, Nichols's insistence on the presence of a "Hindu Hollywood" in 1944 echoes the associations of infiltration and power associated with the term "Jewish Hollywood," a charge that would pit isolationists against interventionists in the arguments about the United States entering the European theater of World War II.[61] There are other links to be made between Hollywood and India on the threshold of war. For example, while wealthy Hollywood studio heads had long been referred to as "moguls," connecting them to courtly opulence and Eastern imperialist rapacity, film industry progressives' support for Indian independence was seen by the FBI as part of a broader campaign of leftist subversion within Hollywood.[62] The most remarkable connection between Hinduism, Hollywood, and India, however, is the racialized characterization of film labor within a climate of intense xenophobia. How did Indian labor come to embody American anti-immigrant sentiment at the same time that Hollywood celebrated a burgeoning Indomania?

At the turn of the twentieth century, state referenda, municipal ordinances, and consumer boycotts rode on a swelling tide of anti-Asian racism in the United States. Even before Naturalization Act of 1870 denied Asians the right to citizenship, Japanese, Chinese, and Indian immigrants had endured a history of systematic exclusion from property ownership. Despite the fact that only seven thousand Indians arrived in the United States from the early 1880s to the end of World War I, Indians played a powerful symbolic role in the formulation of racist state policy. By the turn of the twentieth century, California had systemic problems with its Indian population. For example, a 1909 Federal Immigration Commission's inquiry into Indian laborers settled along the Pacific Coast noted that "the Hindus are regarded as the least desirable, or better the most undesirable, of all the eastern Asiatic races which have come to share our soil."[63] A local newspaper claimed that an Indian's attempt to buy property in 1913 was met with brokers collectively asserting that when "Hindoos and Negroes" settled in a community, they "depreciated [the] value of adjacent property and injured the reputation of the neighborhood and are generally considered as undesirable."[64] In a 1920 report, the California State Board of Control claimed that the "Hindu is the most undesirable immigrant in the state . . . unfit for association with American people."[65] Over the coming decades, the Indian population of the United States plunged as a result of these and other institutionalized forms of racism against Asian immigration. This trend was not to be reversed until well after World War II.[66]

At the same time that resident Indians were systematically excluded from basic labor and property rights in California, Hollywood indulged an Indological fascination. This interest in India was countrywide, activated by high-profile intercultural events such as Swami Vivekananda's trip to the World Parliament of Religions in Chicago in 1893, the founding of the Vedanta Society in New York in 1895, Jiddu Krishnamurti's visit to the United States in 1924, and the burgeoning Theosophy movement. By the 1930s, Swami Prabhavananda had established the headquarters of the Southern California Vedanta Society in the Hollywood Hills, helping to energize LA's engagement with spiritualism and religious uplift. Meher Baba, who visited the United States in 1932, announced through his secretary that he would be willing to enter Hollywood films if that proved "to be the best avenue of approach to the American mind."[67] The modern, "practical" Hinduism espoused by Vivekananda and others helped popularize yoga and other healthful practices as a way for Americans to experience a romanticized India that partially reaffirmed Orientalist fascination.[68] While Hindu holy men framed and translated a commodified spiritualism for the American public, in its fascination with India the United States found an ideal reflection of its own religious priorities.[69] As Wendell Thomas argued in 1930 book *Hinduism Invades America*, "We see a rebound of the West on itself—the stimulus is American, the response Hindu."[70]

Hinduism offered Hollywood a similar kind of exoticized attachment to the world of the Orient. In films from Edison's *Hindoo Fakir* (1902) to D. W. Griffith's *The Hindoo Dagger* (1909), the word "Hindoo" combined a general ethnological interest with a heightened sense of narrative tension that alterity was supposed to signify. Film after film referenced a fascination with Hindu spectacle. Pacific Motion Picture Company's hand-colored *Shalimar* (1912) featured what its writer noted was "a photograph of the eyes of a celebrated Hindoo hypnotist that will put under the hypnotic spell all in the audience who are susceptible to hypnotic suggestion, although the owner is thousands of miles away in his native India."[71] Proto-horror films like Vitagraph's *Reincarnation of Karma* (1912) told the story of a Hindu high priest reincarnated as Leslie Adams in a story of supernatural love and revenge. Ambrosio's *Benares, the Sacred City* (1912) showcased the everyday life of Hindu devotion, and Éclair's educational *Fire* (1913) contained a section on the worship of Agni, the Hindu god of fire. Edison's *Curious Scenes in India* (1913) featured Hindu pilgrims and the involvement of elephants in religious ritual, while Gaumont's *Weekly No. 53* (1913) contained a religious festival sequence where "The Hindus Celebrate," and Éclair's *Anaradhapura, the Birthplace of Buddhism* (1913), featured Indian temple architecture.

Other films construed Hinduism in terms of a mystical orientalism, like Rex's *The Stolen Idol* (1913), which featured an Indian religious artifact that finds its way to New York (decades before the *Indiana Jones* movies). Similarly, the Siva temple of Sun Photoplay's *The Princess of India* (1915) is filled with treasure and depicts hapless temple robbers devoured by prowling wild beasts. Mysticism and murder were a common paring, prominent in the crimes of treacherous Hindu servants against their Christian masters in films like *False Ambition* (George P. Hamilton, 1918) and *Money Mad* (Hobart Henley, 1918).

These stories were produced within Hollywood's nascent studio system, where opportunities abounded, but opportunity was also available to those intrepid enough find "authentic" footage overseas. For example, in 1913 *Motion Picture Story Magazine* told readers about shooting in India and "the Hindu charm" and "the spirit of the Orient" to be found there.[72] Race also served as an index of authenticity. For example, a 1916 *Photoplay* advice column counseled an aspiring actor recently settled in the United States: "Even though you have just arrived in this country from India you should be able perhaps to secure a place as an actor. You see, while you are disqualified for plays requiring Americans, you have the qualification of being a 'natural Indian' and would be valuable just as the Japs are in their roles. Why don't you try the studios of Hollywood and Los Angeles?"[73] Yet ethnic malleability was a constitutive feature in casting nonwhite actors; hence Sessue Hayakawa's character in *The Man Beneath* (William Worthington, 1919), "a high-caste Hindu in love with a white girl," was praised in the press for being "real and unusual enough to be of immediate interest."[74]

As Hollywood grew into a complex assemblage of production practices in the late 1910s, Hinduism helped to bolster American cinema's extraordinary possibilities, framing an entire discourse of the marvelous. Here was an industry worldly enough to embrace all forms of life, while at the same time transcending the differences between them. Early Hollywood deployed Hindu figures to exemplify this simultaneity between the ordinary world and the sensational "dream factory" of the film industry.[75] For example, the Hindu mystic S. Khriju gave astrological readings to Hollywood actors like Lloyd Hughes in the early 1920s. And when Paramount wanted "at least 560 Hindu troopers" for its forthcoming film on the lives of Bengal Lancers in 1934, Serevan Singh, a "high-caste Hindu" and Long Beach fortune-teller, offered his extrasensory credentials to the casting director. When asked how Paramount might reach him in case he got the role, the actor said, "Just think of me when you want me and I shall appear."[76]

While "Hindoos" were listed alongside "Indian" and "Chinese" in the panoply of "racial types" used by the Central Casting Corporation's "Race Casting Director" in the apportionment of film extra work in the mid-1930s,[77] the "Hinduization" of Hollywood catapulted a select few to the ranks of the permanently employed. Lal Chand Mehra, long known as "Hollywood's favorite Hindu" for his roles in *The Charge of the Light Brigade* (1936) and *Gunga Din*, wrote Hindi titles for DeMille's *King of Kings* and served as a technical adviser to *The Black Watch* (John Ford, 1929), a film that was part of an upswing of melodramas set in India. Having served as one of three turban costumers on *The Rains Came* (1939) and an expert on the "many variations of turban twists demanded by caste and locality," Husain Nasri presided as "leader of Hollywood's Hindus."[78] Another costumer, Bhagwan Singh, "Hollywood's very urban turban wrapper-upper," had been tying turbans in American film productions since the mid-1910s, as soon as Hollywood began to pay attention to its Indian market and started hiring technical advisers to avoid "riots in India, the Malay States and diverse sundry other Oriental nations, where they take their turbans seriously."[79] As early as 1915, *Motography* was to praise Singh's technical expertise for the Mutual Film Corporation as an "East India native, familiar with customs and the manners of the Oriental."[80]

While these minor American Indian celebrities played a supporting role in Hollywood's Hindu narrative, the religious identity of Hollywood's most famous Indian star, Sabu, remained in question. Introduced to American audiences in Robert Flaherty and Zoltán Korda's *Elephant Boy* (1937), Sabu was often described as a "Hindu juvenile" or the "Hindu boy actor."[81] Though born into a lower-class Muslim family in Mysore, *Life* magazine nevertheless described Sabu as "the Hindu Mickey Rooney."[82] So prevalent was Sabu's shifting religious biography in Hollywood that the gossip columnist Louella Parsons took it upon herself to correct the record in 1940:

> Sabu, the dark-skinned Mohammedan boy—yes, he is a Mohammedan and not a Hindu—who has been with us everyday, has grown into our hearts on this personal appearance tour. He is a darling and the only thing that irks him is to be called a Hindu. He looked very grave and so sad. I asked his tutor, Austin Menzies, why Sabu disliked to be called a Hindu. "He is afraid," said his tutor, "that they will tear him limb from limb when he goes back to India, for there is a great rivalry there between the Mohammedans and the Hindus."[83]

As Prem Chowdhry notes, the story of Sabu's transformation from the son of an elephant driver to a Hollywood actor helped to justify the civilizational discourse of imperialism. His films present him as a loyal imperial subject, one who has internalized the moral standards of his masters. This capitulation may be the reason that Sabu never achieved great popularity among Indian audiences.[84] In Hollywood, the confusion over Sabu's religious identity renders him a generic marker of an unthreatening and pliant colonial subjectivity—and the United States emerges as the only place that can save him from the savages of his homeland, which, according to Louella Parsons, has fully bought into his misidentified Hinduism. This pliability was confirmed when Sabu was granted American citizenship after enlisting in the U.S. Army Air Forces. Sabu was conferred the right to become an American in an era when most Indians were denied the right to naturalize. At a time when Hollywood's Indological fascination extended to the production of "empire films" designed to battle British cinema for relevance on the subcontinent, Sabu's star text was placed between immigrant success story and Orientalist nativism.[85] On August 21, 1938, the *Washington Post* exemplified the characteristic narration of Sabu's "transformation" with the headline, "From Jungle to Movies—the Tale of Sabu—'Elephant Boy.'"

In Hollywood, though, Hinduism was more than an identity category held by some of its labor force. Beginning in the 1920s, Hinduism became associated with the ongoing transformation of studio labor. In classic orientalist fashion, Hollywood used Hinduism not only as a way to understand India, but also as a way to understand itself. References to Hollywood's labor aristocracy as a "caste system" conflated Hinduism with forms of social life common to Indological fascination and located Hollywood within an unwavering system of social oppression.[86]

Implicated in a European taxonomy of racial and social types and essentialized as quintessentially Indian, the use of caste has been both widespread and contradictory. James Mill insisted in his 1858 *History of British India* that caste "is the first and simplest form of the division of labor," while H. H. Risley's 1909 book *The People of India* claimed that the Indian caste system might evolve into a class structure over time. On the other hand, Gandhi defended the caste system as a means to prevent class warfare by preserving occupational heredity.[87] In Hollywood, however, the concept of caste and its relationship to class was less ambivalent.

In 1923, the Hollywood reporter Myrtle Gebhart noted that "not alone in India does the caste system flourish, but in plebian Hollywood, that gingham child-town now beginning to wear her silks and jewels as though she'd been used to them all her life."[88] For Gebhart, "social caste" was synonymous with the mobility of cliques and partygoing, a means for the "high moguls of filmdom" as well as the members of a "young girl's" social club to recognize one another. As a means of describing Hollywood's social organization, caste was not connected specifically to religion, though Gebhart was sanguine about Hollywood's faddish fascination with Hinduism: "Hollywood is great on fads. For a while it was an interesting Hindu religion, very mysterious, which was supposed to teach its novitiates how to be thin and religious at the same time, according to some old philosophy of India. The religion, when the glamour had worn off, proved to be a very ordinary affair of exercising properly—and lost its appeal."[89]

If Hollywood was a bellwether for national fads, it was also a microcosm of more enduring trends. For the Hollywood film industry, "caste" had come to signify both stratification and immobility within the studio system's social structure, undermining Hollywood's rags-to-riches labor mythology prevalent since the 1910s.[90] In a 1929 column, the photographer H. T. Cowling claimed that film was the one medium that could abolish Hinduism's social structure: "Bang—goes the caste system on the toboggan—what medium will do as much for India in supplanting the antiquated and unjust caste system, as that of motion picture entertainment?"[91] By the early 1930s, John Scott would claim that, "like India, Hollywood's caste system admits of little social climbing in the studios."[92] Like other reporters of his time, Scott shifts between "caste" and "class" as a means of describing the "unwritten rules" that structured the division of labor in Hollywood—between extras, contract players, and stars—that blocked mobility from one set of acting ranks to another.

Beginning in the mid-1930s, with a slew of Hollywood productions set in India, *Washington Post* writer Hubbard Keavy would put caste to a number of uses: to capture Hollywood's "sharp lines of social distinction"; as a general system of grading between A and B pictures, stars, and agents; and as a way to render certain forms of talent invisible in the hierarchy of work.[93] Others were more focused in their determinations. For example, John Chapman's 1941 exposé of the politics of Hollywood's caste system told the story of a model employed at Republic Pictures. While working on the set of a Western, the model made the social error of eating with the cowboy extras rather than the principal players. "It was a terrible thing to do," recalled Chapman, "for Hollywood is a very proper town with a rigid caste system, and the Brahmins are as far apart from the untouchables as a B picture is from a good notice."[94]

None other than Hedda Hopper, Hollywood's infamous gossip columnist, weighed in on the caste question. Like John Scott, Hopper slips between class and caste, but caste signifies both the systematic wage inequity in Hollywood as well as the intractability of social reform: "People tear their hair over the shame of Mother India and the cruelty of her caste system, but it would take a better man than Mahatma Gandhi to bridge the chasm between a $200 a week actor, and one who earns $2,000 . . . The caste system has caused more tragedies in Hollywood than have scandals. It never belonged in America."[95] As Hopper's admonition attests, "caste" functioned as a way of capturing and critiquing the entrenched labor stratification of big-budget cultural production. In fact, the increasing use of the term "caste" to signify inequality in the film industry from the 1920s to the early 1940s maps onto the growing labor–management crisis in Hollywood's "Golden Era."

When Murray Ross's pioneering 1941 study *Stars and Strikes* was published, he could claim with confidence that "Hollywood is a union town."[96] This reversed a long historical trend. As many film historians have shown, film producers were initially drawn to Los Angeles because of its status as an anti-union, open-shop city.[97] Hollywood's transition from a system based on the open shop to one based on collective bargaining over its first quarter-century was enabled by a proliferation of guilds, associations, unions, and societies, often with competing rationalizations and jurisdictions. Ongoing organizing efforts took place in a national climate of economic depression, even as the National Recovery Administration focused on improving labor conditions while protecting monopoly practices in the media industries.[98] Riots, work stoppages, strikes, and other agitations increasingly characterized Hollywood's labor–management relationship as the studio system consolidated. Public consciousness of worker exploitation in the film industry addressed the widening gap between the opulent life of the star and the economic degradation of the film extra. Not surprisingly, when the progressive Indian screenwriter and producer K. A. Abbas visited the United States in 1943, he found that an "entirely new Hollywood," a "Trade Union–conscious Hollywood," was at the forefront of the film industry.[99]

So why was "caste" such a prevalent metaphor for describing Hollywood's labor aristocracy? In fact, there were a number of ways to engage caste as a trope of "Hindu Hollywood." That a modern industry like film production could be so dominated by the "backwardness" of caste signaled Hollywood's social depravity for an American public that still recalled the scandals and moral excesses of the 1920s. At the same time, using "caste" instead of "class" allowed for social commentators and critics to address structural labor inequality without inviting associations with Marxist terminology at a time when Hollywood was popularly assumed to be a communist breeding ground. In other words, caste became a way for writers to identify a labor–management problem without politicizing it. Furthermore, referring to work problems as a "caste system" may have helped to isolate Hollywood's labor unrest from similar tensions in other industries around the country.

Historically, the evocation of caste allowed colonial governmentality to indicate social difference in a society thought not yet mature enough for class difference. Conversely, Hollywood caste was a way to indict the studio system's barbarous primitivism without invoking the Marxian language of class. This dichotomy is apparent as early as 1925 in an article in *Photoplay*, the leading fan magazine of its day. Claiming that "the rugged old movie democracy is fading and Hollywood is putting on the Pekingese," Herbert Howe noted that "the caste system of India is lax compared with that of Hollywood. Charlie Chaplin, who at times inclines towards society bolshevism, once remarked that he could tell to the dime how much a man earned by the place he occupied at a Hollywood party."[100] The cartoon that accompanied the article underscored this point (see fig. 4.3).

Serving as a kind of Weberian shorthand for "status" and "social group," as well as a safer alternative to "class," caste signified immobility as a social force. Yet Hollywood's ethno-national associations with caste seem ironic given the relative marginality of Indian labor in Hollywood as well as the systematic exclusion of Indian Americans in the racialized citizenship and property discourse of the time. Certainly, the predominant use of "caste" to denote the screen labor aristocracy aligns with Hollywood's fascination with colonial India in the 1930s. Yet, outside the film press, the most prevalent use of caste was in terms of African American cultural politics. While W. E. B. Du Bois had famously used "the barriers of caste" as a way to reference American race relations, the association between race and caste had a long history in sociology, letters, and political discourse from Reconstruction to the onset of World War II.[101] As film historian Jane Gaines notes, "caste" designated both the fixed boundaries of racial classification in American everyday life and the generalized "invidious distinctions" that would function in popular genres like film melodrama to "stir emotions and touch raw nerves.[102]

Given its explosive potential, the Hollywood press seems to have dispatched caste by referencing a safely distant Orient, rather than politicizing film industry labor practices within the broader social framework of American race relations. Nevertheless, "caste" as a marker of "Hindu Hollywood" is intertwined with the slow, painful transition toward wage reform that was enormously consequential for women and ethnic minorities looking for work in California and beyond. Kamala Visweswaran notes that globalization "enables the displacement and relocation of apparently stable analytic objects like 'caste' or 'race' to

Figure 4.3. Robert Patterson's cartoon for *Photoplay*,
August 1925, 29. The caption reads, "Now, if you want
to bounce in on the swellest parties, you have to be a
Swami or a Duke."

new contexts."[103] The casting of caste as a key player within labor and
management conflict in prewar Hollywood suggest that there are much
longer time lines of interconnection that precede and anticipate contemporary global transformations.

The alterity of "Hindu Hollywood" in Bombay and the "Hinduization" of Hollywood labor demonstrates how religion marks the hierarchy of work in the film industries at particularly precarious moments in
their history. The popular description of Indian film work as "Hindu"
at the same time that religious caste was used to characterize tensions
between labor and management in interwar Hollywood signals a coincidental trajectory of appropriation, linking the social worlds of Indian
and American labor even as anti-Asian nativist anxieties come to the
fore in the United States. Hollywood's Western parochialism was validated by the invocation of Hinduism in caste and national attribution
in the interwar United States, which addressed structural inequality in
local industrial terms without locating it within broader racialized labor
formations.

However, the affective register also maps more broadly across the
transnational configurations of work between Hollywood and Bombay.
In this chapter's first case study, the promotional discourse of celebrity
tourism masks labor as leisure but also engages the face-work of travel,
creating forms of empathy and identification that are critical to fortify-

ing Hollywood's institutional credibility. Similarly, as my second case study shows, epistolary productions capitalize on attachment through the affective economies of interpersonal investment.

We should be wary, however, of such wholly institutional justifications. After all, the circulation of global labor practice is framed by the play of recognition and encounter. While Hollywood's motivations for institutional consolidation are clear, the navigation of space and difference is a necessarily fraught one. This chapter has traced the film industry's materialization in the cultural politics of work, excavating its practices of global and local sense-making across spaces and histories. At the heart of this excavation is the question of what animates the circulation of these practices across social and cultural spaces of industrial encounter.[104] Underlying this circulation are the practices of identification and expression that characterize forms of laboring subjectivity.

Conclusion

Close Encounters of the Industrial Kind

Contact is capable of transforming both parties worked in
the transaction.
Naoki Sakai, "You Asians: On the Historical Role of the
West and Asia Binary," *South Atlantic Quarterly*, Fall 2000

In March 2013, some thirty years after his last trip to India and on the
heels of his most recent film release, *Lincoln*, Hollywood director Steven
Spielberg visited Mumbai. There was ample cause for his return. After
all, *Lincoln* was coproduced by the Mumbai-based media conglomerate
Reliance Entertainment, which had entered into a merger with Spielberg's banner DreamWorks in 2008.

At the time of the merger, press commentators saw the Indo-
American alignment in the newly christened Reliance DreamWorks as
a fable of "starry-eyed suitors eager and hungry to be part of the fantasy of it all"; proof that when it came to Hollywood, "the myth, more
powerful than any surrounding any other business everywhere, still
attracts."[1] A few years later, Reliance DreamWorks was at full steam,
garnering eleven nominations for *War Horse*, *The Help*, and *Real Steel*
at the 2012 Academy Awards, attended by Reliance chairman Anil
Ambani.

In 2013, Spielberg traveled to Mumbai to meet Ambani and take part
in a number of events commemorating the success of *Lincoln* and the
Reliance–DreamWorks partnership. At an exclusive "master class" event
organized by Reliance, Spielberg participated in a question-and-answer
session with Amitabh Bachchan, Hindi cinema's iconic star. In the audience were over sixty members of an elite Indian film fraternity, whose
names were distributed to the press days in advance. In a series of exchanges with Bachchan, Spielberg freely admitted that he knew "not so

much" about Indian cinema, suggesting both commercial and cultural reasons for his lack of familiarity: "We in the U.S. need to be exposed to other cultures . . . DreamWorks and Reliance, led by Anil Ambani and his team, have that goal to build the cultural bridge. We are actually doing that this very moment." Elaborating on the DreamWorks merger with Reliance and his own relationship with Ambani, Spielberg continued: "For one, this has brought me to India. We were introduced at the Cannes film festival. In 2008, as the economic turmoil hit, Reliance continued to support us. We will never forget this. They believe in loyalty and freedom as much as we do. We speak the same language."[2] With this formulation, Spielberg cast the Reliance DreamWorks partnership as a shared vernacular project—when it came to the business of media, Hollywood and Mumbai spoke in the same tongue. What the *Hollywood Reporter* called "Spielberg's Close Encounter with Bollywood" was, then, less a meeting between alien species and more of a homecoming.

At the outset of this book, I suggested that we suspend such familiar tropes of contact in favor of more textured, "entangled" accounts. While the metaphor of "closeness" suggests the appositeness of encounter in contemporary global media, if we dig down deeper and further back, we might uncover more nuanced formulations of proximity and distance. In this conclusion, I offer one last archeology of Hollywood.

Steven Spielberg's father, who passed his World War II stories onto his son, was posted in Karachi and outside Calcutta as a B-25 radio operator. Arnold Spielberg senior also flew combat missions to Imphal as part of the early Burma Campaign, striking against Japanese targets as well as the anticolonial Indian National Army. For years, rumors persisted that Spielberg junior would make a film about the Burma Campaign.

However, when Steven Spielberg went on his first trip to India in 1977, it was for more practical reasons than visiting the place of his father's wartime memories. Columbia Pictures, the producers of *Close Encounters of the Third Kind* (1977), had amassed significant, unrepatriable box-office profits in India and was obliged to spend the money domestically. Spielberg and the studio decided to use the funds for a shoot just outside Bombay (doubling as Dharamsala), for the scene where villagers point to the sky in collective acknowledgment of alien visitation. Prior to filming, the production's camera equipment was impounded by Indian customs officials suspicious of unauthorized resale, much to the ire of the director. Once the equipment was released, the film's Indian production manager, Baba Shaik, spent hours coordinating two thousand extras to point in the same direction at the same time.[3]

The director François Truffaut, in India to act in the *Close Encounters* crowd scene as the French scientist Claude Lacombe, had once worked for Roberto Rossellini on the Italian documentary *India* (1958). Rossellini had been inspired to shoot the film after hearing Jean Renoir's stories about shooting in India for *The River* (1951).[4] Filmed in India with the assistance of Satyajit Ray and Subratra Mitra, *The River* inspired Hollywood to think about future Indo-American coproductions. Among the films that materialized out of this interest, the inaugural Merchant Ivory production, *The Householder* (1963), was the first feature produced in India by an American–Indian company and was acquired for worldwide release by Columbia Pictures, the company behind Spielberg's *Close Encounters*.

Spielberg was back in India in 1983 to scout locations for *Indiana Jones and the Temple of Doom*, the prequel to the hugely successful *Raiders of the Lost Ark* (1981). As before, he was frustrated by tax and equipment clearances mandated by Indian location shooting policy. Indian authorities also objected to the film's dialogue, which included the words "Thuggee" and "Maharajah." Fed up, and claiming that Indian rivers were too polluted for shooting anyway, Spielberg left India to shoot three weeks worth of exterior shots in Sri Lanka. On set in Sri Lanka, Spielberg asked Chandran Ratnam, owner of Film Location Services, to exhort the extras in their native language for the cameras. Ratnam objected that it would not be in Hindi, to which Amrish Puri, playing the cult leader Mola Ram, said, "Chandran, who the hell will know the difference?"[5]

Amrish Puri had initially declined the part of Mola Ram, finding that Spielberg's film was too reminiscent of a depraved commercial Hindi cinema. He was finally convinced to take the role by Richard Attenborough, who had directed Puri in *Gandhi* (1982). A third of *Gandhi's* US$22 million budget had been subsidized by the Indian National Film Development Corporation, which allowed film profits to be fully repatriated without limit out of India. Columbia Pictures purchased *Gandhi* for worldwide distribution, planning simultaneous openings in London,

Delhi, and Washington DC, and released 100 of the total 150 Indian prints dubbed in Hindi.

Indiana Jones and the Temple of Doom is set in 1935, a year after Columbia established local offices in Burma, India, and Ceylon. That was also the release year for two key "empire" films, *Clive of India* and *Lives of a Bengal Lancer*. Both films are set against a British empire in decline and feature vaguely disguised caricatures of Indian anticolonial nationalism. These films, along with *Gunga Din* (1939)—whose Thuggee high priest is a clear antecedent for *Temple of Doom*'s Mola Ram—led to calls from the Indian National Congress for a boycott of American cinema. If the boycott controversy complicated Hollywood's plans in India it proved fortuitous for Baburao Patel, the enterprising and self-promoting editor of *filmindia*, who used the uproar to cement a national reputation for his magazine in the late 1930s. The *New York Times*, commenting on Patel's recent visit to Hollywood, reinforced the protests of Congress against the "unsympathetic treatment accorded the Indians in several recent pictures," but Patel was careful to acknowledge that "we import 250 American pictures annually, and last year the producers took a net profit of $2,000,000 out of India."[6]

At the same time, Ram Bagai, *filmindia*'s "Staff Correspondent in Hollywood," exhorted his Indian readers to submit story ideas directly to Hollywood: "I have been asked by Hollywood producers to 'please bring back some Indian stories—something really Indian. We are ready to make films on India—the real India—but we know so little of that India. It's up to you and India to show us!'"[7] Hollywood's problems with "inauthentic" Indian stories were reinforced when *Gunga Din* was banned in India. Still, Hollywood was able to take advantage of the controversy over "empire" films when it released *The Rains Came* (1939)—with the ethnically malleable Tyrone Power cast as an Indian doctor—and it was advertised as the first "pro-India picture from Hollywood." As Karla Rae Fuller notes, the Caucasian face made to appear Asian is a critical part of the history of Hollywood representation, casting impersonation as central to the Western imagination of the Orient.[8]

The political debates over Hollywood's representation of the subcontinent, and the drama of authenticity staged in the travels of journalists and film texts, clearly informs the setting of *Temple of Doom*, which narrates this history as a screen memory of colonial encounter. So it's not surprising that *Temple of Doom*'s phantasmagoric travelogue, rehashing the caricatured indigeneity of colonial travel genres, was itself referenced in campy fashion in the Hindi B-film *Shaitan Tantrik* (1999).

Around the time he left India to film *Temple of Doom* in Sri Lanka in 1983, Spielberg reconciled with his former girlfriend, actress Amy Irving, then shooting in India for the HBO miniseries *The Far Pavilions* (1984), in which she played the Indian princess Anjuli. The same year, director Satyajit Ray attempted to file a plagiarism suit against Spielberg, claiming that the story for an earlier Spielberg film, *E.T. the Extra-Terrestrial* (1982), had been lifted from his script *The Alien*, which he had submitted to Hollywood in 1967. Responding to a number of infringement claims around *E.T.*, though not Ray's in particular, Spielberg said, "It's the people you've never heard of who crawl out of the woodwork like cockroaches to sue you."[9]

Even if he decided to make the film based on *The Alien*, Ray insisted that "people will think that I have borrowed from the American film whereas exactly the opposite has been the case."[10] Ray's criticism of Spielberg extended to his opinion of *Temple of Doom*, which Ray saw while in London in 1984. Ray described the film as "absolutely haywire, unbelievably bad."[11] The film was initially banned in India, vilified by the U.S. National Asian American Telecommunications Association, and protested at a Seattle movie theater in a demonstration led by a Pakistan-born political science professor who carried a placard labeling Spielberg and executive producer George Lucas "Raiders of the Third World."[12]

The history of Spielberg in India is clearly one of troubled as well as close encounters. However, by the time of his third visit to India, thirty years after the aborted *Temple of Doom* shoot, the Indian film establishment was in a charitable frame of mind. A few weeks after Spielberg's *Lincoln* event in Mumbai, the 2013 Academy Awards feted another set of Indo-American film relations. *Lincoln*, along with the India-themed *Life of Pi* (2012), was up for the Best Picture award. When *Life of Pi* won, it generated hopes for increased location shooting in India and confirmed the "crossover" appeal of Bombay cinema stars like Irfan Khan and Tabu. This was the first time since *Slumdog Millionaire*'s success at the 2009 Oscars that a major international release fueled such high hopes around Indian coproduction.

In fact, the Spielberg tributes didn't come solely from Hollywood. In 2013, a nineteen-year-old Bangalore resident named Krishna Bala Shenoi made a seventy-five-second tribute to Spielberg's films, painstakingly animating sequences from *Jaws* to *Lincoln* frame by frame in a rotoscoping process that took four months to complete. The short animated tribute has generated more than fifty-seven thousand YouTube hits.[13] At the time, Shenoi served as a "special correspondent" for the *Chicago Sun Times*, attached to film critic Roger Ebert, who posted the tribute on the newspaper's blog. Spielberg's makeup designer forwarded the clip to Spielberg, who wrote Shenoi a handwritten note of thanks: "Krishna Shenoi is surely one of the most gifted young filmmakers and writers on the internet. I have a good feeling about Krishna. Remember his name. I suspect you may hear it again. A born filmmaker, a prize product of the generation born into a world of video cameras. Could be the next Spielberg."[14]

The itineraries of influence, controversy, and rejection formed by *Temple of Doom*'s Indian intertexts frame screen practice and culture as they circulate through the politics of encounter. In many ways, the film's biography anticipates the literal and figurative movements of Hollywood as its first century in India comes to a close. All the key themes of this complex story are present: geopolitics and development, primitivism and fecundity, mimicry and masquerade, caricature and barbarism, individual desires and frustrations, institutional difficulties and chaotic bureaucracies, and underneath it all, the tantalizing possibility of collaboration.

Tracing Hollywood in India—one of the few remaining places in the world where it plays as a secondary cinema—presents challenges and opportunities for comparative media research. Many of the characterizations that substantiate global Hollywood—cultural imperialism, narrative ubiquity, distributional hegemony, market saturation, state subsidy, and the logic of numerical calculation—cannot be uniformly applied in the Indian context. This does not mean that Hollywood is insignificant in India, nor does it deny the extension of structural features that define Hollywood across global and local predicaments. Quite simply, attending to Hollywood in India allows for the asking of different kinds of questions.

Two decades ago, Bollywood film star Shah Rukh Khan insisted that "soon Hollywood will come to us."[15] *Orienting Hollywood* has shown how Hollywood has been traveling to India for a century. In the early 1920s, Florence Burgess Meehan, who would scout shooting locations in South and Southeast Asia, claimed that "the Orient receives the camera-man gladly and warmly . . . it loves the moving pictures and that 'gifted child of the gods' who carries a Bell and Howell is all but revered in most places."[16] The Western camera was a talisman, with its reverence stra-tegically cast as aspiration for the Indian film industries. Yet, India also offered a study in contrasts, with Hollywood as the standard of com-parison. Margit Kelen, writing in the pages of *Travel* magazine in 1934, wondered, "Did India have its Hollywood and who were its great stars and the big directors?" "I found my answer," she wrote, "in a squalid suburb of Bombay. Here in an enclosure set off from the neighboring huts by a stone wall was India's motion picture capital. It was scarcely an impressive place."[17]

Orienting Hollywood has focused on such figural descriptions as a way to capture the movement of screen objects and events through dif-ferent material circuits and environments. "Figures" refers both to those enumerated forms of commodity travel (e.g., systems of transnational exchange, imports, and exports) as well as those informal processes through which translocal movement is imagined and engendered. In macroeconomic calculations of the balance of trade, figures are nor-mally evoked to reference cross-border commodity flows. In this book, I've tried to move beyond this formal arithmetic and retain the collo-quial sense of the verb *figure* as a way of "working things out."

The art historian Richard Schiff proposes a tripartite understanding of the term *figure*—as the materiality of the object, the forming of a the-matic, and the ghostly forms that nonetheless exercise real force.[18] As artifact, act, and imaginary, figures are objects, practices of reflection, and accounts of movement. Figures are real, rhetorical, and representa-tive. Throughout this book, I have cast the figures through which Holly-wood has encountered and made sense of Bombay media ecologies (and vice versa). In many ways, *Orienting Hollywood* is a catalog of figures imagined and materialized through various itineraries of contact, draw-ing the historical into contemporary practice.

There is no shortage of ways in which Hollywood figures itself in India. The built environment frames the festival, the video parlor and the multiplex, the hoarding and the film poster, the on-location shoot, the art market, and the bazaar as figures through which Hollywood encounters Indian media ecologies. Written forms, like trade and industry policy, film reviews, fiction, biographies, film course syllabi, and the artist manifesto locate and resituate Hollywood in India. Geopolitics informs the ways in which television, color production and processing, immigration, and censorship institute Hollywood in particular ways. To these figures of transit we might add vegetarianism and fast food, *tikas* and *tikkis*, jewelry, henna, kohl, vermilion, *mehndi* and *bindis*, kissing, blue jeans and bikinis, rain-drenched cotton, turbans, autorickshaws, tantric yoga and the mysticism of self-help, award shows and beauty pageants, transnational child adoption, talk shows, and dance sequences—all are global and local stagings through which Hollywood "takes place" in the Indian mediascape.

Engaging these figures helps "provincialize" Hollywood in the process of framing commodity transit, taking up the forms of circulation that constitute the cultural politics of encounter.[19] Looking at the ways in which Hollywood materializes in forms of encounter, excavating its practices of global and local sense-making, implicating contemporary movements within older figurations of exchange, allows for a certain flexibility in analysis. Provincializing Hollywood—locating an account of its material existence in specific places and times, understanding the diverse ways that Hollywood is imagined, vernacularized, and figured in everyday screen practice—defies the grammar of mobility through which the narrative of global domination is most often communicated. Such provincialization is a form of reorientation, but it is also a form of location. In his call to "unsettle cinema," Bhrigupati Singh asks that we understand cinema as a "socially embedded set of practices," shifting "away from the fictionality of cinema as a formal 'text' towards its *fictive* quality, its being 'made up' as a form."[20] Part of a larger shift within contemporary critical media studies to move the problematic of textuality beyond the boundaries of the frame, *Orienting Hollywood* has focused on the ways in which screen objects and practices are figured through their transit.

This focus on transit is the reason why *Orienting Hollywood* is indebted to methodologies that have considered movement as an analytic and an imaginary. For example, communication and media studies have addressed the historical role of circulation and transport in instituting the infrastructure of information and transforming its meanings.[21] Similarly, influenced by more anthropological accounts of the commodity, transnational cultural studies has addressed "the question of travel" to think through the histories of displacement in public culture.[22] More recent approaches, influenced by science studies' conceptualizations of objects, actors, and agents, have framed the ordering of cultural and social life in terms of assemblages made up by "semiotic, material, and social flows."[23]

At the heart of this study is the consideration of what happens when one industry takes from another and how this exchange is both transactional and constitutive. As Lesley Stern puts it, "It is only through an engagement with particular sites of encounter and mediation between the filmic and the social that the double inflection of cinematic movement can be adequately apprehended, and that the 'transnational' can be realized as a useful critical tool."[24] If nothing else, *Orienting Hollywood* asks that we understand this multifaceted drama of industry encounter on a transnational stage.

As we have seen throughout this book, as artifacts, industries, and concepts, Hollywood and Bombay cinema are on the move. The intensities of invention and encounter animated by this transit have challenged the uniformity of both industries. Throughout its many case studies, *Orienting Hollywood* has followed the networks of film practice in the American and Indian mediascape, tracing the biographies and movements of commodities assembled under the sign of "Hollywood" and "Bombay cinema."

NOTES

INTRODUCTION

1 Quoted in Nyay Bhushan, "Bollywood Star Shah Rukh Khan: 'It's Good to See Hollywood Producing Indian Films,'" *Hollywood Reporter*, July 26, 2013.

2 I use "Bombay cinema" as a catchall term to refer to the mainstream commercial Hindi film industry centered in Mumbai because Bombay is the historical name of a city and it is still in common usage. The name of the city was officially changed, as part of a project of chauvinist nativism (and not without significant and ongoing controversy), from Bombay to Mumbai in 1995. This was part of a wider trend of renaming Indian cities over the past two decades: hence, Trivandrum to Thiruvananthapuram (in 1991), Calcutta to Kolkata (in 2001), and Bangalore to Bengaluru. Following popular convention, when speaking of the city itself I refer to "Bombay" in pre-1995 history and "Mumbai" after that.

3 For a fascinating account of Hollywood's role in Lux soap advertising in India and the economy of whiteness engaged by the Indian beauty industry, see Sabeena Gadihoke, "Selling Soap and Stardom: The Story of Lux," *Tasveer Ghar: A Digital Archive of South Asian Popular Visual Culture*, available at http://tasveerghar.net/cmsdesk/essay/104/.

4 Sumita Chakravarty, *National Identity in Indian Popular Cinema, 1947–1987* (Austin: University of Texas Press, 1993), 15; and Ravi Vasudevan, "National Pasts and Futures: Indian Cinema," *Screen* 41, no. 2 (2000): 123.

5 For a sense of these policy challenges from the 1960s to the early 1980s, see Manjunath Pendakur, "Dynamics of Cultural Policy Making: The U.S. Film Industry in India," *Journal of Communication* 35, no. 4 (1985): 52–72.

6 Jeremy Latchman quoted in Rohan Swamy, "Hollywood Films Starring India," *Indian Express*, June 3, 2012.

7 As Rajesh Sawhney, the president of RBE (the Indian media conglomerate that acquired a stake in DreamWorks), put it, "If you have global ambitions, then Hollywood is the right starting point." Quoted in Nandani Lakshman and Ronald Grover, "Why India's Reliance Is Going Hollywood," *Businessweek*, June 18, 2008.

8 Eric Johnston, "The Motion Picture as a Stimulus to Culture," *Filmfare*, March 14, 1958, 51.

9 "Movies Abroad: The New Maharajahs," *Time*, January 5, 1959.

10 Ibid.

11 Ulf Hannerz, *Cultural Complexity: Studies in the Social Organization of Meaning* (New York: Columbia University Press, 1992).

12 Rachana Dubey, "Mission Impossible 4 to Be Shot in India," *Hindustan Times*, November 15, 2010.

13 Rubina A. Khan, "Tom Kaun? Junior Artists Paid Rs. 150 to Play Screaming Fans of Tom Cruise at Airport!" *Firstpost*, December 4, 2011, available at http://www.firstpost.com/bollywood/junior-artists-paid-3-to-play-screaming-fans-of-tom-cruise-at-mumbai-airport-147578.html.

14 Mehul Thakkar, "200 Screaming Fans to Welcome Tom, at Only Rs.300 per Head," *Mumbai Mirror*, December 4, 2011.

15 Erving Goffman, *The Presentation of Self in Everyday Life* (New York: Anchor, 1959). In his work on the globalization of Chinese media, Michael Curtin notes that business relationships between film buyers and sellers "cannot be reduced to simple mathematics. Instead, it's a complex negotiation of finances and face, requiring each party to feel the relationship is mutually beneficial over the long term." See *Playing to the World's Biggest Audience: The Globalization of Chinese Film and TV* (Berkeley: University of California Press, 2007), 89.

16 Erving Goffman, *Interaction Ritual: Essays in Face-to-Face Behavior* (Garden City, NY: Doubleday, 1967), 28.

17 Erving Goffman, *Behavior in Public Places: Notes on the Social Organization of Gatherings* (New York: Free Press, 1963), 168.

18 BRICS is "not a policy bloc at all," notes Yasheng Huang, a professor or global economics and management at the Massachusetts Institute of Technology. "It's really a photo op. It is really this idea that the West is no longer or should no longer be viewed as the only center of gravity." See Jim Yardley, "For Group of 5 Nations, Acronym Is Easy, but Common Ground Is Hard," *New York Times*, March 28, 2012.

19 See Andre Gunder Frank, *ReOrient: Global Economy in the Asian Age* (Berkeley: University of California Press, 1998).

20 See, for example, Parag Khanna, *The Second World: How Emerging Powers Are Redefining Global Competition in the Twenty-First Century* (New York: Random House, 2009); and Fareed Zakaria, *The Post-American World* (New York: Norton, 2008).

21 See James Curran and Myung-Jin Park, eds., *De-Westernizing Media Studies* (New York: Routledge, 2000); and Michael Curtin and Hemant Shah, eds., *Reorienting Global Communication: India and Chinese Media beyond Borders* (Urbana: University of Illinois Press, 2010).

22 Panna Shah, *The Indian Film* (1950; repr., Westport, CT: Greenwood Press, 1981), 23. Shah's book is based on her 1949 doctoral thesis under the supervision of Govind S. Ghurye, the well-known Indian social scientist at Bombay University. For an appraisal of Ghurye's role in the development of Indian sociology, see Carol Upadhya, "The Idea of Indian Society: G. S. Ghurye and the Making of Indian Sociology," in *Anthropology in the East: Founders of Indian Sociology and Anthropology*, ed. Patricia Uberoi, Nandani Sundar, and Satish Deshpande (Calcutta: Seagull Books, 2007), 194–255.

23 For a history of the movement and its internal contradictions, see Manu Goswami, "Territorial Nativism: *Swadeshi* and *Swaraj*," in *Producing India: From Colonial Economy to National Space* (Chicago: University of Chicago Press, 2004), 242–76.

24 Quoted in Ashish Rajadhyaksha, "The Epic Melodrama: Themes of Nationality in Indian Cinema," *Journal of Arts and Ideas* 25–26 (1993): 66.

25 Quoted in Nyay Bhushan, "MPAA Chairman Chris Dodd Pushes for Indian Film Industry to Fight against Piracy," *Hollywood Reporter*, March 14, 2012.

26 Arab Amusement's advertisement, *Moving Picture World*, June 1, 1913.

27 Marc Edmund Jones, "The Kalem Studios in California," *Moving Picture World*, February 7, 1914.

28 Edward Said, *Orientalism* (New York: Pantheon, 1978), 54.

29 Mary Louise Pratt, *Imperial Eyes: Travel Writing and Transculturation* (New York: Routledge, 2008), 7.

30 Homay King, *Lost in Translation: Orientalism, Cinema, and the Enigmatic Signifier* (Durham: Duke University Press, 2010).

31 Jeanette Roan, *Envisioning Asia: On Location, Travel, and the Cinematic Geography of U.S. Orientalism* (Ann Arbor: University of Michigan Press, 2010).

32 Sara Ahmed, *Queer Phenomenology: Orientations, Objects, Others* (Durham: Duke University Press, 2006).

33 "The Far East on the American Screen," *Memorandum (Institute of Pacific Relations, American Council)* 2, no. 6 (1933): 1.

34 Kaushik Bhaumik, "Lost in Translation: A Few Vagaries of the Alphabet Game Played between Bombay Cinema and Hollywood," in *World Cinema's "Dialogues" with Hollywood*, ed. Paul Cooke (Houndmills: Palgrave Macmillan, 2007), 202.

35 Heather Tyrell, "Bollywood versus Hollywood: Battle of the Dream Factories," in *Cultural and Global Change*, ed. Tracey Skelton and Tim Allen (New York: Routledge, 1999), 263.

36 Lalitha Gopalan, "'Hum Aapke Hain Koun?': Cinephilia and Indian Films," in *Asian Cinemas: A Reader and Guide*, ed. Dimitris Eleftheriotis and Gary Needham (Honolulu: University of Hawai'i Press, 2006), 320.

37 Raminder Kaur and Ajay Sinha, eds., *Bollyworld: Popular Indian Cinema through a Transnational Lens* (Thousand Oaks, CA: Sage, 2005), 15.

38 Carla Power and Sudip Mazumdar, "Bollywood Goes Global," *Newsweek*, February 28, 2000.

39 Such inversions can recast historical configurations in strange ways beyond film and media. For example, in 2010, Bombay-born Sanjiv Mehta was granted permission by the British Treasury to use the East India Company name and trademark to leverage upmarket products in his luxury Mayfair shop. Newspapers around the world were taken by Mehta's commitment to serve as "curator and custodian" of a brand "created by history," seeing a story of postcolonial redemption. See David Wilkes, "The East India Company to Resume Trading—but This Time under Indian Control," *Daily Mail*, August 2, 2010.

40 For a comprehensive history of these media corporatization initiatives, see Aswin Punathambekar, *From Bombay to Bollywood: The Making of a Global Media Industry* (New York: NYU Press, 2013).

41 "Remarks by the President to the Joint Session of the Indian Parliament in New Delhi, India," November 8, 2010, available at http://www.whitehouse.gov/ the-press-office/2010/11/08/. remarks-president-joint-session-indian-parliament-new-delhi-india.

42 See Vikas Bajaj, "Foreign Investment Ebbs in India," *New York Times*, February 25, 2011; Jack Ewing and Vikas Bajaj, "Enercon Loses a Business in India, a Red Flag for Foreign Investors," *New York Times*, March 24, 2011.

43 Das quoted in Anita Raghavan, *The Billionaire's Apprentice: The Rise of the Indian–American Elite and the Fall of the Galleon Hedge Fund* (New York: Business Plus, 2013), 415. For a boosterish account of India's economic rise, see Gurcharan Das, *India Unbound: From Independence to the Global Information Age* (Delhi: Penguin, 2000).

44 Gerben Bakker, *Entertainment Industrialized: The Emergence of the International Film Industry, 1890–1940* (Cambridge: Cambridge University Press, 2008), 4.

45 Manuel Castells, *Communication Power* (New York: Oxford University Press, 2009), 92.

46 Susan Stanford Friedman, "Why Not Compare?" *PMLA* 126, no. 3 (2011): 753–62.

47 Mieke Bal, *Traveling Concepts in the Humanities: A Rough Guide* (Toronto: University of Toronto Press, 2002), 24.

48 N. Katherine Hayles, *How We Think: Digital Media and Contemporary Technogenesis* (Chicago: University of Chicago Press, 2012).

49 Daniel C. Hallin and Paolo Mancini, *Comparative Media Systems: Three Models of Media and Politics* (New York: Cambridge University Press, 2004).

50 Max Weber, *Economy and Society: An Outline of Interpretive Sociology*, ed. and trans. Guenther Roth and Claus Wittich (Berkeley: University of California Press, 1978), 19.

51 Sonia Livingstone, "On the Challenges of Cross-National Comparative Media Research," *European Journal of Communication* 18, no. 4 (2003): 477–500.

52 For an assessment of this history and the possibilities of recuperation in the work of comparative scholars like Benedict Anderson, see H. D. Harootunian, "Ghostly Comparisons: Anderson's Telescope," *Diacritics* 29, no. 4 (1999): 135–49.

53 For a critique of the "modular" form of the national, see Partha Chatterjee, *Nationalist Thought and the Colonial World: A Derivative Discourse* (Tokyo: Zed Books, 1986). For a sense of how these modular forms have been "refortified" under contemporary neoliberal regimes, see Manu Goswami, "Rethinking the Modular Form: Toward a Sociohistorical Conception of Nationalism," *Comparative Studies in Society and History* 44, no. 4 (2002): 770–99.

54 For an in-depth consideration of "the national" as it is deployed across the media industries, see Nitin Govil, "Thinking Nationally: Domicile, Distinction, and

Dysfunction in Global Media Exchange," in *Media Industries: History, Theory, and Method*, ed. Jennifer Holt and Alisa Perren (Malden, MA: Blackwell, 2009), 132–43.

55 See Tom O'Regan, *Australian National Cinema* (New York: Routledge, 1996).

56 See Woongjae Ryoo, "The Political Economy of the Global Mediascape: The Case of the South Korean Film Industry," *Media, Culture and Society* 30, no. 6 (2008): 873–89.

57 William Mazzarella, "Locations: Advertising and the New *Swadeshi*," in *Shoveling Smoke: Advertising and Globalization in Contemporary India* (Durham: Duke University Press, 2003), 3–14.

58 Eric Cazdyn, *The Flash of Capital: Film and Geopolitics in Japan* (Durham: Duke University Press, 2002), 1.

59 Kuan-Hsing Chen, *Asia as Method: Toward Deimperialization* (Durham: Duke University Press, 2010), 223.

60 Rey Chow, *Entanglements; or, Transmedial Thinking of Capture* (Durham: Duke University Press, 2012), 11.

61 For an engagement of "disjunct, yet adjacent histories and temporalites" that elude dominant critical traditions, see Arjun Appadurai, "Spectral Housing and Urban Cleansing: Notes on Millennial Mumbai," *Public Culture* 12, no. 3 (2000): 627–51.

62 Letter from U. S. Gupta to K. R. S., January 20, 1960, Warner Brothers Archives, University of Southern California.

63 MPEA Memo 530, "India—Import Duty," August 6, 1963, Warner Brothers Archives, University of Southern California.

64 Paul Willemen, "For a Comparative Film Studies," *Inter-Asia Cultural Studies* 6, no. 1 (2005): 103.

65 For more on the concepts of "occasion" and "occasionality," rooted in arts and aesthetics, see Hans-Georg Gadamer, *Truth and Method*, trans. Joel Weinsheimer and Donald G. Marshall (London: Bloomsbury, 1989). For an extension of "occasion" into novelistic genres and the literary marketplace—what he calls "the practical circumstances governing the composition and reception of a piece of speech or writing"—see Ian Hunter, "Providence and Profit: Speculations in the Genre Market," *Southern Review* 22, no. 3 (1989): 211–23. Similarly, in his discussion of media texts and spectators, Toby Miller suggests that occasionality "details the conditions under which a text is made, circulated, received, interpreted, and criticized . . . a life remade again and again by institutions, discourses, and practices of distribution and reception." See Toby Miller and Robert Stam, *A Companion to Film Theory* (Malden, MA: Blackwell, 1999), 4.

66 Rita Felski and Susan Friedman, "Introduction," *New Literary History* 40, no. 3 (2009): v–ix (italics added).

67 I borrow this "orbital" framework from Valerie Hartouni. See her introduction to *Visualizing Atrocity: Arendt, Evil, and the Optics of Thoughtlessness* (New York: NYU Press, 2012).

68 Kent A. Ono, "Retracing an Intellectual Course in Asian American Studies," in *A Companion to Asian American Studies*, ed. Kent A. Ono (Malden, MA: Blackwell, 2005), 12.

69 Akiko Takeyama, "The Art of Seduction and Affect Economy: Neoliberal Class Struggle and Gender Politics in a Tokyo Host Club" (Ph.D. diss., University of Illinois–Champaign, 2008).

70 See Ann Laura Stoler, ed., *Haunted by Empire: Geographies of Intimacy in North American History* (Durham: Duke University Press, 2006).

71 See Sara Ahmed, "Affective Economies," *Social Text* 22, no. 2 (2004): 117–39.

CHAPTER 1. FRAMING THE COPY

1 Lawrence Liang, "Porous Legalities and Avenues of Participation," in *Sarai Reader 2005: Bare Acts*, ed. Monica Narula et al. (New Delhi: Sarai, 2005), 6–17.

2 See, for example, the conclusion to Toby Miller, Nitin Govil, John McMurria, Richard Maxwell, and Ting Wang, *Global Hollywood 2* (London: British Film Institute, 2005); Eduardo Moisés Peñalver and Sonia K. Katyal, *Property Outlaws: How Squatters, Pirates and Protesters Improve the Law of Ownership* (New Haven: Yale University Press, 2010); and Marcus Boon, *In Praise of Copying* (Cambridge: Harvard University Press, 2010).

3 See Daniel Miller, ed., *Materiality* (Durham: Duke University Press, 2005), 1–50.

4 See Yingjin Zhang, "Playing with Intertextuality and Contextuality: Film Piracy on and off the Chinese Screen," in *Cinema, Law, and the State in Asia*, ed. Corey K. Creekmur and Mark Sidel (New York: Palgrave Macmillan, 2007), 213–30. See also Shujen Wang, *Framing Piracy: Globalization and Film Distribution in Greater China* (Lanham, MD: Rowman and Littlefield, 2003).

5 Henry R. Luce, "The American Century," *Life*, February 1941.

6 See Giovanni Arrighi, Po-Keung Hui, Ho-fung Hung, and Mark Selden, "Historical Capitalism, East and West," in *The Resurgence of East Asia: 500, 150 and 50 Year Perspectives*, ed. Giovanni Arrighi, Takeshi Hamashita, and Mark Selden (New York: Routledge, 2003), 259–333.

7 Ashis Nandy, *The Romance of the State and the Fate of Dissent in the Tropics* (New Delhi: Oxford University Press, 2003); see also Ziauddin Sardar, *Islam, Postmodernism and Other Futures: A Ziauddin Sardar Reader* (London: Pluto Press, 2003).

8 Quoted in Pradip Chakravarty, "The Political Economy of Mass Media Development in India, 1947–1984" (Ph.D. diss., University of Illinois at Urbana–Champaign, 1994), 107. In a book published the previous year, Lerner had suggested that efficient global communication needed East–West cooperation, although the recognition of Western superiority could spur development. In his famous discussion of international cooperation based on Western largesse, Lerner reveals the central conceit of developmental discourse: "This is precisely the function of the Western model—to convey to the developing Eastern nations a heuristic model (or 'picture') of what they may become." Daniel Lerner,

"International Cooperation and Communication in National Development," in *Communication and Change in the Developing Countries,* ed. Daniel Lerner and Wilbur Schramm (Honolulu: East–West Press, 1967), 120–21. Lerner's formulation is not wholly instrumentalist, however. Transmitting an idealized snapshot of Western modernity is crucial to the communication process and dependent on empathy, which Lerner defines as the "capacity to see oneself in the other fellow's situation." The possibilities for transcending xenophobia turn on a "psychic mechanism that equips individuals to operate efficiently in a rapidly changing society which requires both mobility and participation" (117). However, critics vilified this form of developmental communication for what Herb Schiller called a "mechanics of cultural leveling." Schiller's excoriation of developmentalism in *Mass Communications and American Empire,* using the powerful language of cultural imperialism, would lay bare the annexation of the "have-not states" by the agents of commercialism and homogenization. Herbert I. Schiller, "The Developing World under Electronic Siege," in *Mass Communications and American Empire* (New York: Augustus M. Kelley, 1969), 109–25.

9 For a critique of these and other initiatives in the use of satellite communication for postcolonial Indian development, see Shanti Kumar, *Gandhi Meets Primetime: Globalization and Nationalism in Indian Television* (Urbana: University of Illinois Press, 2006), 93–118.

10 E. P. Menon, "The Future of the Indian Film Industry," in *The Pictureworld Souvenir of the Indian Motion Picture Congress and Exhibition: Silver Jubilee Year of the Indian Film Industry, 1913–1938* (Bombay: Indian Motion Picture Congress and Exhibition, 1938), 43. Hollywood has served as an industrial model that the Indian media industries have endeavored to emulate. As B. D. Garga insists, "The imitation of Hollywood permeated most aspects of Indian film production, the star myth included." *So Many Cinemas: The Motion Picture in India* (Bombay: Eminence, 1996), 55. Extending this idea, Neepa Majumdar's work on female stardom in early Indian sound cinema shows that the emulation of Hollywood was integral to the consolidation of the Indian star system. Indian stars were often nicknamed with Hollywood epithets according to physical resemblance, notoriety, and the extent of their public circulation. The "translocation" of Hollywood stardom to India created a standard for enhancing publicity and improving acting practice predicated on the ideal of Hollywood efficiency. See Neepa Majumdar, *Wanted Cultured Ladies Only! Female Stardom and Cinema in India, 1930s–1950s* (Urbana: University of Illinois Press, 2009).

11 Ravi Vasudevan, "National Pasts and Futures: Indian Cinema," *Screen* 41, no. 1 (2000): 123; Sumita Chakravarty, *National Identity in Indian Popular Cinema, 1947–1987* (Austin: University of Texas Press, 1993), 15.

12 Kripa Singh, *India: A Market for American Products: A Bird's Eye View* (Detroit, 1934), 18.

13 William D. Allen, "World's Second Biggest Filmmaker: A Report from India on Her Film Industry," *Films in Review* 1 (February 1950): 7.

14 For more on this "unfinished" concept of Bombay cinema in relation to Western industry in particular, see Madhava Prasad, *The Ideology of the Hindi Film: A Historical Construction* (New York: Oxford University Press, 1998); and Nitin Govil, "Bollywood and the Frictions of Global Mobility," in *Media on the Move: Global Flow and Contra-Flow*, ed. Daya Thussu (London: Routledge, 2007), 84–98. The origins of the Indian film industry reflect the overdetermined nature of influence in commodity circulation. The origins of Indian cinema are often narrated through biographical legends that celebrate the heroic exploits of entrepreneurial men, suggesting that film practice was borrowed rather than invented. These stories begin with Maurice Sestier, who represented the French Lumière brothers, who demonstrated their Cinématographe at Bombay's Watson's Hotel in July 1896. Over the next few years, Indian scenic footage was shot by European cameramen for exhibition in the country and around the world. By the late 1890s, however, Indian filmmakers like H. S. Bhatvadekar, F. B. Thanawala, and Harilal Sen were filming Indian scenes for local audiences, using camera equipment bought from foreign sales agents, as Indian exhibitors continued to import European pictures. Cinema may have arrived in India from the outside, but it engaged with cultural traditions already transformed by modern encounter. Cinema as a public culture integrated popular arts and practices—from literature, dance, music, theater, photography, magic, and the visual arts—with myth, religion, spectacle, nationalism, the colonial condition, and the synesthesia of everyday urban life. At the same time, cinema was part of a shifting network of tinkerers and practitioners, amateur photographic clubs and studios, and legal and non-legal trade circuits of equipment and technology that cast the net of Indian film practice through a wider transnational space. See Sudhir Mahadevan's account of these networks and trade practices of early Indian film culture in "Traveling Showmen, Makeshift Cinemas: The Bioscopewallah and Early Cinema History in India," *Bioscope* 1, no. 1 (2010): 27–47.

15 Stephen McDowell, *Globalization, Liberalization and Policy Change* (London: Macmillan, 1997).

16 Madhava Prasad, "The State in/of Cinema," in *Wages of Freedom: Fifty Years of the Indian Nation-State*, ed. Partha Chatterjee (Oxford: New Delhi, 1998), 126.

17 Manjunath Pendakur, *Indian Popular Cinema: Industry, Ideology, and Consciousness* (Cresskill, NJ: Hampton Press, 2003), 59.

18 As Ashish Rajadhyaksha notes, Hindi cinema's "ability to do battle with Hollywood, important as it may be . . . pales into insignificance compared with its ability to use Hollywood in order to battle its delegitimation at the hands of the Indian state." *Indian Cinema in the Time of Celluloid: From Bollywood to the Emergency* (Bloomington: Indiana University Press, 2009), 16.

19 K. S. Hirlekar, *The Place of Film in National Planning* (Bombay: Visual Education Society, 1939), 1, 9.

20 *Report of the Indian Film Industry's Mission to Europe and America* (Bombay: Avanti Prakashan, 1946), 59. While Hollywood's close alignment with the

American state was recognized as critical to its success, some were less positive than Hirlekar about using Hollywood as a standard for industrial imitation. Indian cinema's industrial problem, critic Chidananda Das Gupta suggests, actually lay in its *imperfect* imitation of Hollywood. While "Hollywood is our guru," he argues, "in imitating Hollywood, the mass film in India has landed itself in a star system without studio control, formula film-making without Hollywood's variety of formulas, [and] an annual investment of some 85 million dollars without Hollywood's audience research or other organizational safeguards." Chidananda Das Gupta, "Indian Cinema Today," *Film Quarterly* 22, no. 4 (1969): 31.

21 Julio García Espinosa, "For an Imperfect Cinema," trans. Julianne Burton, *Jump Cut* 20 (1979): 24–26.

22 K. A. Abbas, "Creativity Comes First," in *Symposium on Cinema in Developing Countries* (New Delhi: Ministry of Information and Broadcasting Publications Division, 1979), 49.

23 Ibid., 50.

24 See, for example, Sean MacBride, ed., *Many Voices, One World: Towards a New More Just and More Efficient World Information and Communication Order* (Paris: UNESCO, 1980).

25 Adrian Johns, *Piracy: The Intellectual Property Wars from Gutenberg to Gates* (Chicago: University of Chicago Press, 2009).

26 Phil Hazlewood, "Indian Film Industry Wants More Awareness over Piracy," *Agence-France-Press*, August 22, 2010.

27 Ashish Rajadhyaksha, "International Seminar on the Production and Distribution of Films in Developing Countries," UNESCO Report CC-88/WS/2920, December 1988.

28 B. K. Karanjia, "The Low Priority of Piracy," *Screen*, May 18, 1984. Reprinted in B. K. Karanjia, *A Many-Splendoured Cinema* (Bombay: New Thacker's Fine Art Press, 1986), 181–83.

29 Aziz Haniffa, "Hollywood Accuses India of Piracy," *India Abroad*, April 7, 1989.

30 "Estimates Place Piracy Losses at $300 Million to India's Film Industry," *Variety*, September 19, 1984.

31 The interests of the MPAA and the United States do not run in lockstep and punishment does not always suit the geopolitical economy at the time. For example, in 2005, the MPAA lobbied the Office of the U.S. Trade Representative (USTR) to review China's copyright enforcement policies, but the American studios were dismayed that the USTR declined to impose trade sanctions against China.

32 India had folded copyright into national legal policy, from its first copyright act in 1914, modeled on Britain's 1911 act, to the 1957 Copyright Act and the various amendments introduced to conform to the obligations of belonging to multilateral legal agreements like the Berne Convention and the Universal Copyright Convention. The Copyright Act of 1984 implemented specific language against

video piracy. For a history of copyright law in India, see Priti H. Joshi, "Copyright Problems in India Affecting Hollywood and "Bollywood,"" *Suffolk Transnational Law Review* 26, no. 2 (2003): 295–322.

33 See Ravi Sundaram, "Uncanny Networks: Pirate, Urban and New Globalisation," *Economic and Political Weekly* 39, no. 1 (2004): 64–71. For an account of antipiracy initiatives at the local, regional, and national levels, see Nupur Jain, "Anti-piracy Enforcement Efforts Made by the Bombay Film Industry: A Report and Assessment of Present Ideas and Practices," Sarai Research Report, February 25, 2009. Piracy prosecutions are rare but receive massive media coverage, as in the July 2006 jailing of Samath Abdul Amir Khan and Mukesh Satish for six-month sentences. Both men were also fined over $1,000 each for selling pirated Indian and American films on the street.

34 James Ulmer, "In Transit: India Tries to Defend against Video Pirates," *Hollywood Reporter*, November 13, 1992.

35 Roshmila Bhattacharya, "Three-Pronged Attack on Piracy: FMC–FFI to Join Hands with U.S. Agency," *Screen*, August 2, 1996.

36 Uma da Cunha, "MPA Reps Lobby Locals to Stem Piracy in India," *Variety*, July 29, 1996.

37 For an affective tracing of these degradations in the fidelity of the copy, see Lucas Hilderbrand, *Inherent Vice: Bootleg Histories of Videotape and Copyright* (Durham: Duke University Press, 2010).

38 See Pradip Ninan Thomas, "Uncommon Futures: Interpreting IP Contestations in India," in *Intellectual Property Rights and Communications in Asia*, ed. Pradip Ninan Thomas and Jan Servaes (New Delhi: Sage, 2006), 174–90.

39 See Prashant Iyengar, "Fake Facts: An Incredulous Look at Piracy Statistics in India," *Alternative Law Forum*, February 19, 2009; see also Nitin Govil, "Size Matters," *BioScope: South Asian Screen Studies* 1, no. 2 (2010): 105–9.

40 See Majid Yar, "The Global 'Epidemic' of Movie 'Piracy': Crime-Wave or Social Construction?" *Media, Culture and Society* 27, no. 5 (2005): 677–96.

41 Kris Olds and Nigel Thrift, "Cultures on the Brink: Reengineering the Soul of Capitalism—on a Global Scale," in *Global Assemblages: Technology, Politics, and Ethics as Anthropological Problems*, ed. Aihwa Ong and Steven Collier (Malden, MA: Blackwell, 2005), 270–90. When representatives of the American and Indian film industries agreed on joint plans to eradicate film piracy in April 2008, it was seen as definitive proof that the relationship between Hollywood and Bollywood had reached a new stage. The agreement, between the U.S.—India Business Council (USIBC) and the Federation of Indian Chambers of Commerce and Industry (FICCI), was announced on the heels of Ernst and Young's report, "The Effects of Counterfeiting and Piracy on India's Entertainment Industry," which claimed that the Indian entertainment industries lost US$4 billion and 820,000 jobs to media piracy every year. Again, in March 2010, the MPAA joined with seven Indian companies to combine the goals of

protecting U.S. intellectual property overseas and nurturing the growth of Indian media industries.

42 Reports like the USTR 301 are a "name and shame" strategy to get national governments and markets to crack down on intellectual property infringement. It is not a surprise then that officials from Canada, Israel, Spain, and South Korea and representatives from the dozens of other named countries criticize the report for overstating piracy losses and for the somewhat arbitrary nature of its analysis. Michael Geist, "Could the Piracy Blacklist Backfire?" *BBC News*, May 5, 2009.

43 "2010 Special 301 Report," Office of the U.S. Trade Representative, April 30, 2010, 9.

44 See John Frow, *Time and Commodity Culture: Essays in Cultural Theory and Postmodernity* (Oxford: Clarendon Press, 1997).

45 See, for example, Edwin L. C. Lai, "International Intellectual Property Protection and the Rate of Product Innovation," *Journal of Development Economics* 55 (1998): 133–53; and Belay Seyoum, "The Impact of Intellectual Property Rights on Foreign Direct Investment," *Columbia Journal of World Business* 31, no. 1 (1996): 50–59.

46 Peter Avery, *The Economic Impact of Counterfeiting and Piracy* (Paris: Organisation for Economic Co-operation and Development, 2008), 138.

47 Susan Ronald, *The Pirate Queen: Queen Elizabeth I, Her Pirate Adventurers, and the Dawn of Empire* (New York: HarperCollins, 2007).

48 Doron Ben-Atar, *Trade Secrets: Intellectual Piracy and the Origins of American Industrial Power* (New Haven: Yale University Press, 2004).

49 Jane Gaines, "Early Cinema's Heyday of Copying," *Cultural Studies* 20, nos. 2–3 (2006): 227–44.

50 See A. Coskun Samli, *In Search of an Equitable, Sustainable Globalization: A Bittersweet Dilemma* (Westport, CT: Quorum Books, 2002); and Peter Drahos, "Doing Deals with Al Capone: Paying Protection Money for Intellectual Property in the Global Knowledge Economy," in *Intellectual Property and Information Wealth: Issues and Practices in the Digital Age*, ed. Peter K. Yu (Westport, CT: Praeger, 2007), 141–58.

51 Ackbar Abbas, "Faking Globalization," in *Other Cities, Other Worlds: Urban Imaginaries in a Globalizing Age*, ed. Andreas Huyssen (Durham: Duke University Press, 2008), 260.

52 Otto Kurz, *Fakes* (New York: Dover, 1967). While the temporality of piracy resonates with immediacy and the shortcut, the duration of copyright vacillates between the nanosecond of storage and the perpetuity of authorship. Even the law, as Sarah Harding notes, is indebted to a linear concept of the past in the doctrine of precedent, but also points toward a future informed by a constantly reforming legal system. Sandra Harding, "Perpetual Property," *Florida Law Review* 61 (2009): 285–329. See also Carol J. Greenhouse, "Just in Time: Temporality and the Cultural Legitimation of Law," *Yale Law Journal* 98 (1989): 1631–51; and Frow, *Time and Commodity Culture.*

53 Quoted in Randeep Ramesh, "Bollywood Falls for the Power of Merchandising," *The Guardian*, October 1, 2008. In addition, the novelist Barbara Taylor, who filed a copyright petition against the producers of an Indian television soap opera, complained that Hindi cinema takes part in "stealing, pirating properties every hour on the hour." Quoted in K. M. Gopakumar and V. K. Unni, "Perspectives on Copyright: The 'Karishma' Controversy," *Economic and Political Weekly*, July 12, 2003, 2935.

54 Quoted in Penny Pagano, "Valenti: Film Industry's Master Lobbyist," *Los Angeles Times*, September 3, 1985.

55 Michael T. Malloy, "India: Hollywood of World," *Los Angeles Times*, September 5, 1974, 114.

56 See Nitin Govil, "War in the Age of Pirate Reproduction," in *Sarai Reader 2004: Crisis/Media*, ed. Ravi Vasudevan et al. (New Delhi: Sarai, 2004), 378–83. For example, in 2009, the RAND Corporation released a report that linked Indian crime boss Dawood Ibrahim's D-Company syndicate to film piracy. D-Company had "leveraged rackets in the film industry to vertically expand into piracy," using its Dubai headquarters to coordinate pirate distribution networks from the Gulf to Pakistan. See Gregory T. Treverton et al., *Film Piracy, Organized Crime, and Terrorism* (Santa Monica, CA: RAND Safety and Justice Program and the Global Risk and Security Center, 2009). While the equation of piracy and terrorism rationalizes the need for greater state security, piracy also informs possible reconciliation. In 2003, with burgeoning peace initiatives underway between India and Pakistan, it was thought that a rapprochement between the two nations could help curb Indian film piracy in Pakistan, then estimated to cost the India US$35 million a year. Banned for decades in Pakistan after 1954, Indian films' popularity was driven by piracy, and the Bombay industry was looking forward to making it legitimate. As one producer/distributor put it, "Pakistanis are like Indians when it comes to movies. Let peace be established and give us one year. We will become another Hollywood." Vashu Bhagnani quoted in Bryan Pearson, "Piracy Hurts B'wood Profits," *Variety*, May 12, 2003. With their business hurt by piracy and Indian television satellite bleeding in from border cities, Pakistani theater owners also wanted the forty-year ban on Indian films lifted.

57 Ziauddin Sardar, *The Consumption of Kuala Lumpur* (London: Reaktion Books, 2000).

58 Lawrence Liang, "Cinema, Citizenship, and the Illegal City," *Inter-Asia Cultural Studies* 6, no. 3 (2005): 18.

59 Ravi Sundaram, *Pirate Modernity: Delhi's Media Urbanism* (New York: Routledge, 2010).

60 Brian Larkin, *Signal and Noise: Media, Infrastructure, and Urban Culture in Nigeria* (Durham: Duke University Press, 2008).

61 Sardar, *Consumption of Kuala Lumpur*, 89.

62 "United States Films in India," *New York Times*, April 9, 1922.

63 See, for example, "Bombay to Enter Film Production," *Los Angeles Times*, November 8, 1925.

64 For an account of these distinctions, as well as practices that crossed over, see Priya Jaikumar, "Hollywood and the Multiple Constituencies of Colonial India," in *Hollywood Abroad: Audiences and Cultural Exchange*, ed. Melvyn Stokes and Richard Maltby (London: British Film Institute, 2004), 78–98.

65 Valerie Wagg, "Dadar: India's Hollywood," *Chicago Daily Tribune*, July 21, 1946.

66 Rajinder Dudrah, *Bollywood: Sociology Goes to the Movies* (New Delhi: Sage, 2006), 34–35.

67 Stephen Teo, "Film and Globalization: From Hollywood to Bollywood," in *The Routledge International Handbook of Globalization Studies*, ed. Bryan S. Turner (New York: Routledge, 2010), 418.

68 Charles Ramírez Berg, *Cinema of Solitude: A Critical Study of Mexican Film, 1967–1983* (Austin: University of Texas Press, 1992), 15. For the now classic analysis of the dialectic of distinction and derivation in the modularity of "the national," see Partha Chatterjee, *Nationalist Thought and the Colonial World: A Derivative Discourse* (Minneapolis: University of Minnesota Press, 1993).

69 See Tom O'Regan, *Australian National Cinema* (London: Routledge, 1996).

70 William van der Heide, *Malaysian Cinema, Asian Film: Border Crossings* (Amsterdam: Amsterdam University Press, 2002). Furthermore, national cinema's position in avowed opposition to Hollywood underestimates the ways in which the American film industries have solicited the support of the U.S. government. While *The Economist* maintains that "the world's best films are produced by America's unsubsidized industry," the government has provided decades of export assistance, support for media conglomeration, and local subsidies for film production, while Hollywood contributions have flowed into the coffers of both Republican and Democratic election campaigns. In addition to disavowing Hollywood as a kind of national culture, national cinema's opposition between an authentic local culture and Hollywood hegemony begs, as Ravi Vasudevan says, "the question whether Hollywood is, indeed, as unified a phenomenon as the formulation requires it to be." "British Films and Tax Relief," *The Economist*, February 28, 2004; Ravi Vasudevan, "The Meanings of 'Bollywood,'" *Journal of the Moving Image* 7 (December 2008), available at http://www.jmionline.org/articles/2008/the_meanings_of_bollywood.pdf.

71 Quoted in "Fans in India Like Double Movie Bills," *Hollywood Citizen News*, September 3, 1940.

72 Quoted in "H'w'd, India Exchange Pix Views," *Variety*, October 7, 1952.

73 Alex Perry, "India Incorporated: Bombay's Boom," *Time*, June 26, 2006.

74 Quoted in Rama Lakshmi, "Bollywood, Hollywood Tightening Film Ties," *Washington Post*, March 7, 2009.

75 Edwin Lord Weeks, "Street Life in India," *Harper's New Monthly Magazine*, August 1890.

76 Gyan Prakash, "Mumbai: The Modern City in Ruins," in *Other Cities, Other Worlds: Urban Imaginaries in a Globalizing Age*, ed. Andreas Huyssen (Durham: Duke University Press, 2008), 195–96. See also Gyan Prakash, *Mumbai Fables* (Princeton: Princeton University Press, 2010).

77 Sujata Patel, "Bombay and Mumbai: Identities, Politics, and Populism," in *Bombay and Mumbai: The City in Transition*, ed. Sujata Patel and Jim Masselos (New Delhi: Oxford University Press, 2003), 3–30. Furthermore, Bombay's regional identity was claimed by both Maharashtra and Gujarat after independence. A home for Muslim populations displaced by Partition, and a model and metaphor for Indian cosmopolitanism, Bombay has also been ripped apart by communal hatred and violence. The city's mutability was ossified in its official renaming as "Mumbai" in 1995, after a long nativist campaign by various conservative Hindu political parties. Mapping an urban imaginary across the skyscraper and the slum, Bombay functions as an allegory of urban planning and disintegration, spatial order and sprawl. For Hindi cinema, Bombay has mapped the collision between popular melodrama and, more recently, the grotesque, informing both the utopian vision of Indian cosmopolitanism and the dystopian nightmares of a modern urban life in crisis. See Ranjani Mazumdar, "Friction, Collision, and the Grotesque," in *Noir Urbanism: Dystopic Images of the Modern City*, ed. Gyan Prakash (Princeton: Princeton University Press, 2010), 150–85.

78 Given the silent and early sound era's flows of equipment, actors, practitioners, and industrialists, Shuddhabrata Sengupta suggests that the invocation of "Bombay or even Hindi cinema in the 1920s and 30s is premature." "Reflected Readings in Available Light: Cameramen in the Shadows of Hindi Cinema," in *Bollyworld: Popular Indian Cinema through a Transnational Lens*, ed. Raminder Kaur and Ajay J. Sinha (New Delhi: Sage, 2005), 122.

79 J. B. H. Wadia, "Those Were the Days," *Cinema Vision* 1, no. 1 (1980): 95; Ashish Rajadhyaksha, "The Curious Case of Bombay's Hindi Cinema: The Career of Indigenous 'Exhibition,'" *Journal of the Moving Image* 5 (December 2006), available at http://www.jmionline.org/articles/2006/the_curious_case_of_bombays_hindi_cinema_the_career_of_indigenous.pdf.

80 In an article about the supposed decline of traditional Indian dance troupes written under a Bombay byline, Tom Treanor wrote about the "diseased commercialism" of the "Hollywood of India." Tom Treanor, "The Home Front," *Los Angeles Times*, May 14, 1943. Bombay's quantitative substantiation as Hollywood's Indian equivalent was common enough by 1950 that an Indian "Who's Who" directory could claim that "early [cinema] development took place in Bombay, which can today be called the chiefly 'Hollywood of India.' About 80 to 90 per cent of the total annual production of Indian films comes from Bombay studios, the balance coming from Madras and to a small extent Calcutta." *The Times of India Directory and Year Book and Who's Who* (Bombay: Bennett, Coleman & Co. 1950), 186.

81 S. M. Akhtar, Gurcharan Singh, and Kewal Krishan Dewett, *Indian Economics* (Delhi: S. Chand, 1946), 319.

82 Furthermore, a 1931 *Times of India* advertisement for the Bangalore-based Surya
    Film Company's *Kingdom of Love* is captioned with "India's Hollywood makes
    another fine film." Priya Jaikumar, "Hollywood and the Multiple Constituencies of
    Colonial India," 82.

83 Jack Howard, "The Film in India," \ *Quarterly Review of Film, Radio, and
    Television* 6, no. 3 (1952): 220–21.

84 *The Reporter* 5 (1951) 32.

85 Harrison Rhodes, "The High Kingdom of the Movies," *Harper's Monthly
    Magazine*, April 1920, 640–53; Katherine Fullerton Gerould, "Hollywood: an
    American State of Mind," *Harpers Monthly Magazine*, May 1923, 689–95.

86 Rachel Field, *To See Ourselves* (New York: Macmillan, 1937), 134.

87 Carey McWilliams, *Southern California: An Island on the Land* (1946; repr., Salt
    Lake City: Peregrine Smith Books, 1973), 339.

88 Ibid., 334.

89 Quoted in David Bordwell, Janet Staiger, and Kristin Thompson, *The Classical
    Hollywood Cinema: Film Style and Mode of Production to 1960* (London:
    Routledge, 1985), xiii

90 Sallie A. Marston, Keith Woodward, and John Paul Jones, "Flattening Ontologies
    of Globalization: The Nollywood Case," *Globalizations* 4, no. 1 (2007): 45–63.
    UNESCO's Institute of Statistics released an "International Survey on Feature
    Film Statistics" in May 2009 which ranked India and Nigeria ahead of the United
    States in terms of numbers of feature-length video and film productions. The
    report's referencing of Indian and Nigerian film/video industries as Bollywood
    and Nollywood testifies to the existence of quantitatively significant cultural
    industries, media sectors qualified by the mark of local and/as national
    distinction.

91 Keating, who did not visited India until he was ten years into the twenty-two-
    volume *Inspector Ghote* series, finally reached the subcontinent for the first time
    just prior to writing *Filmi*. This lack of physical familiarity with the Indian urban
    landscape, Gary Hausladen suggests, is the reason why the *Ghote* series is weak
    "in narrative description of landscape, more heavily emphasizing cultural and
    institutional characteristics of place." Ironically, some critics claim that Keating's
    novels grew *more* superficial after the author's contact with the reality that his
    books fictionalize. As the first of these "post-India" Ghote novels, *Filmi* is more
    clearly informed by the author's Indian travels, but suffers from a newly found
    glibness. Like "Bollywood" itself, the novel is caught between the fiction of a real
    place and the suspension of a physical veracity that more fully signifies its reality.
    Gary J. Hausladen, *Places for Dead Bodies* (Austin: University of Texas Press,
    2000), 144; Meera Tamaya, *H. R. F. Keating, Post-colonial Detection: A Critical
    Study* (Bowling Green: Bowling Green State University Press, 1993).

92 H. R. F. Keating, *Filmi, Filmi, Inspector Ghote* (Chicago: Academy Publishers,
    1976), 45.

93 Madhava Prasad, "This Thing Called Bollywood," *Seminar* 525 (May 2003): 17–20.

94 Deming notes, "In passing it might be explained that our Calcutta studio was located in the suburb of Tollygunge . . . Tolly being a proper name, and Gunge meaning locality. After studying the advantages of HOLLYGUNGE we decided on TOLLYWOOD. There being two studios present in that locality, and several more projected, the name seems appropriate." Wilford E. Deming, "Talking Pictures in India," *American Cinematographer*, March 1932, 10.

95 Prasad, "This Thing Called Bollywood," 17.

96 Jyotika Virdi, *The Cinematic Imagination: Indian Popular Films as Social History* (New Delhi: Permanent Black, 2003), 21.

97 Priya Jaikumar, "Bollywood Spectaculars," *World Literature Today* 77 (October 2003).

98 Ashish Rajadhyaksha, "The 'Bollywoodization' of the Indian Cinema: Cultural Nationalism in a Global Era," *Inter-Asia Cultural Studies* 4, no. 4 (2003): 25–39.

99 See Anna Tsing, *Friction: An Ethnography of Global Connection* (Princeton: Princeton University Press, 2005).

100 The producers, "having decided to make a film about a robbery . . . simply stole their plot [and the] vault they raided belongs to Quentin Tarantino," claimed one critic, while another noted that *Kaante*, "for all its apparent conceptual audacity, borrows without transforming." "A Bollywood Heist That's Gone to the Dogs," *Sydney Morning Herald*, February 20, 2003, 17; Philippa Hawker, "Tarantino Homage Dogs Bollywood Gangster Musical," *The Age*, February 13, 2003, 4. For a time, there was a Facebook page that asked people to join if they thought that "Sanjay Gupta is a thief" at http://www.facebook.com/group.php?gid=7492062570.

101 By the time *Kaante* was released, director Sanjay Gupta was already well-known for his Hindi remakes of Hollywood films: *Aatish* (1995) revisits *State of Grace* (1990); *Khauff* (2000) retries *The Juror* (1996) with additional testimony provided by *Witness* (1985); and *Jung* (2000) recalibrates *Desperate Measures* (1998).

102 Sanjay Gupta quoted in Zainal Alam Kadir, "Six in the Bag, More on the Horizon for K3G," *New Straits Times*, March 29, 2002.

103 Sandeep Unnithan, "Action Films: Tech Tonic," *India Today*, September 25, 2001.

104 The film was released worldwide on December 20, 2002, with eight hundred prints (two hundred overseas). It opened to full houses in India, requiring extra showings, grossing close to Rs.100 million in the opening week, while collections dipped in the second. The film debuted in the United States with a $425,000 box-office take over its opening weekend release on twenty-six screens. It reached #7 in the U.K. box office, playing on thirty screens to a opening weekend gross of over UK£100,000 and its per-screen average was second only to *The Lord of the Rings: The Two Towers* premiere. After the film's box office success, more Hollywood-based Hindi films were planned, including co-productions with LA-based production houses.

105 Komal Nahta quoted in Aparita Bhandari, "Crunch Time in Bollywood," *Toronto Star*, January 24, 2003.

106 Ashish Saksena quoted in Bryan Pearson, "English-Lingo Pix Trump Bollywood," *Variety*, November 11–17, 2002.

107 Not only did the *Kaante*'s promotional campaign reference the film's "reimagining" of *Reservoir Dogs*, but the main police detective in the film is named MacQuarrie, in tribute to Christopher McQuarrie, the writer of *The Usual Suspects*, another clear antecedent for the Hindi film. *The Usual Suspects* was remade in Hindi a few years later as *Chocolate* (Vivek Agnihotri, 2005).

108 For a critique of these changing financial practices, see Tejaswini Ganti, *Producing Bollywood: Inside the Contemporary Hindi Film Industry* (Durham: Duke University Press, 2012).

109 Michelle R. Nelson and Narayan Devanathan, "Brand Placements Bollywood Style," *Journal of Consumer Behavior* 5 (May–June 2006): 211–21.

110 Sanjay Bhutiani quoted in Bill Britt, "Madison + Vine: Content, Commerce Deals Offer Answers in Overseas Markets; Role of Integration Booms in Europe, Asia, Latin America," *Advertising Age*, October 21, 2002.

111 Aswin Punathambekar, *From Bombay to Bollywood: The Making of a Global Media Industry* (New York: NYU Press, 2013), 83–92.

112 Arijit Biswas and Anindya Sen, "Coke vs. Pepsi: Local and Global Strategies," *Economic and Political Weekly* 34, no. 26 (1999): 1701–8.

113 Controversy has beset this market recapture. For example, in 2003 farmers alleged that Coke and Pepsi contained high pesticide levels and sprayed their crops with soda as an inexpensive insect retardant.

114 Ashis Nandy, "The Philosophy of Coca-Cola," in *Dissenting Knowledges, Open Futures: The Multiple Selves and Strange Destinations of Ashis Nandy*, ed. Vinay Lal (New Delhi: Oxford University Press, 2000), 203.

115 Neelam Sidhar Wright, "'Tom Cruise? Tarantino? E.T.? . . . Indian!': Innovation through Imitation in the Cross-Cultural Bollywood Remake," *Scope* 15 (November 2009). Derek Elley claims that the film's strange color grading, which bathes Los Angeles in yellow, recalls *Bad Boys* (1995). In fact, *Kaante* was the first Indian feature to use Digital Intermediary color correction, processed in the United States. Derek Elley, "Bollywood Tackles Tarantino," *Variety*, January 6, 2003.

116 Dave Kehr, "Shot in Los Angeles, but Bombay All the Way," *New York Times*, December 20, 2002.

117 Indu Ramachandani, ed., *The Encyclopedia of Hindi Cinema* (New Delhi: Encyclopedia Britannica [India]), 2003), 437.

118 Ravi Vasudevan, "Addressing the Spectator of a 'Third World' National Cinema: The Bombay Social Film of the 1940s and 1950s," *Screen* 36, no. 4 (1995): 308; Rosie Thomas, "Indian Cinema: Pleasures and Popularity," *Screen* 26, nos. 3–4 (1985): 117

119 See, for example, Heidi Pauwels, ed., *Indian Literature and Popular Cinema: Recasting Classics* (New York: Routledge, 2007), 1–16; and Vijay Mishra, *Bollywood Cinema: Temples of Desire* (New York: Routledge, 2002).

120 Y. A. Fazalbhoy, "Improvement of Film Industry's Position: Wanted Rationalisation," in *The Pictureworld Souvenir of the Indian Motion Picture Congress and Exhibition*, 69.

121 Quoted in Gautaman Bhaskaran, "Aping Hollywood," *The Hindu*, August 22, 2003.

122 Quoted in Claire M. Wilkinson-Weber, "A Need for Redress: Costume in Some Recent Hindi Film Remakes," *BioScope: South Asian Screen Studies* 1, no. 2 (July 2010): 140.

123 John Harlow, "When Producers in India Say 'That's a Take,' They Mean It," *The Australian*, September 16, 2002.

124 Robert Trumbull, "Movies Are Booming: In Bombay," *New York Times Magazine*, July 5, 1953. Hollywood-style music also made an appearance in 1950s cinema, as new technologies facilitated the recording of larger symphonic ensembles, allowing Hindi soundtracks to feature chromatic movement, whole-tone scales, metrical ambiguity, and other mainstays of Hollywood scores. See Anna Morcom, *Hindi Film Songs and the Cinema* (Aldershot: Ashgate, 2007).

125 As of 1990, the only time a Hollywood company successfully sued an Indian producer for an illegal remake was when Warner Brothers took the producers of *Khoon Khoon* (1973) to court for remaking *Dirty Harry* (1971) scene by scene. Warner received US$50,000 in punitive damages against the producers of the film, Eagle Films, who thought twice after they decided to remake Billy Wilder's *Irma la Douce* (1963); they contacted United Artists soon after losing the suit to Warner and obtained remake rights. Arthur Pais, "4 'Ghosts' Meet 3 'Pretty Women' in India's Ripoffs," *Variety*, November 12, 1990.

126 Ramola T. Badam, "Bollywood May Have Lost the Plot," *The Advertiser*, June 16, 2003.

127 In an interview about "official adaptations," Johar says, "We have gone legal we have gone legal on a remake by officially adopting the Hollywood film *Stepmom* and getting the rights for the Elvis song 'Jailhouse Rock.' I would be open to other legal remakes but only when opportunity knocks. I am not going to go looking for it. There is an art to adaption. Lifting scenes does not make a Hindi film. You have to chop and change scenes." Udita Jhunjhunwala, "Karan Johar on 'We Are Family,'" *Express News Service*, August 28, 2010.

128 Quoted in Anupama Chopra, "Bollywood Soars Toward Hollywood," *New York Times*, March 5, 2010.

129 Prasad, "This Thing Called Bollywood," 17–20.

130 Patricia Aufderheide, "Made in Hong Kong: Translation and Transmutation," in *Play It Again, Sam: Retakes on Remakes*, ed. Andrew Horton and Stuart Y. McDougal (Berkeley: University of California Press, 1998), 191.

131 Chakravarty, *National Identity in Indian Popular Cinema*, 15–16.

132 Tejaswini Ganti, "Casting Culture: The Social Life of Hindi Film Production in Contemporary India" (Ph.D. diss., New York University, 2000), 342–43.

133 Sheila J. Nayar, "The Values of Fantasy: Indian Popular Cinema through Western Scripts," *Journal of Popular Culture* 31, no. 1 (1997): 74–75.

134 "Bollywood Stars, Hollywood Suspects," *Indian Express*, September 30, 2001. The terrorism intertexts don't end with the trip to the United States. Ironically, two other stars of the film, Sanjay Dutt and Mahesh Manjrekar, were implicated in colluding with underworld boss Chota Shakeel when Mumbai courts released a taped cell-phone conversation in August 2002. Not only had Sanjay Dutt spent an extended period in jail under the Terrorist and Disruptive Activities Act for possession of firearms, but Hindi film financier Bharat Shah had just been convicted for his links with Chota Shakeel. *Kaante*'s delayed release was rumored to be a consequence of negative publicity from the taped conversations and underworld links. In the interim, pirated DVDs and VCDs of the film were in wide circulation. Rounding out its associations with communal terror, members of the right-wing political party Shiv Sena protested *Kaante*'s fascination with the United States. Party members tore down promotional posters and threatened to release poisonous snakes into any movie theater that dared to show the film during its then-planned September release. Reportedly, Bombay's Shiv Sena boss insisted that a Jaipur Shiv Sena group was agitating against the film and cleared the film for exhibition in the city.

135 Srinivas, "The Quentin Conversation," *Passion for Cinema*, April 25, 2007, accessed July 11, 2010, at http://passionforcinema.com/the-quentin-conversation/.

136 Celia Lury, *Cultural Rights: Technology, Legality and Personality* (New York: Routledge, 1993), 4.

137 Naoki Sakai, "You Asians: On the Historical Role of the West and Asia Binary," *South Atlantic Quarterly* 99, no. 4 (2000): 798.

CHAPTER 2. MANAGING EXCHANGE

1 Hamish McDonald, *Mahabharata in Polyester: The Making of the World's Richest Brothers and Their Feud* (Sydney: New South, 2010).

2 Suketu Mehta, "Welcome to Bollywood," *National Geographic* 207, no. 2 (2005): 52–69.

3 While Reliance owns the Indian rights for the films that it coproduces, it also represents a new way of taking advantage of Hollywood marquee recognition for first-look projects, bypassing Hollywood studios by signing deals directly with stars and independent producers and then using these deals to catapult cofinancing agreements with the majors. Done this way, major deals can be made more quickly and without the extensive back-and-forth of typical media negotiations. See Michael Fleming and Ali Jaafar, "H'Wood Sign of Change," *Variety*, December 6, 2009. In 2010, Reliance Broadcast Network signed a deal with CBS Studios International to launch three English-language channels in India. Reliance has also had talks with Universal Studios to build a billion-dollar theme park and resort in India.

4 One could imagine that Reliance would have been less confident about its Hollywood investments after the difficulty with the DreamWorks deal. However, when the debt-ridden Hollywood studio Metro-Goldwyn-Mayer (MGM) offered itself up for sale in early 2010, Reliance entered the bidding. Reliance was most interested in acquiring MGM's huge film library, leveraging content from profitable franchises like *James Bond* and *The Pink Panther*. While Reliance didn't buy MGM in the end, the fact it could contend for the ownership of multiple Hollywood studios was a demonstration of the newfound investment power of Indian media capital.

5 For an account of the recent proliferation of statistics in Indian film industry discourse and practice, see Nitin Govil, "Size Matters," *BioScope: South Asian Screen Studies* 1, no. 2 (2010): 105–9.

6 Because of nonalignment, postwar India's national imaginary was always tied to a certain vision of global political modernity. Despite India's advocacy of geopolitical neutrality, forms of fealty remained, particularly to Soviet Union, but also to the United States. The United States loaned India billions of dollars worth of food, which India could not pay for in dollars because it lacked enough foreign exchange reserves. By the mid-1960s, the United States had accumulated over US$2 billion worth of blocked rupees in India, most of which came from the sale of "surplus agricultural commodities" like food, grain, and edible oil. It was estimated that American rupee holdings and credits were equal to almost *half* the money in circulation in India. There was a scramble to spend this "blocked money" in India by increasing diplomatic travel in India, helping to fund the United States Information Agency's book program, and other initiatives. See Thomas F. Brady, "U.S. and India Sign $398 Million Food Agreement," *New York Times*, October 1, 1964. U.S. congressional representatives criticized blocked funds for forcing the expenditure of funds "only in very limited ways which are conducive to waste and extravagance on the part of our own government." "Rep. Anderson Wants Bit of Aid Returned," *Chicago Daily Tribune*, September 17, 1962.

7 While only a part of a wider economy of Indian cultural export at the time, film drove revenue in ancillary industries as well. In the 1960s, for example, overseas sales of playback singer Lata Mangeshkar's extensive recordings brought in valuable foreign exchange.

8 There were extensive union protests in the early 1950s, led by organizations like the International Alliance of Theatrical and Stage Employees and Motion Picture Operators of the United States and Canada. In its 1952 convention, the group argued against the proliferation of what were known even back then as "runaway productions," where Hollywood studios used blocked funds to hire foreign workers to work on location. See J. D. Spiro, "Hollywood Dossier." *New York Times*, August 3, 1952. At the time, over two dozen Hollywood films were being shot abroad, building on the success of John Huston's *The African Queen*, much of which was shot in England. This was part of an emerging independent

production model in Hollywood. Eric Hoyt describes a 1951 amendment to the U.S. income tax code, which "exempt[ed] income taxes on monies earned if the taxpayer resided abroad for seventeen out of eighteen consecutive months. Congress intended the so-called 'eighteen months exemption' to be an incentive for construction and oil workers working abroad in the postwar years. But top Hollywood talent quickly discovered ways to utilize the exemption for their own advantage—traveling abroad to make movies either with independent financing or the 'frozen funds' of studios. Galvanized by the prospect of earning hundreds of thousands of dollars in untaxed earnings, William Wyler traveled to Europe in 1952 to produce and direct *Roman Holiday* for Paramount." Eric Hoyt, "Hollywood and the Income Tax, 1929–1955," *Film History* 22, no. 1 (2010): 15.

9 Hollywood's late 1950s peak in India is perhaps best represented by the remarkable success of Cecil B. DeMille's *The Ten Commandments*, which ran for thirty-one weeks "House Full" at the Regal in Bombay in 1958. At the time, out of the 3,500 theaters in India, two hundred ran Hollywood pictures in morning shows only (fifty showed foreign films exclusively) and American films were thought to draw 3 percent of India's film-going audience. *The Ten Commandments* established a then all-time earnings record for a foreign film in India. The film's success was all the more remarkable as its Indian profits were 100 percent remittable back to the United States because it was imported prior to new remittance restrictions. See the cable from G. C. Vietheer to the MPEA Foreign Finance Committee, August 10, 1959, Warner Brothers Archives, University of Southern California. There were other notable Hollywood successes—*Ben-Hur* ran for twenty-six weeks in Bombay and *My Fair Lady* for twenty-seven weeks, but profits from these films were subject to new remittance restrictions.

10 See Peter Lev, *The Fifties: Transforming the Screen, 1950–1959* (Berkeley: University of California Press, 2003).

11 MPEA Memo, "Consolidated," 1957. All the memoranda cited in this section are available at the Warner Brothers Archive at the University of Southern California.

12 Thomas F. Brady, "On Indian Film," *New York Times*, December 1, 1963.

13 MPEA, Memo 573, "India: Uses for Blocked Funds," August 19, 1959.

14 See the specific request made the by New York distribution office for Warner Brothers in Norman H. Moray to Cedric Francis (letter), August 10, 1956.

15 "India: Uses for Blocked Funds."

16 "Indian Jewelry for Sale," *Times of India*, July 6, 1963.

17 "RM" Letter to Jack E. Dagal, December 28, 1964.

18 MPEA Memo 412, August 10, 1964.

19 Daryl D'Monte, "Import of Feature Films: Bungling All the Way," *Times of India*, December 15, 1978.

20 For an account that links the proliferation of Hindi genres to capital investment in the Bombay industry, see Madhav Prasad, *Ideology of the Hindi Film: A Historical Construction* (New Delhi: Oxford University Press, 2000).

21 See Valentina Vitali, *Hindi Action Cinema: Industries, Narratives, Bodies* (New Delhi: Oxford University Press, 2008), 134–44.

22 In the late 1960s, rupee devaluation gave the false appearance of growing export earnings. In addition, the East African market, which a few years before accounted for 20–25 percent of export earnings, was contracting due to film import restrictions being set up in Kenya and threatened in Tanzania, and the marked exodus of much of the Indian diaspora at that time. See "No Pat on the Back," *Times of India*, December 1, 1968.

23 For an account of these "global" Hindi films, see Ranjani Mazumdar, "Aviation, Touring and Dreaming in 1960s Bombay Cinema," *BioScope: South Asian Screen Studies* 2, no. 2 (2011): 129–55.

24 "Miss a Location!" *Filmfare*, April 29, 1966.

25 "End Hollywood Monopoly, Demands Tariq," *Blitz*, January 3, 1970.

26 Neil G. Caward, "The Toast of Death," *Motography*, August 21, 1915.

27 "The World in Hollywood," *Popular Mechanics Magazine*, November 1935.

28 Quoted in Peter Noble, "Indian Culture Fused with Western Technology," *Screen International*, June 18, 1977.

29 For an account of the priorities of this kind of "global localization," see Koichi Iwabuchi, *Recentering Globalization: Popular Culture and Japanese Transnationalism* (Durham: Duke University Press, 2002). For an account of some of the problems of these corporate localization strategies in the construction of a predictable market and in the inculcation of stable forms of commodity consumption, see John Sinclair, "Globalization and the Advertising Industry in China," *Chinese Journal of Communication* 1, vol. 1 (2008): 77–90.

30 Uma da Cunha, "Asia TV Sales: Uphill for U.S. Firms," *Variety*, February 20, 1994.

31 Melissa Butcher, *Transnational Television, Cultural Identity and Change: When STAR Came to India* (New Delhi: Sage, 2003), 16.

32 Todd Miller quoted in Magz Osborne, "AXN: Evolution," *Television Asia* 14, no. 10 (2007): 42.

33 Quoted in Nicole LaPorte, "Sony Betting Big on Bollywood," *Variety*, October 20, 2005.

34 Anand Giridharadas, "Hollywood Starts Making Bollywood Films in India," *New York Times*, August 8, 2007.

35 Vajir Singh and Princy Jain, "King Khan Rules, Ranbir Retreats," *Hindustan Times*, November 10, 2007.

36 Quoted in Renee Montagne, "In Mumbai, Hollywood Gambles—and Gets Burned," *National Public Radio*, December 12, 2007.

37 Jason Anderson, "Hollywood's Bollywood Raid Disappoints," *The Globe and Mail*, November 12, 2007.

38 Quoted in Anil Sinanan, "Give Us Some of that Bolly Lolly," *The Times*, November 8, 2007.

39 Quoted in "Hollywood's Bollywood Fails to Score," *Toronto Star*, December 7, 2007.

40 Quoted in Anusha Subramanian, "Hollywood in Bollywood," *Business Today*, November 4, 2007.

41 Warner had also recently announced an Abu Dhabi deal to make films for Arabic-speaking audiences, with future plans to partner with a Russian company.

42 Quoted in Nyay Bhushan, "Warner Bros. Shooting Indian Prod'n in China," *Hollywood Reporter*, August 22, 2007.

43 Quoted in Surender Bhatani, "Beijing Olympics Led Nikhil Advani to Shoot in Bangkok," *Indo-Asian News Service*, December 4, 2008.

44 Richard Fox quoted in Dominic Wells, "Riches of the East," *The Times*, January 3, 2009.

45 Folke Fröbel, Jürgen Heinrichs, and Otto Kreye, *The New International Division of Labour: Structural Unemployment in the Industrialised Countries and Industrialization in Developing Countries*, trans. Pete Burgess (Cambridge: Cambridge University Press, 1980).

46 See Vivian Lin, "Women Electronics Workers in Southeast Asia: The Emergence of a Working Class," in *Global Restructuring and Territorial Development*, ed. Jeffrey Henderson and Manuel Castells (London: Sage, 1987), 112–35.

47 See Toby Miller, "Hollywood and the World," in *The Oxford Guide to Film Studies*, ed. John Hill and Pamela Church Gibson (New York: Oxford University Press, 1998), 371–81.

48 See Toby Miller, Nitin Govil, John McMurria, and Richard Maxwell, *Global Hollywood* (London: British Film Institute, 2001), 44–82.

49 Ibid., 82.

50 Saskia Sassen, *The Mobility of Labor and Capital: A Study in International Investment and Labor Flow* (Cambridge: Cambridge University Press, 1988), 36.

51 See R. T. Ford, "Law's Territory: A History of Jurisdiction," *Michigan Law Review* 97 (February 1999): 843–930.

52 For more on the media industries' strategic evocation of the national, see Nitin Govil, "Thinking Nationally: Domicile, Distinction, and Dysfunction in Global Media Exchange," in *Media Industries: History, Theory, and Method*, ed. Jennifer Holt and Alisa Perren (Malden, MA: Blackwell, 2009), 132–43.

53 U.S. Department of Commerce, "The Migration of U.S. Film and Television Production" (Washington, D.C., 2001), 4, available at http://www.ita.doc.gov/media/migration11901.pdf.

54 See Jon May and Nigel Thrift, eds., *TimeSpace: Geographies of Temporality* (New York: Routledge, 2001).

55 In January 2009, on the heels of an announcement by newly elected president Barack Obama that promised to keep more jobs in the United States, Warner Brothers announced that it would cut 10 percent of its global workforce and outsource jobs to Poland and India. Indeed, with growing unemployment in the United States, outsourcing has become a hot-button election issue. The international flight of American manufacturing and service jobs that fueled technology speculation and bloated the Internet bubble at the end of the twentieth century is

now widely viewed as part of a general anemic employment outlook at the beginning of the twenty-first. Proponents of outsourcing attribute its benefits in developed and emerging economies to a number of factors: reduced labor costs; the possibilities of new markets and revenue streams that (theoretically) generate new employment in emerging markets; opportunities to repatriate earnings for U.S. firms with overseas workforces; and the idea that displaced U.S. workers might be freed from repetitive production tasks in order to focus on innovation. Meanwhile, emerging economies absorb the influx of these displaced lower-paying jobs from the West. In time, it is imagined, jobs in the emerging economies will also cycle upward in terms of wage, skill, and productivity as they reap the benefits of increased employment and consumption. For a characteristically optimistic view, see Jagdish N. Bhagwati, *In Defense of Globalization* (New York: Oxford University Press, 2004).

56 Hollywood has started to use Indian legal labor as its back office as well. Fox, Sony, and Universal are contracting copyright, contract, insurance, and tax processing work to Indian films like the Mysore-based SDD Global Solutions. SDD Global is also the India arm of British Channel 4's U.S. legal counsel, and conducted part of the legal research that led to the successful dismissal of a libel case involving *Da Ali G Show* in the California Court of Appeals.

57 "Madras Picture Executive to Study Hollywood Ideas," *Los Angeles Times*, November 15, 1928.

58 F. W. Fox, "Khan Ends Visit: India's DeMille Lauds Hollywood," *Hollywood Citizen News*, March 5, 1947.

59 See Ranjani Mazumdar, "Women and the City: Fashion, Dance and Desire in Popular Bombay Cinema," in *Kapital and Karma: Kunsthalle Vienna Catalogue on Contemporary Indian Art* (Ostfildern: Hatje Cantz, 2002). Indian multimedia firms are part of a much larger Asian outsourcing community, most with long histories in 2D animation production. Hollywood has also sent traditional animation storyboarding and background finishing tasks to South Korea since the 1980s. When the IMF crisis and the strong U.S. dollar in the late 1990s cut local production costs, Chinese companies emerged as competitors to Korean outsourcing, but quality problems meant that work continued to be sent to South Korean firms. However, since the early 2000s, Indian forms have emerged as a significant competitor to the East Asian animation houses.

60 India's animation industry is seen by industry professionals to be akin to Japan's Studio Ghibli thirty years ago, poised to explode into global prominence with marquee films made by maverick directors. See Patrick Frater, "Bollymation Boom," *Variety*, June 2, 2008. However, influenced by the lucrative promises of Hollywood's outsourcing to India, Singapore's Media Development Authority recently invested US$165 million into the local animation industry.

61 Rhythm & Hues, which has worked on films like *Garfield: A Tail of Two Kitties*, *The Chronicles of Narnia*, and *The Golden Compass*, relied on Indian local talent

as well as expatriate employees, but claimed to treat its entire dispersed workforce as a unified whole without regard for local cost savings. "We don't differentiate between locations," notes one of its managing directors. Prashant Buyyala quoted in Aishah Mustapha, "New Value: Creative Content Gets Its Rhythm," *The Edge Malaysia*, January 11, 2010.

62 Michael Curtin and John Vanderhoef, "A Vanishing Piece of the Pi: The Globalization of Visual Effects Labor," *Television and New Media*, Winter 2014, 1–21.

63 See Vincent Mosco, "Loose Ends: The Death of Distance, the End of Politics," in *The Digital Sublime: Myth, Power, Cyberspace* (Cambridge: MIT Press, 2004), 85–116.

64 See Deirdre Boden and Harvey L. Molotch, "The Compulsion of Proximity," in *NowHere: Space, Time, and Modernity*, ed. Roger Friedland and Deirdre Boden (Berkeley: University of California Press, 1994), 257–86.

65 For a discussion of the cultural and symbolic pressures of co-presence in the Indian animation and special effects industry, as well as background into the political economy of Hollywood outsourcing, see Nitin Govil, "Hollywood's Effects, Bollywood FX," in *Contracting out Hollywood: Runaway Productions and Foreign Location Shooting*, ed. Greg Elmer and Mike Gasher (Lanham, MD: Rowman and Littlefield, 2005), 92–114.

66 Quoted in Ellen Wolff, "VISFX—Filmmaker's Notebooks: Coleman and Edland, Impressions of India," *Millimeter: The Magazine of Motion Picture and Television Production* 28, no. 2 (2000).

67 John Labrie quoted in Erika Kinetz, "Special Effects Outsourcing Grows in India," *Associated Press Financial Wire*, June 18, 2009.

68 Patrick von Sychowski quoted in Rhys Blakely, "Bollywood Mogul Offers Sweetheart Deal on 3-D Makeovers of Classic Films," *The Times*, February 12, 2010.

69 Jyoti Deshpande quoted in Patrick Frater, "F/X Biz Computes into Future Takeoff," *Variety*, March 17, 2008.

70 Yogi Aggarwal, "'Slumdog' Shows the Way for More Foreign Investment," *Business Times Singapore*, March 6, 2009.

71 Shanti Kumar, "Mapping Tollywood: The Cultural Geography of 'Ramoji Film City' in Hyderabad," in *Reorienting Global Communication: India and Chinese Media beyond Borders*, ed. Michael Curtin and Hemant Shah (Urbana: University of Illinois Press, 2010), 105.

CHAPTER 3. THE THEATER OF INFLUENCE

1 See the comments of Sir Vithaldas Thackersey, the education reformer and philanthropist, in "Films in India," *Wid's Daily*, August 18, 1919.

2 Arvind Adiga, *The White Tiger* (New York: Free Press, 2000), 173.

3 For an account of these kinds of spaces, see Tim Cresswell, *On the Move: Mobility in the Modern Western World* (New York: Routledge, 2006).

4 *Back in the Spotlight: FICCI/KPMG Indian Media and Entertainment Industry Report* (New Delhi: FICCI/KPMG, 2010), 27.

5 O. R. Geyer, "The Golden Age of the Pictures," *Photoplay*, June 1920.

6 "Zukor Planned Theater Conquest in Foreign Countries, Trial Shows," *Film Daily*, May 1, 1923.

7 From April 1925 to March 1926, film imports into India were at almost 14 million feet in total length, up from 9.5 million feet in 1924–25 and just over 7 million feet in 1923–24. But from April to November alone in 1926, imports were already at well over 11 million feet, indicating a very lucrative year ahead for Hollywood, since over 90 percent of imported films were of American manufacture. "India Imports Up," *Film Daily*, March 2, 1927.

8 C. J. North, "Our Foreign Trade in Motion Pictures," *The Annals of the American Academy of Political and Social Science, No. 217: The Motion Picture in Its Economic and Social Aspects* (Philadelphia, 1926), 106.

9 Kaushik Bhaumik, "The Emergence of the Bombay Film Industry, 1913–1936" (Ph.D. diss., Oxford University, 2002), 36.

10 For more detail on Hollywood's problems (and alignments) with British cinema in India, see Priya Jaikumar, *Cinema at the End of Empire: A Politics of Transition in Britain and India* (Durham: Duke University Press, 2006); and Brian Larkin, "Circulating Empires: Colonial Authority and the Immoral, Subversive Problem of American Film," in *Globalizing American Studies*, ed. Brian T. Edwards and Dilip Parameshwar Gaonkar (Chicago: University of Chicago Press, 2010), 155–83.

11 "Move to Displace American Films in India; Princes Offer $5,000,000 to Aid British Output," *New York Times*, September 13, 1926.

12 Erik Barnouw and S. Krishnaswamy, *Indian Film* (New York: Oxford University Press, 1980), 65.

13 "Seek India Chain," *Film Daily*, March 27, 1927.

14 "Madan's Offer," *Film Daily*, May 10, 1927.

15 "India Deal On," *Film Daily*, June 23, 1927.

16 *Report of the Indian Cinematograph Committee, 1927–28* (Madras: Government Press, 1928).

17 "American Film Invasion. Mr. Madan Fears. Reply to Criticism of Indian Industry," *Times of India*, November 10, 1928.

18 L. Prouse-Knox, "American Film Invasion: U.S. Corporation Representatives Reply to Mr. Madan," *Times of India*, November 12, 1928.

19 "Motion Pictures in India," *New York Times*, April 15, 1928, 118.

20 Eripa Singh, *India: A Market for American Products: A Bird's Eye View* (publisher unknown, ca. mid-1930s), 19. Pamphlet available at Special Collections, Academy of Motion Picture Arts and Sciences, Margaret Herrick Library, Los Angeles.

21 The Regal is also credited as the first theater in India to house an underground parking lot, the first to use neon signs, the first to use uniformed staff, and the first to install Cinemascope. David Vinnels and Brent Skelly, *Bollywood Showplaces: Cinema Theatres in India* (Cambridge: E&E Plumridge, 2002), 96.

22   "Bombay Theatremen Aid Civic Activities: Exhibitors and Managers Participate in Social and Public Life," *Motion Picture Herald*, August 7, 1937.

23   "New Delhi Visitor Says Film Industry Plays Vital Role in India," *Hollywood Citizen News*, July 18, 1947.

24   V. Doraiswamy, "India," *Motion Picture Herald*, December 25, 1963.

25   For example, the Apsara theater was built in Bombay in 1964, with the largest seating capacity of Indian theaters at the time and intriguing architectural flourishes such as a walkway that rose over a waterfall. The new 70mm Hoopalee Cinema in Gujarat was thought to have cost over US$1 million, with seating for over a thousand patrons (Fox's *Can Can* was the opening feature). The air-conditioned Safire theater in Madras housed a cinema, art theater, and continuous screening theater all under one roof, designed with the latest architectural innovations.

26   "India Favors Easier Credits to Multiply Rural Theatres," *Variety*, May 12, 1976.

27   "Indian Film Finance Corp. Wears Many Cinema Hats," *Variety*, February 9, 1977. UNESCO estimated that a country the size of India should have had a minimum of 37,000 theaters to support the population, yet in the late 1970s, the total number of both hardtop and mobile theaters stood at 9,700. "India Film Prod. Is up but Quality Remains Dubious," *Variety*, January 3, 1979.

28   "U.S. Majors Curbed in India, but Market Has Big Potential," *Variety*, February 2, 1977.

29   Douglas Gomery, "Building a Movie Theatre Giant: The Rise of Cineplex Odeon," in *Hollywood in the Age of Television*, ed. Tino Balio (Boston: Unwin Hyman, 1990), 377–91. CO opened theaters across the United States using techniques that are now commonplace in the multiplex trade: automatic platter systems to increase projectionist efficiency (contributing to the rise of part-time labor); soundproofing to prevent theater audio spillover; and rotating single films across smaller screens as attendance dropped during the course of its theatrical run. Thomas Guback points out that the subsequent multiplex boom of the 1980s was based on the cost savings of part-time employment, leasing deals with real estate and shopping center developers, and the exhibitors' short-term investment of cash before a portion of the profits have to be turned over to the distributors. These leasing deals translated into modest investment upfront (for furnishing and equipment) and relatively predictable cash flows unburdened by the long-term debt of all-out land ownership. See Thomas Guback, "The Evolution of the Motion Picture Theatre Business in the 1980s," *Journal of Communication* 37, no. 2 (1987): 60–77.

30   Charles Acland, *Screen Traffic: Movies, Multiplexes, and Global Culture* (Durham: Duke University Press, 2003), 129.

31   Ibid., 139.

32   Suresh Nair, "Hollywood Waits as Hindi Films Hog Theatres," *Times of India*, November 10, 1995.

33   Manjunath Pendakur, *Indian Popular Cinema: Industry, Ideology, and Consciousness* (Cresskill, NJ: Hampton Press, 2003), 22.

34 Jivraj Burman, "10-Screen Multiplexes Coming up in India," *Screen*, September 2, 1994.

35 "A Welcome Idea," *Screen*, September 2, 1994.

36 Mike Macclesfield quoted in Nabeel Abbas, "Double Takes," *Times of India*, January 10, 1995.

37 "The Romance Is Over," *Screen*, August 30, 1996.

38 Vaijayanti Kulkarni-Apte, "Multiplexes New Target of *Swadeshi-Wallahs*," *Times of India*, November 28, 1995.

39 There were other problems as well. Warner Brothers parted ways with its Indian licensee at the end of 1995 when the Indian firm, Magnasound, decided to concentrate on Hindi pop music after the success of a number of Bombay film releases had boosted the Hindi music retail sector.

40 Sudipto Dey, "Multiplexes Coming up to Woo Cine Buffs," *Times of India*, November 21, 2001.

41 Adlabs began by advertising film processing, moved onto documentary and feature films, and now has interests in the film processing in Western India. In addition to running multiplexes and IMAX theaters like the one in Bombay's Wadala, Adlabs processes the majority of releases for Western India. See Kaveree Bamzai, "Bollywood: Brave New Directions," *India Today*, November 29, 2003.

42 Kwanchai Rungfapaisarn, "On the Big Screen: IMAX Forecasts Rapid Growth in Region," *The Nation* (Thailand), November 29, 2001. IMAX Canada finalized a conversion process that could blow up any 35mm film into the IMAX format, facilitating Hollywood spectacle as a means of differentiation from local cinematic forms.

43 Bryan Pearson, "H'wood Speaks to Middle Class," *Variety*, August 26, 2002.

44 "IMAX Theatre Steaming Ahead," *Times of India*, August 3, 2002.

45 Roger Ebert, "Calcutta Serious about Films," *Chicago-Sun Times*, November 16, 1999; see also Roger Ebert, "Finding Nirvana in a Calcutta Theater," *Chicago-Sun-Times*, November 18, 1999.

46 "Lighthouse to Lighten Up," *The Statesman* (India), February 13, 2002.

47 Jhimli Mukherjee Pandey, "Lighthouse Gives Way to Multiplex," *Times of India*, March 9, 2002.

48 Tim Birchenough, "Healthy B.O. Should Fuel Multiplex," *Variety*, September 8, 2003.

49 See Federation of Indian Chambers of Commerce and Industry, *The Indian Entertainment Industry: Strategy and Vision* (New Delhi: FICCI, 2001), 31–38.

50 Ashoke Nag, "Plexes Pump B.O. Volume," *Variety*, March 8, 2004.

51 John Robertson, "A Patron's Experience: From Start to Finish," *Cinema Systems*, February 2004, 30–34.

52 "The Multiplex Revolution," *Cinema Systems*, May–June 2002, 51.

53 Susan Davis, "The Theme Park: Global Industry and Cultural Form." *Media, Culture and Society* 18, no. 3 (1996): 402.

54 Ibid., 403.

55 Dipayan Baishya and Moinak Mitra, "Management Usher: Suits in the Multiplex," *Business Today*, January 4, 2004.

56 Interview with Shravan Shroff, December 22, 2000. All further unattributed quotes are taken from this and subsequent interviews, e-mails, and phone conversations.

57 Similarly, Shroff notes that the Indian multiplex trade is "very similar to the hotel business." Many of the new generation of multiplex owners are drawn from the leisure and hospitality business.

58 James L. Watson, "McDonald's in Hong Kong," in *Golden Arches East: McDonald's in East Asia*, ed. James L. Watson (Stanford: Stanford University Press, 1997), 90.

59 Responding to a question on the types of audiences one might see at a Shringar multiplex, Shroff notes: "I would say that even the Rs.80 ticket factors out the lower class . . . if I want to get those people, I'd have to price tickets at Rs.50, but given my investment in the project, I can't. Given where my project is located, I can't, because that's not a clientele I want to attract. The clientele I want to attract in that area would pay me Rs.100 or Rs.150." Concentrating his multiplex investment in Maharashtra, Shroff is able to take advantage of a lack of local ordinances that mandate a certain number of cinema seats be reserved for the poor (as they are in Delhi, for example).

60 At the same time that multiplexes have been planned as distribution support for foreign film, they are also possible supports for Indian alternative and art cinema. The National Film Development Corporation has built a number of dedicated art-film mini-theatres in India. But with the decline of film clubs and societies, some in the Indian parallel cinema scene have begun to lobby multiplex owners to rent their "theatres to film clubs at low rates for periodic screenings of non-mainstream films" at times "when the theatre is not in use, like in the mornings." In order to qualify for exemption on entertainment taxes, many states require at least one screen in a multiplex to be reserved at some time during the month for regional films. Shringar's folding of regional Hindi cinemas in the rubric of "world cinema" also satisfies this cultural policy mandate. See Gunvanthi Balaram, "Gov't Building Two Small Theatres," *Times of India*, August 20, 2002.

61 Adrian Athique, "Leisure Capital in the New Economy: The Rapid Rise of the Multiplex in India," *Contemporary South Asia* 17, no. 2 (2009): 123–40.

62 Brian Carvalho, "Small Towns, Big Business," *Business Today*, July 18, 2004.

63 Gary Edgerton, "The Multiplex: The Modern American Motion Picture Theatre as Message," in *Exhibition, the Film Reader*, ed. Ina Rae Hark (New York: Routledge, 2002), 163–64.

64 "Movies, *Masti* but No Multiplexes in the City," *Times of India*, December 15, 2002.

65 See S. V. Srinivas, "Is There a Public in the Cinema Hall?" *Framework* 42 (Summer 2000), available at http://www.frameworkonline.com/Issue42/42svs. html. Srinivas notes that "Dalits (members of the formerly 'untouchable'

castes) were physically prevented by theatre managers from entering the Balcony or the highest class [of seats] in parts of Andhra Pradesh as late as the 1950s in order to avoid displeasing the predominantly upper caste customers there."

66 Charles Acland, "Cinemagoing and the Rise of the Megaplex," *Television and New Media* 1, no. 4 (2000): 375–402.

67 William Mazzarella, *Shoveling Smoke: Advertising and Globalization in Contemporary India* (Durham: Duke University Press, 2003), 3–14.

68 Ibid., 256.

69 Igor Kopytoff, "The Cultural Biography of Things: Commoditization as Process," in *The Social Life of Things: Commodities in Cultural Perspective*, ed. Arjun Appadurai (Cambridge: Cambridge University Press, 1986), 64–91.

70 Ravi Vasudevan, "Cinema in Urban Space," *Seminar* 525 (May 2003), available at http://www.india-seminar.com/2003/525/525%20ravi%20vasudevan.htm.

71 Letter from B. N. Nadkarni to Carl Schaefer, August 10, 1963.

72 Faizan Ahmed, Puloma Pal, and Ravi Vasudevan, "Interview with Rajesh Khanna." Research conducted for the Sarai project "Publics and Practices in the History of the Present: Old and New Media in Contemporary India," Sarai Centre for the Study of Developing Societies, 2003.

73 Ipsita Sahu, "From the Ruins of Chanakya: Film Exhibition and Urban Memory" (M.Phil. diss., Jawaharlal Nehru University, 2011).

74 Vinnels and Skelly, *Bollywood Showplaces*, 181

75 A battle between the Chanakya proprietors and the New Delhi Municipal Council over who originally came up with the multiplex idea caused additional friction. Sandeep Joshi, "Curtain down for Chanakya," *The Hindu*, January 18, 2002.

76 Sudipto Dey, "Multiplexes Coming up to Woo Cine Buffs," *Times of India*, November 21, 2001.

77 Hamari Jamatia, "Now Screening: Chanakya Razed," *Indian Express*, December 9, 2009.

78 Harish V. Nair, "Decks Cleared for Multiplex at Chanakya," *Hindustan Times*, January 13, 2009.

79 See Tarun Bhaskar et al., "An Optimization Model for Personalized Promotions in Multiplexes," *Journal of Promotion Management* 15, nos. 1–2 (2009): 229–46.

80 Timothy Mitchell, "The Stage of Modernity," in *Questions of Modernity*, ed. Timothy Mitchell (Toronto: University of Toronto Press, 1994), 1.

81 Charles Jencks, *Le Corbusier and the Continual Revolution in Architecture* (New York: Monacelli Press, 2000), 210.

82 See Miriam Hansen, "Vernacular Modernism: Tracking Cinema on a Global Scale," in *World Cinemas, Transnational Perspectives*, ed. Natasa Durovicova and Kathleen Newman (New York: Routledge, 2007), 287–314.

83 Ravi Kalia, *Chandigarh: The Making of an Indian City* (New Delhi: Oxford University Press, 1999).

84 Gautam Bhatia, "Indian Archetypes," *Architectural Review* 5 (May 1995): 74.

85 For a sense of the intimate association between ruin and modernity, see Julia Hell and Andreas Schönle, eds., *Ruins of Modernity* (Durham: Duke University Press, 2010).

86 Curt Gambetta, "Concrete and the 'Technical Imagination': The Politics of Architectural Making in Post-independence Bangalore," conference talk delivered at "Metropolis and Micropolitics: South Asia's Sutured Cities," University of Washington, May 15, 2009.

87 Ibid. See also Curt Gambetta, "Material Movement: Cement and the Globalization of Material Technologies," *Scapegoat: Landscape/Architecture/Political Economy* 2 (2011): 26–28.

88 P. C. Varghese, *Advanced Reinforced Concrete Design* (New Delhi: Prentice Hall of India, 2006), 434.

89 Marc Augé, *Non-places: Introduction to an Anthropology of Supermodernity*, trans. John Howe (New York: Verso, 1995).

90 Ackbar Abbas, *Hong Kong: Culture and the Politics of Disappearance* (Minneapolis: University of Minnesota Press, 1997).

91 See "UN Members Laughed and Applauded at 'Lage Raho . . . ,'" *Glamsham*, http://www.glamsham.com/movies/scoops/06/nov/14_lage_raho_munna_bhai_rajkumar_hirani.asp.

92 Ashis Nandy, "The Lure of 'Normal' Politics: Gandhi and the Battle for Popular Culture of Politics in India," *South Asian Popular Culture* 5, no. 2 (2007): 167–78.

93 Joseph Lelyveld, *Great Soul: Mahatma Gandhi and His Struggle with India* (New York: Knopf, 2011), 349.

94 William Mazzarella, "Branding the Mahatma: The Untimely Provocation of Gandhian Publicity," *Cultural Anthropology* 25, no. 1 (2010): 2.

95 Sheela Reddy, "Gandhi, a Second Coming," *Outlook*, September 11, 2006.

96 As David Nasaw describes the transformation of disparate strangers into the sociability of the audience in the American movie picture palace of the 1920s, it was "not only the experience they shared in common" that united the audience, but "also the recognition that in sharing it, they were deserving of this privilege." *Going Out: The Rise and Fall of Public Amusements* (New York: Basic Books, 1993), 238.

97 Lakshmi Srinivas, "Cinema Halls, Locality and Urban Life," *Ethnography* 11, no. 1 (2010): 201.

CHAPTER 4. ECONOMIES OF DEVOTION

1 Michael Hardt and Antonio Negri, *Multitude: War and Democracy in the Age of Empire* (New York: Penguin, 2004), 108.

2 Luc Boltanksi and Eve Chiapello, *The New Spirit of Capitalism* (New York: Verso, 2005).

3 Akiko Takeyama, "The Art of Seduction and Affect Economy: Neoliberal Class Struggle and Gender Politics in a Tokyo Host Club" (Ph.D. diss., University of Illinois–Champaign, 2008).

4   See Ann Laura Stoler, ed., *Haunted by Empire: Geographies of Intimacy in North American History* (Durham: Duke University Press, 2006).

5   See Sara Ahmed, "Affective Economies." *Social Text* 22, no. 2 (2004): 117–39.

6   Quoted in Stardust Gonsalves, "Unexpected Windfall for Sally Field–Goldie Hawn Fans," *Screen*, March 18, 1994, 1. The banal appraisals of Hollywood stars have proliferated to the point that they have become their own trope of inter-industry contact, crystallizing the exchange between the worlds of labor and leisure. For example, visiting Bombay to meet with the members of the Tibetan Youth Congress and to promote AIDS awareness, the actor Richard Gere claimed that "India is like an older and wiser brother to Tibet and is even more important as Buddha was born on this soil. "Richard Gere to Visit Mumbai," *Screen*, April 3 1998, 1. At an AIDS awareness press conference during the same trip, Gere was bedecked in a *bindi*, firming up his message with the validating presence of Indian actress Shabana Azmi, who joined him on stage. See Uma da Cunha, "Richard Gere's War on AIDS," *Screen*, April 17, 1998. Da Cunha claims that "what is disarmingly unexpected and a bonus is Gere's lack of a screen ego or vain mannerisms associated with superstardom."

7   Chris Rojek, *Celebrity* (London: Reaktion Books, 2001). Extending Rojek, we are fascinated with celebrity religion because it seems to compensate for the lack of substance associated with stardom. The flash of the paparazzi camera marks our initiation as acolytes into the rites of celebrity worship. We revere stars even as they pray to other "heavenly bodies." Ironically, Richard Dyer's influential text on stardom does not elaborate on the question of celebrity faith, noting only that religion is among the many "social categories in which people are placed and through which they have to make sense of their lives." See Richard Dyer, *Heavenly Bodies: Film Stars and Society* (New York: Routledge, 200), 16.

8   For more on the emergence of the Hollywood's international division of cultural labor, see Toby Miller, Nitin Govil, John McMurria, Richard Maxwell, and Ting Wang, *Global Hollywood 2* (London: BFI, 2005).

9   Ernest Sternberg, "Phantasmagoric Labor: The New Economies of Self-Presentation," *Futures* 30, no. 1 (1998): 3–28.

10 For more on the commodity logic of self-branding, see Sarah Banet-Weiser, *Authentic™: Political Possibility in a Brand Culture* (New York: NYU Press, 2012).

11 For more on the industries of circulation, repackaging, and repurposing that enable the "afterlife" of media commodities, see Shawn Shimpach, *Television in Transition: The Life and Afterlife of the Narrative Action Hero* (Malden, MA: Blackwell, 2010).

12 See, for example, "Hindus in U.S. Admire Julia Roberts for Sporting *Bindi* during Taj Mahal Visit," *Asian News International*, January 26, 2009; and "Hindus Warmly Welcome Julia Roberts to Hinduism," *Hindustan Times*, August 5, 2010.

13 Georgina Littlejohn, "'I'm a Hindu': Julia Roberts Reveals That She Converted to the Religion While Making Her New Film Eat, Pray, Love," *Daily Mail*, August 6, 2010.

14 Inderpal Grewal, *Transnational America: Feminisms, Diasporas, Neoliberalisms* (Durham: Duke University Press, 2005).

15 Erving Goffman, *Interaction Ritual: Essays in Face-to-Face Behavior* (New York: Pantheon, 1967), 12.

16 Michael Curtin, *Playing to the World's Biggest Audience: The Globalization of Chinese Film and Television* (Berkeley: University of California Press, 2007), 299.

17 "Face-work" is sometimes a literal matter of faces. Films like the English-language *Bride & Prejudice* are designed to promote Aishwarya Rai's global appeal, mapped onto her "crossover" looks as a way of entering into Hollywood's generically Asian stardom. See Goldie Asuri, "Ash-Coloured Whiteness: The Transfiguration of Aishwarya Rai," *South Asian Popular Culture* 6, no. 2 (2008): 109–23. Since the 1990s, the international success of Indian fashion models have been recognized for their "global look." The positioning machinery of stardom promotes this look as an exoticism divorced from geographic location. Contemporary Indian female stardom is central to driving this branding of "ethnic ambiguity." See Shobita Dhar, "The Dotboomers," *Outlook*, November 1, 2004.

18 Serena Menon, "I Would Like to Sing and Dance in Bollywood," *Hindustan Times*, September 28, 2010; Prashant Singh, "India 'Feels Like Being at Home' to Travolta," *India Today*, September 28, 2010. As Hollywood stars continue to be won over by working in India—joining Western celebrities like Lindsay Lohan, Katy Perry, Kylie Minogue, and Jessica Simpson in declaring their Indian admiration—the public management of celebrity becomes more precarious, subject to dissolution by scandal. So, for example, the controversy over the suspected racial epithets of two of Angelina Jolie's white British bodyguards during the shooting of *A Mighty Heart* in India in 2006 led to Johnny Depp's refusal to shoot Warner's upcoming *Shantaram* on location in India. Depp reportedly asked director Mira Nair if the Bombay-set film could be shot in Mexico instead. Amid this hullabaloo, widely reported in the Indian and international press and confirmed by some of the film's cast, the friendship between Depp and Jolie's husband, Brad Pitt, was cemented by the intimacies of offence, overriding any and all other rationalizations of *Shantaram*'s numerous delays. Similarly, Hindi film star Shah Rukh Khan's detention at Newark Airport while promoting a film on racial profiling among Muslim communities in 2009, which generated a host of anti-American headlines in the Indian press, demonstrates how the Hollywood–Bombay media relationship is increasingly predicated on the public instabilities of star (im)mobility.

19 Quoted in Simi Horwitz, "From Bollywood to Hollywood: Four South Asian Actors on the Art of Crossing Over," *Backstage*, February 25, 2010.

20 For example, as Kareena Kapoor says of Hollywood, "To get a role there you have to give screen tests, park yourself there for about seven to eight months, and then maybe you get a two-bit role. I'd rather enjoy the best of Bollywood." Quoted in Zakia Uddin, "Kareena Kapoor: 'SRK Is Our Tom Cruise,'" *Digital Spy*, March 25, 2011.

21 Danae Clark, *Negotiating Hollywood: The Cultural Politics of Actors' Labor* (Minneapolis: University of Minnesota Press, 1995), 2.

22 For example, in 1935, the *Los Angeles Times* reported that the wife and daughters of "a noted Hindu surgeon" were impressed with Hollywood, finding that "Los Angeles closely resembles Bombay and Southern California is similar to India." See "Bombay Trio Visit in City," *Los Angeles Times*, August 17, 1935. Society parties served as meeting grounds between American and Indian celebrity, such as those thrown for wealthy Bombay financier Dinshaw Petit earlier in 1935, attended by "practically everybody" from Hollywood. See T. Marshall Kester, "Parties for India Financier Top Cinema Social Efforts," *Los Angeles Times*, March 3, 1935.

23 Grace Kinglsey, "Movie Gossip: Indian Prince Studies Movies," *Los Angeles Times*, February 24, 1915.

24 Similarly, the marriage of Prince Satish Chandra Singh to LA dancer Doris Booth was covered by the press because he came "to Hollywood to study the motion picture industry" in the early 1930s. See "Dancer Weds Hindu Prince: Husband to Open Film Studio in India," *Los Angeles Times*, January 7, 1933.

25 "Prince and Bride to See Studios," *Los Angeles Times*, July 17, 1936.

26 Christina Klein, *Cold War Orientalism: Asia in the Middlebrow Imagination, 1945–1961* (Berkeley: University of California Press, 2003).

27 Harold A. Gould, "U.S.–Indian Relations: The Early Phase," in *The Hope and the Reality; U.S. Indian Relations from Roosevelt to Reagan*, ed. Harold A. Gould and Sumit Ganguly (Boulder, CO: Westview Press, 1992), 21.

28 Harold Isaacs, *Images of Asia: American Views of China and India* (New York: Capricorn, 1962), 379–83.

29 Frank Capra, *The Name above the Title: An Autobiography* (New York: Macmillan, 1971), 430.

30 A few months after he returned to the United States, Capra helped organize a four-week, eight-city tour of the United States for a visiting Indian film delegation.

31 W. E. Sikes, "American Movies in India," *Christian Century*, August 13, 1930, 992–93.

32 See Neepa Majumdar, *Wanted: Cultured Ladies Only! Female Stardom and Cinema in India, 1930s–1950s* (Urbana: University of Illinois Press, 2009).

33 Louis Ogull, "He Tells Uncle Sam!" *Filmindia*, October 1939.

34 These interpersonal gestures of reciprocity are not always staged for public consumption in the pages of film magazines. For instance, when K. M. Modi of Western India Theatres asked the director of International Relations at Warner Brothers to supply 8x10 autographed photos of Natalie Wood and Suzanne Pleshette in the 1960s, Warner Brothers obliged, throwing in a autographed Rex Harrison photo as an added gesture of goodwill. See the Warner Brother's Archive at the University of Southern California for the account of this exchange. The stars themselves were not above collecting autographs of one another: as the *Times of India* reported during an Indian film delegation visit to Hollywood in

1952, "Nargis was collecting signatures of her American colleagues while Greer Garson made sure that she got those of her newly won Indian friends." See "Film Delegate Welcomed," *Times of India*, October 9, 1952.

35 "Polly Perkins Says," *Wid's Daily*, January 11, 1919.

36 Sylvia Norris, "Film Letter from Hollywood," *Filmfare*, June 6, 1958. See also Bunny Reuben, *Mehboob, India's DeMille: The First Biography* (New Delhi: Indus, 1994).

37 "Letter to the Editor," *Moving Picture News*, January 28, 1911.

38 See S. R. Kantebet, "Letter to the President of the Academy of Motion Picture Arts and Sciences," September 15, 1932, archived at the Margaret Herrick Library, Academy of Motion Picture Arts and Sciences, Los Angeles. Sixty-five years later, P. K. Nair, assistant curator of the National Film Archive of India, would write a letter, published in a 1968 issue of *Cineaste*, welcoming "donations of films and ancillary film material like books, journals, stills, publicity posters, programme notes, pamphlets, press books, etc." See "National Film Archive of India," *Cineaste* 2, no. 2 (1968–69): 19.

39 Bernard Simon, "Scenarios to the Office Boy," *North American Review* 232, no. 1 (1931): 82.

40 Phil M. Daly, "And That's That," *Film Daily*, August 22, 1926.

41 G. S. Sengar, "Letter to Jack L. Warner," April 4, 1964. This and the other letters and memos referenced below are archived at the Warner Brothers Collection, University of Southern California, Los Angeles.

42 Carl Schaefer, "Letter to Gulab Singh Sengar," April 17, 1964.

43 Manharlal H. Chawda, "Letter to Rtn. Jack L. Warner," August 14, 1964. "Rtn." refers to "Rotarian."

44 S. Gupta, "What Makes Rotary Go in India." *The Rotarian* 82, no. 2 (1953): 6. Gupta wrote this article as the vice president of the Rotary Club of Jamshedpur.

45 Memo to Carl Schaefer, August 26, 1964.

46 Suketu Mehta, *Maximum City: Bombay Lost and Found* (New Delhi: Penguin, 2004), 376–77.

47 Subhash Jha, "The Hollywood Movie Rip-offs Are Here," June 19, 2005, available at http://www.bollywood.com/hollywood-movie-rip-offs-are-here.

48 The eating of Hollywood, under the authority of Ravana, the ten-headed demon king of Lanka in the Hindu epic *Ramayana*, engenders a heterogeneous multiplicity—an alternative cosmology of cultural production. Furthermore, locating Hollywood within an alternative universe of cultural production where authenticity is de-sacralized shares something with contemporary feminist theorizations of critical reinvention, while the trope of regurgitation and reinvention is common to postcolonial mimesis. For example, Meaghan Morris notes that "essays are cantankerous: they like to take received ideas of About, chew them up and spit them out in little pieces which have changed." And Gayatri Spivak considers that critical reinvention is predicated on a politics of "swallowing and eating." See Meaghan Morris, "On the 'On' of *On Photography*," in *The Pirate's Fiancée:*

Feminism, Reading, Postmodernism (New York: Verso, 1988), 151; and Howard Winant, "Gayatri Spivak on the Politics of the Subaltern," *Socialist Review* 20, no. 3 (1990): 85–97.

49 Quoted in "D. G. Phalke, Dossier: Swadeshi Moving Pictures," *Continuum* 2, no. 1 (1988): 51–73.

50 K. A. Abbas, "The 'Filum' in India," *Life and Letters To-day* 24 (1940): 186. Similarly, the government-owned broadcasting network was named Doordarshan in the late 1950s, from *darshan*, the Sanskrit word for "sight," denoting the practices of mystical perception.

51 There were accounts that avoided the obvious religious metaphors, such as that of Mae Tinee, who wrote in 1926 that the recently founded Sharda Film Company in Bombay was "making a valiant attempt to rival the practical monopoly of Los Angeles." See Mae Tinee, "The Movies in India," *Chicago Tribune*, March 28, 1926.

52 Beverley Nichols, *Verdict on India* (New York: Harcourt, Brace and Company, 1944). Nichols was already a well-known British writer and confidant (and possibly lover) of Somerset Maugham when he wrote his *Verdict*. Maugham had traveled to India in 1938 on a three-month journey that would influence his portrayal of Indian mysticism in *The Razor's Edge*, published in 1944. Nichol's *Verdict*, a kind of Indian travelogue published the same year, could not have been more different. Traveling to India as a correspondent for Allied Newspapers during World War II, Nichols continued to write on India as an "independent observer." In this way, Nichols was similar to Katherine Mayo, who had insisted on her status as a "volunteer unsubsidized, uncommitted, and unattached," "neither an idle busybody nor a political agent, but merely an ordinary American seeking facts to lay before my own people." The "fact" that Mayo came to India with an open mind was supposed to add credence to her vituperative condemnation of South Asia in the book *Mother India*, published in 1927 and a clear influence on Nichols. Katherine Mayo, *Mother India* (New York: Harcourt, Brace and Company, 1927), 11–13. For a critique of Mayo's barely disguised political motivations, see Mrinalini Sinha, *Specters of Mother India: The Global Restructuring of an Empire* (Durham: Duke University Press, 2006). There was some talk in the early 1930s about a Hollywood film adaptation of Mayo's book.

53 Nichols, *Verdict on India*, 106.

54 "Hindus Find Film Making as 'Screwy' as Hollywood," *Hollywood Reporter*, January 10, 1941.

55 "Hindu Hollywood," *Chicago Daily Tribune*, April 2, 1939, H7.

56 John MacCormac, "'Shiraz,' a Hindu Film," *New York Times*, October 7, 1928, 7. Writing about the success of a Hindi-dubbed version of *Bambi*, Donald Nelson wrote that Disney had, for the first time, penetrated the "native Hindu market." Donald M. Nelson, "The Independent Producer," *Annals of the American Academy of Political and Social Science* 254 (November 1947): 53.

57 "India Will Make Bid for Attention in Film Medium," *Los Angeles Times*, August 28, 1935, 23. For Hollywood, like most of the United States, almost anything

Indian was generically marked as "Hindu." So the fashion trend sweeping Hollywood's period of high colonial fascination in the 1930s was a "Dhoti-Turkish-Hindu-Indian fad"; the one thousand extras brought in for the massive production of *Clive of India* were "Hindus living in various parts of California and the Middle West," and stars like the Bombay-born actress Merle Oberon were noted as "one-half Indian (Hindu, not Dakota)." See "Bizarre Fashions Hit by Hollywood," *Washington Post*, June 30, 1935; "Mr. Zanuck Itemizes the Cost of a 'Million Dollar Picture,'" *Washington Post*, March 3, 1935; and Francis Fink, "Films Import World's Biggest Stars: Hollywood's 'Buyers' Travel in Search of Talent," *Washington Post*, January 13, 1935.

58 See Francesca Orsini, *The Hindi Public Sphere, 1920–1940: Language and Literature in the Age of Nationalism* (New Delhi: Oxford University Press, 2002).

59 See Debashree Mukherjee's dissertation on the Bombay film industry in the 1940s, "Writing Cinema, Writing the Cinema" (M.Phil. diss., School of Arts and Aesthetics, Jawaharlal Nehru University, 2009).

60 On the other hand, for a segment of the Bombay film press, it was Hollywood that had compromised the essential Hinduism of Indian culture. *Filmindia*, an English-language film monthly almost solely the provenance of its self-promoting editor and publisher, Baburao Patel, insisted on cinema as "an index of Indian life," providing a kind of ethical instruction in the exercise of national civic vitality. See Kavita Daiya, *Violent Belongings: Partition, Gender, and Postcolonial Nationalism in India* (Philadelphia: Temple University Press, 2008), 114. Though Islam was the primary culprit in Patel's vitriolic communalism, he also included Hollywood in a long line of cultural compromises, from the "nine centuries of inescapable Mogul influence" though "two hundred years of British rule." Writing a few years after *Verdict on India*'s evocation of Bombay as a "Hindu Hollywood," Patel holds Hollywood responsible for the pollution of Hindu civic virtue, invoking a gendered nationalism: "Esther Williams wore perhaps a hundred different swim-suits in M.G.M.'s 'Bathing Beauty.' Two years later, Nalini Jaywant, a respectable married Hindu lady in private life, also wore a scanty swim-suit as seen in her recent picture . . . when Duhshasan tried to strip Draupadi, the Queen of the Pandavas, and see a little more of her skin, millions of warriors went to war and ended a civilization where such an outrage could even be attempted. There won't be a Mahabarat over Nalini Jaywant, for, it seems, that no longer do we consider a women's person as a sacred trust of man. And these days Indian women themselves strip faster than men require. Thanks to Hollywood and its American poison!" See Baburao Patel, "Rape of Our Heritage," *Filmindia*, July 4, 1951. Interestingly, Patel's movement from a long-standing commitment to conflating "politics, filmdom, and sex" toward a more publicly expressed Hindu revivalism is expressed through the instrument of Hollywood. For a mapping of Patel's trajectory, told in Manto's own inimitable style, see Saadat Hasan Manto, "Babu Rao Patel: Soft-Hearted Iconoclast," in *Stars from Another Sky: The Bombay Film World of the 1940s*, trans. Khalid Hasan (New Delhi: Penguin, 1998), 182–94.

61 While claims of a Jewish control of American media have been popular since the 1880s, Charles Lindbergh's anti-Semitic writings and speeches in the late 1930s exacerbated these tensions. The 1941 Propaganda Hearings of the U.S. Congress charged that the Jewish domination of Hollywood had created a number of pro-interventionist films. See Steven A. Carr, *Hollywood and Anti-Semitism: A Cultural History up to World War II* (Austin: University of Texas Press, 2001).

62 See John Sbardellati, "Brassbound G-men and Celluloid Reds: The FBI's Search for Communist Propaganda in Wartime Hollywood," *Film History* 20, no. 4 (2008): 412–36.

63 Quoted in Karen Leonard, *Making Ethnic Choices: California's Punjabi Mexican Americans* (Philadelphia: Temple University Press), 24.

64 Quoted in Joan M. Jensen, "Apartheid: Pacific Coast Style," *Pacific Historical Review* 38 (August 1969): 335–40.

65 Bill Ong Hing, *Defining America through Immigration Policy* (Philadelphia: Temple University Press, 2004), 45. In 1923, the Supreme Court denied an Oregon-settled Punjabi Sikh's request for naturalized American citizenship. Bhagat Singh Thind had claimed that his Aryan descent qualified him as a Caucasian, exempting him from the Exclusion Act of 1917, which had denied naturalization to Indians. See "Court Rules Hindu Not a 'White Person,'" *New York Times*, February 20, 1923.

66 For the remarkable history of Indian labor migration and settlement in the United States, primarily on the West Coast, see Nayan Shah, *Stranger Intimacy: Contesting Race, Sexuality, and the Law in the North American West* (Berkeley: University of California Press, 2011).

67 "Hindu 'Messiah' Lands in East," *Los Angeles Times*, May 20, 1932.

68 See Stephanie Syman, *The Subtle Body: The Story of Yoga in America* (New York: Farrar, Strauss and Giroux, 2010). For another account of the popular reception of Hinduism in the United States, see Robert Love, *The Great Oom: The Improbable Birth of Yoga in America* (New York: Viking, 2010).

69 See Kirin Narayan, "Refractions of the Field at Home: American Representations of Hindu Holy Men in the 19th and 20th Centuries," *Cultural Anthropology* 8, no. 4 (1993): 476–509.

70 Wendell Thomas, *Hinduism Invades America* (New York: Beacon, 1930), 247.

71 "New Scale for Photoplaywrights," *Moving Picture World*, June 15, 1912.

72 Peter Wade, "A Girdle of Film Round the World," *Motion Picture Story Magazine*, August 1913.

73 "Questions and Answers," *Photoplay Magazine*, January 1916.

74 "Race Prejudice Theme of Hayakawa Subject," *Wid's Daily*, July 13 1919.

75 The designation of Hollywood as a "dream factory" comes from Hortense Powdermaker's famous attribution made in *Hollywood, the Dream Factory* (1950; repr., New York: Arno Press 1979).

76 "India Lancers Being Hunted in Hollywood," *Washington Post*, August 12, 1934; George Shaffer, "Here's a Way to Land a Job as Film 'Extra': Hindu Reads Mind to

Get Role," *Chicago Daily Tribune*, September 12, 1934; Kirtley Baskette, "Making a Man's Picture," *Photoplay Magazine*, January 1935.

77 Harry Levette, "Don't Forget All Else for Movie Chance Says Scribe," *Chicago Defender*, January 5, 1935.

78 Lucie Neville, "Temperament Tantrums Trouble!" *Washington Post*, September 10, 1939. Neville goes on to describe Hollywood's taxonomy of racialized types and the prejudices associated with their labor: "There's scarcely a Chinese in Hollywood who can be coaxed onto a horse. Most Hawaiians are unable to swim. Proud Sikhs from India will not tolerate defeat, or even honorable death, in movie battles. There are African natives who must fortify themselves with banana beer before a scene, and who really want to kill each other once they get into the spirit of the drama. American Negroes have gone on strike rather than go barefoot. And American Indians just won't understand English."

79 Ted Gill, "Turban Expert Holds Filmdom Job 27 Years," *Washington Post*, August 4, 1940; Nelson B. Bell, "Bizarre Jobs Sprout in Some Fertile Minds," *Washington Post*, August 18, 1940.

80 "Big Increase in Horsley Activities: More Talent Engaged," *Motography*, December 25, 1915. Casting Hollywood "Hindus" was not without its challenges. For example, in casting the Hindu ascetic in *Son of India* (1931), the producers were looking for someone who "must look the part physically without too obvious a make-up. He must have a recognizably spiritual quality to his face, manner and voice. He must look very frail, but must be actually physically strong. And above all, he must have had both stage and screen experience . . . to express subtle nuances in both pantomime and with spoken word." Nathalie Bucknall, "Casting," in *The World Film Encyclopedia: A Universal Screen Guide*, ed. Clarence Winchester (London: Amalgamated Press, 1933), 437

81 See Edwin Schallert, "Hindu Boy Rated Unique Discovery in Kipling Feature from Abroad," *Los Angeles Times*, March 27, 1937; Norbert Lusk, "Unusual Jungle Film in New York: Hindu Juvenile Stars in 'Elephant Boy,' a Story of India," *Los Angeles Times*, April 11, 1937; "Dorothy Lamour and Sabu Boost Sale of Stamps," *Chicago Tribune*, February 4, 1942.

82 "*The Jungle Book*: New Movie Is Made about Mowgli the Man-Cub, Whom Rudyard Kipling Created Here in Vermont," *Life*, March 16, 1942.

83 Louella O. Parsons, "Sabu—the 1940 Thief of Baghdad—an Accomplished Actor," *Washington Post*, October 20, 1940.

84 Prem Chowdhry, *Colonial India and the Making of Empire Cinema: Image, Ideology and Identity* (New Delhi: Vistaar, 2000), 90–91.

85 Gayatri Gopinath, *Impossible Desires: Queer Diasporas and South Asian Public Cultures* (Durham: Duke University Press, 2005), 67. For a thorough examination of "empire cinema" in interwar geopolitics, see Priya Jaikumar, *Cinema at the End of Empire: A Politics of Transition in Britain and India* (Durham: Duke University Press, 2006).

86 See Ron Inden, "Orientalist Constructions of India," *Modern Asian Studies* 20, no. 3 (1986): 401–46.

87 Ronald Inden, "India in Asia: The Caste Society," in *Imagining India* (London:, 1990), 57; see also Nicholas Dirks, *Castes of Mind: Colonialism and the Making of Modern India* (New Delhi: Permanent Black, 2002).

88 Myrtle Gebhart, "Caste Rules in Hollywood: Many Different Social Planes Are Developing in the Life of the Cinema Players," *Los Angeles Times*, October 7, 1923.

89 Ibid., 36. Anthony Slide describes an ironic ending to Gebhart's writing career as she became obsessed with astrology in the late 1920s. Anthony Slide, *Inside the Hollywood Star Machine: A History of Star Makers, Fabricators, and Gossip Mongers* (Jackson: University of Mississippi Press, 2010).

90 See Shelley Stamp, "'It's a Long Way to Filmland': Starlets, Screen Hopefuls, and Extras in Early Hollywood," in *American Cinema's Transitional Era: Audiences, Institutions, Practices*, ed. Charlie Keil and Shelley Stamp (Berkeley: University of California Press, 2004), 332–52.

91 H. T. Cowling, "India's New Magic," *International Photographer*, May 1929.

92 John Scott, "Hindu Caste System Has Parallel among Actors: Yawning Gaps Separate Star From 'Unwashed' Extra, while Social Climber Stranded at Start," *Los Angeles Times*, February 28, 1932.

93 Hubbard Keavy, "Hollywood's Social Code Is Unique: Caste System Covers Extras, Bit Players, Heroines Alike," *Washington Post*, October 25, 1936; Hubbard Keavy, "All Is A and B in Hollywood Caste System," *Washington Post*, September 3, 1938; and Hubbard Keavy, "Caste System in Hollywood Keeps Best Talent Buried," *Washington Post*, April 20, 1941. Similarly, Douglas Churchill, writing about independent production in Hollywood, wrote about the spiraling ambitions of photographers, "camera Brahmins" taking their place in "the caste system [that was] taking hold of all branches of the industry." See Douglas W. Churchill, "Hollywood Anxiously Clocks a Dark Horse," *New York Times*, August 16, 1936.

94 John Chapman, "Looking at Hollywood: Models in the Movies," *Chicago Daily Tribune*, June 8, 1941.

95 Hedda Hopper, "On Hollywood's Caste and Class System," *Washington Post*, December 18, 1938. See also Hedda Hopper, "Pay-Check Caste Rules Film Society: Hollywood Recognizes Lone Aristocracy of Earning Capacity," *Los Angeles Times*, December 18, 1938.

96 Murray Ross, *Star and Strikes: Unionization of Hollywood* (1941; repr., New York: Arno Press, 1967), 3.

97 See, for example, Denise McKenna, "The City That Made the Pictures Move: Gender, Labor, and the Film Industry in Los Angeles, 1908–1917" (Ph.D. diss., New York University, 2008); Robert Sklar, *Movie-Made America: A Cultural History of American Movies* (New York: Vintage, 1994); and Michael Nielsen, "Toward a Workers' History of the U.S. Film Industry," in *The Critical Communications Review, Volume 1: Labor, the Working Class, and the Media*, ed. Vincent Mosco and Janet Wasko (Norwood, NJ: Ablex, 1983), 47–84.

98 See Clark, *Negotiating Hollywood*.

99 K. A. Abbas, *An Indian Looks at America* (Bombay: Thacker and Co., 1943), 38.

100 Herbert H. Howe, "Hollywood in a High Hat," *Photoplay*, August 1925.

101 See W. E. B. Du Bois, *The Souls of Black Folk* (1903; repr., New York: Norton, 1999). For a fascinating discussion of the sociological and historical debate over the association of caste and race, see Kamala Visweswaran, *Un/common Cultures: Racism and the Rearticulation of Cultural Difference* (Durham: Duke University Press, 2010). For an argument against the caste theory of race that delimits its political efficacy in social transformation, see Oliver Cromwell Cox, *Caste, Class, and Race: A Study in Social Dynamics* (New York: Monthly Review Press, 1959). For a placement of Cox within the history of black radical thought, see Nikhil Pal Singh, *Black Is a Country: Race and the Unfinished Struggle for Democracy* (Cambridge: Harvard University Press, 2004). In the 1940s, B. R. Ambedkar, India's prominent Dalit leader, and W. E. B. Du Bois exchanged correspondence addressing the applicability of "untouchable" rights to racial politics in the United States. For an analysis of this remarkable exchange, see S. D. Kapoor, "B. R. Ambedkar, W. E. B. Dubois and the Process of Liberation," *Economic and Political Weekly* 38, nos. 51–52 (2003): 5344–49; and Visweswaran, *Un/common Cultures*.

102 Jane Gaines, "*The Scar of Shame*: Skin Color and Caste in Black Silent Melodrama," *Cinema Journal* 26, no. 4 (1987): 3–21.

103 Visweswaran, *Un/Common Cultures*, 5.

104 Dilip Gaonkar and Elizabeth Povinelli, "Technologies of Public Forms: Circulation, Transfiguration, Recognition," *Public Culture* 15, no. 3 (2003): 392.

CONCLUSION

1 Nicole LaPorte, *The Men Who Would Be King: An Almost Epic Tale of the Moguls, Movies, and a Company Called DreamWorks* (Boston: Houghton Mifflin, 2010), 443.

2 Nyay Bushan, "Steven Spielberg's Close Encounter with Bollywood," *Hollywood Reporter*, March 11, 2013.

3 Ray Morton, *Close Encounters of the Third Kind: The Making of Steven Spielberg's Classic Film* (New York: Applause, 2007).

4 Dileep Padgaonkar, *Under Her Spell: Roberto Rossellini in India* (New Delhi: Penguin, 2008).

5 Nirupama Subramanian, "Dream Locales in Lanka," *The Hindu*, April 17, 2005.

6 Thomas M. Pryor, "Hollywood's Far Eastern Problem," *New York Times*, September 10, 1939.

7 Ram Bagai, "Hollywood Wants India Stories," *Bombay Chronicle*, April 4, 1940.

8 Karla Rae Fuller, *Hollywood Goes Oriental: CaucAsian Performance in American Film* (Detroit: Wayne State University Press, 2010).

9 Joseph McBride, *Steven Spielberg: A Biography* (New York: Da Capo Press, 1997), 334.

10 "E.T. Story Taken from Ray's 'The Alien' Claims Director," *India-West*, April 1, 1983.

11 Quoted in Andrew Robinson, *Satyajit Ray: The Inner Eye* (New York: I. B. Tauris, 2004), 9.

12 "30 Seattle Picketers See Bias in 'Indiana Jones,'" *New York Times*, July 17, 1984.

13 "Steven Spielberg—Animated Tribute (2012)," February 25, 2013, available at http://www.youtube.com/watch?v=mabUieoeTQ8.

14 See "Spielberg Writes Indian Film Student Handwritten Letter," March 8, 2013, available at http://us.shalomlife.com/culture/18910/spielberg-writes-indian-film-student-handwritten-letter/. For a full account of the exchange, see Shenoi's blog at http://krishnabalashenoi.wordpress.com/.

15 Quoted in "The Hundred Luminaries," *Movie International*, February 1996.

16 Florence Burgess Meehan, "Off the Beaten Track with a Camera," *American Cinematographer*, August 13, 1921.

17 Margit Kelen, "Hollywood in India: Gods of the Hindus on the Silver Screen," *Travel*, February 1934, 38.

18 Richard Schiff, "Afterward: Figuration," in *Critical Terms for Art History*, ed. Robert S. Nelson and Richard Schiff (Chicago: University of Chicago Press, 1996), 479–85.

19 Like other borrowers of this term, especially Miriam Hansen, I should acknowledge that this use of "provincialize" is indebted to Dipesh Chakrabarty's formulation in *Provincializing Europe* (Princeton: Princeton University Press, 2007).

20 Bhrigupati Singh, "Introduction to *Unsettling Cinema*: The Problem," *Seminar* 525 (2003): 12–17.

21 See, for example, Armand Mattelart, *The Invention of Communication*, trans. Susan Emanuel (Minneapolis: University of Minnesota Press, 1996).

22 See Caren Kaplan, *Questions of Travel* (Durham: Duke University Press, 1996).

23 See Tony Bennett and Patrick Joyce, eds., *Material Powers: Cultural Studies, History and the Material Turn* (New York: Routledge, 2010).

24 Lesley Stern, "How Movies Move (Between Hong Kong and Bulawayo, between Screen and Stage)," in *World Cinemas, Transnational Perspectives*, ed. Natasa Durovicova and Kathleen Newman (New York: Routledge, 2010), 189.

INDEX

ABOUT THE AUTHOR

Nitin Govil is Assistant Professor of Critical Studies in the School of Cinematic Arts at the University of Southern California. He is a coauthor of *Global Hollywood* (2001), *Global Hollywood 2* (2005), and *The Indian Film Industry* (2015).